BEFORE THE
REVOLUTION

VICTORIA GONZÁLEZ-RIVERA

BEFORE THE
REVOLUTION

WOMEN'S RIGHTS AND RIGHT-WING
POLITICS IN NICARAGUA, 1821–1979

THE PENNSYLVANIA STATE UNIVERSITY PRESS
UNIVERSITY PARK, PENNSYLVANIA

Lyrics by Carlos Mejía Godoy in chapter 6
reproduced by permission.

Library of Congress Cataloging-in-Publication Data

Gonzalez-Rivera, Victoria, 1969–
Before the revolution : women's rights and right-wing politics
in Nicaragua, 1821–1979 / Victoria Gonzalez-Rivera.
p.   cm.
Includes bibliographical references and index.
Summary: "An exploration of the history of feminist activism
in Nicaragua.Looks at the role of women in conservative
politics and the Somoza regime"—Provided by publisher.
ISBN 978-0-271-04870-3 (cloth : alk. paper)
ISBN 978-0-271-04871-0 (pbk. : alk. paper)
1. Women—Political activity—Nicaragua—History.
2. Women—Suffrage—Nicaragua—History.
3. Feminism—Nicaragua—History.
4. Women's right—Nicaragua—History.
5. Nicaragua—Politics and government.
I. Title.

HQ1236.5.N5G66 2011
305.42097285—dc23
2011019665

The Pennsylvania State University Press is a member of
the Association of American University Presses.

It is the policy of The Pennsylvania State University
Press to use acid-free paper. Publications on uncoated
stock satisfy the minimum requirements of American
National Standard for Information Sciences—
Permanence of Paper for Printed Library Material,
ANSI Z39.48–1992.

CONTENTS

ILLUSTRATIONS

PREFACE

> We cannot live without stories. Our need for stories of our lives is so huge, so intense, so fundamental, that we would lose our humanity if we stopped trying to tell stories of who we think we are. And even more important, if we stopped wanting to listen to each other's stories.
> —*Ruth Behar,* Translated Woman

The story I tell in this book is a heartbreaker. I document the rise of first-wave feminism in Nicaragua during the first decades of the twentieth century and the movement's co-optation by a U.S.–backed dictator. I then address the reasons why so many working- and middle-class women in this small and poor country felt compelled to support a right-wing dictatorship over the course of almost half a century. I tell how, believing itself to be the rebel child of the leftist Sandinista patriarchs, second-wave feminism developed in Nicaragua in the early 1990s completely unaware of its foremothers' existence. And how, in 1996, with the heirs of the Liberal right-wing dictatorship back in power, a new Liberal women's movement emerged, with no memory of women ever organizing on behalf of the Somozas. I couldn't have made this story up even if I'd tried.

The interpretation put forth in this book seeks to replace the previous one, which held that Nicaraguan women were not active in politics until the late 1970s, when they mobilized, often as mothers, to support the Sandinista revolution, which brought an end to the Somoza dictatorship. Previous scholars had also held that Nicaraguan women first embraced feminism in the early 1990s, and that, before then, they had simply suffered at the hands of their men as *sufridas*.

Before the Revolution tells an entirely different story. Many of the arguments it presents, which constitute my particular take on Nicaraguan women's history, are now, thirty years after the Somozas' defeat, largely accepted as "what happened" by scholars and activists in the United States and Nicaragua alike.[1] Indeed, the story I tell has become a somewhat familiar one. I have published (in English and Spanish) many of my general arguments in several different articles and book chapters and have presented my work at over a dozen conferences throughout the world. But fifteen years ago, when I first started to publicly share my conclusions on the history of Nicaraguan women, they were considered sheer heresy, "counterintuitive" at best. In the next few pages, I outline some of the ways in which my research findings were first received, both in Nicaragua and the United States. I pay particular attention to the reasons why my audiences were dissatisfied with what they heard in my presentations.

Reactions to My Research

Although today it is much in vogue among feminists and the leftist intelligentsia to criticize the Sandinistas, back in 1994, it was still taboo in many circles. It was even worse to humanize anyone who had ties to the Somozas. Thus my conclusions at first elicited some highly negative reactions, particularly among nonfeminist Sandinista women and men. Some Nicaraguans were upset with me because I was arguing that feminism was not a foreign import. Others were upset because I was taking credit away from the Sandinistas for "awakening" women to their inner power. Still others were outraged that I was making the Somoza dictatorship palatable by ignoring the "fact" that working-class Somocista women had either been duped or coerced into Somocismo. And some were both confused and saddened: they conceded that many women had supported the Somozas, but could not understand why that was important. Wasn't their story as Sandinista revolutionaries more meaningful? What kind of scholar would choose to write about evil people? My father, in fact a devout anti-Somocista activist, died without ever fully understanding why, among all the topics I could have picked to study, I picked this one.

Some additional issues were at play, especially—though not only—in the United States. It seemed to me that some U.S. activists and scholars could not get beyond the stereotypes of the *mujer sufrida* and the macho man, stereotypes that are often embraced by Nicaraguans themselves even today. According to these stereotypes, Nicaraguan men are and traditionally have been more sexist than other (white) men. Therefore, it follows that Nicaraguan women are and traditionally have been more oppressed than other (white) women, that they are and were, indeed, mujeres sufridas. In the minds of many, this stereotype came to replace the reality of Nicaraguan first-wave feminists who demanded the right to vote, the right to an education, and the right to choose motherhood.

Not surprisingly, most of those who promoted the stereotypes of the overly sexist Nicaraguan man and the superoppressed Nicaraguan woman did so in good faith. Apparently unaware of the international nature of first-wave feminism, they believed that the collective struggle against sexist oppression could only have originated in Europe and the United States. Most important, however, they had not done the extensive archival research or asked the sorts of questions that would have elicited historically accurate information on this topic.

In Nicaragua there was also, understandably, some distrust of first-wave feminists by those on the Left who actually knew of their existence. Nicaraguan nonfeminist leftists who were involved in politics in the late 1940s and the 1950s viewed feminists with suspicion because of their seemingly ambiguous relationship with the Somozas, a point I address in the chapters to follow. Ironically, Somocistas of that same generation also distrusted first-wave feminists—but because of their independent streak.

Second-wave feminists, on the other hand, suffered from an almost complete historical amnesia for totally different reasons. First, they were too young to have personally known first-wave feminists—women like Josefa Toledo de Aguerri, who in her prime was Nicaragua's foremost feminist, before being reduced to simply a "famous educator." Second, some leading figures in the late-twentieth-century feminist movement were not from Nicaragua and thus were initially unaware of local histories. Third, these feminists had been preoccupied with more pressing issues, such as their relationship to the FSLN and to the revolution. And, finally, few of them were professional historians; those who had academic degrees tended to be sociologists, psychologists, journalists, writers, or medical professionals. Once they heard what I had to say, however, they were very open to hearing more.

On its face, my version of Nicaraguan history made no sense to many academics in the United States nor to many college students (and even a few feminists) who heard me speak on campuses throughout Managua in the mid-1990s. Why would thousands of poor women mobilize "against their own interest" (in support of a right-wing dictatorship), only to give their overwhelming support to the Sandinista revolution? How could this possibly be true? One conclusion was that someone had to be lying. Or perhaps Nicaraguan women were schizophrenics.

What This Book Seeks to Do

Before the Revolution seeks to piece together, for the first time ever, a comprehensive history of some Nicaraguan women from 1821 through 1979. By no means the whole story, it is just the tip of the iceberg. And though I call it a "story," it tells many stories: it is a small part of an ongoing conversation about Nicaragua's past, present, and future between those in and out of academia, between men and women on the many Lefts and the many Rights, inside and outside Nicaragua, and across generations.

Where I Fit In

Who we are, who we think we are, and who others think we are profoundly influence what we write. This deceptively simple point bears repeating, for it has not been said often enough in relation to what has been written about Nicaragua and about Nicaraguans.

What I put forth here is thus also a story of how we—a broad, collective, transnational "we"—have imagined Nicaraguan women's past and present from our own specific and uniquely complicated locations. It is, inevitably, not only the history of Nicaraguan women between 1821 and 1979, but also my own history, my own story, and a reflection of the ways in which academic, social, and political relations between individual Nicaraguans and white U.S. Americans have impacted Nicaragua's versions of its past and others' versions of its past.

My version of Nicaraguan history, by necessity, rests on decades of constant dialogue between U.S. Americans and Nicaraguans, between academics and activists, and on a lifetime of crossing cultural, linguistic, and geographic borders. It is a reflection on my childhood experiences in Nicaragua and how those experiences led me to the questions and issues I address in this book. But even though my background influenced both the issues I chose to focus on and those I chose to ignore, I do not believe it inevitably led me to the conclusions I make. Nor do I mean to suggest that only someone of my background could have written such a text (faults and all) or to imply that my background necessarily made it better, only that my particular experiences produced this particular text. I hope—and expect—that other scholars from all sorts of different backgrounds will challenge and improve on what I present here, which is, like so many pioneering works, simply a rough draft.

My Childhood

As the child of a Nicaraguan man and a white U.S. American woman in the 1970s and 1980s, I was not alone. But my experience was rare enough. My parents hoped my siblings and I would be "citizens of the world." We ended up being children of war instead, like all the other Nicaraguans of our generation.

Born in 1969, I lived through the last years of the Somoza dictatorship, the insurrection of 1978, the revolution of 1979, and the Contra
war of the early 1980s. I led a middle-class, twice-mestiza, small-town girl
life in a place that was in many ways still a "frontier" society before 1979
and a war zone after that. Matagalpa, the birthplace of Carlos Fonseca
Amador and Tomás Borge, co-founders of the FSLN, had a population of
approximately 40,000 in 1979, the year I turned ten.[2] Many of the adults
around me depended financially on commercial trade with the people
who until recently had been called "indios" (Indians) but were now called
simply "campesinos" (peasants). Racial tensions lay just below the sur-
face, masked by the myth of *mestizaje* that still pervades contemporary
Nicaragua in spite of the best efforts of scholars such as Jeffrey Gould and
the indigenous communities themselves, some of which to this day lie
just miles away from the center of town.[3]

I attended the best school for girls in Matagalpa, the girls-only K–12
Colegio San José, run by the Mexican order of Josephine sisters. Like
many of my classmates, I was light skinned. By coincidence, we shared
the German/English–Nicaraguan heritage that characterizes a significant minority of the Matagalpa population, both rich and poor. My father,
however, did not come from that particular background or from any
recent immigrant stock.[4] He was a third- or fourth-generation *mata-
galpino,* with deep roots in León, a colonial city hours west of Matagalpa.

My Father

Given up for dead soon after birth, it was only when my father started
crying that he was taken out of a box from under the bed where his sick
mother lay. After losing his mother at an early age, he was raised by
cousins. In 1970, he would become one of only two pediatricians in our
town, a huge achievement since neither one of his parents and none of
his siblings had gone to college.[5]

Active in politics in the 1970s, my father was a member of the anti-
Somocista Conservative Party, like many of his paternal relatives. Only a
handful of his relatives were Somocistas and, ironically, he was quite
close to some of them, as was I. Like most other Nicaraguans, my father
had relatives and friends across the political spectrum. He had a socialist
half brother, a Liberal anti-Somocista cousin, and many Sandinista nieces
and nephews. Several relatives held high-level posts locally and nationally, the Somocistas in the 1970s and the Sandinistas in the 1980s. My
father, however, was active only in local politics.

Though at first he had supported the Sandinista revolution, he became disillusioned early on. He grew to hate the Sandinistas' authoritarian tendencies. To him, the revolutionary slogan "¡Dirección Nacional ordene!" (National Directorate, give us your orders!), shouted constantly at most political rallies, symbolized the subjugation of the Nicaraguan people by their new dictators. He longed for "pure" revolutionary leaders like "el Che" and Carlos Fonseca, untainted by power and corruption. But he stopped short of supporting the counterrevolutionary offensive against the Sandinistas and the U.S.–sponsored Contra war of the 1980s, having no illusions about U.S. politicians and their vision for Nicaragua, and possibly also because so many in the Contra leadership were his former Somocista foes.

Like many—if not most—Nicaraguans, my father's political identity was complex, and it changed over time. It was also deeply affected by Nicaragua's long-standing relationship with the United States, even though he never lived here. In fact, he came to this country only twice, once when he got married in 1967 and a second time when he visited my brother, my sister, and me in 1985. Although he neither spoke nor understood English, he interacted with many white U.S. Americans over the decades and had a brother who lived in the United States for more than thirty years.

I was not surprised to find out that my father was touched by the death of Ben Linder, whose body he examined as one of several coroners in north central Nicaragua during 1987. Linder was a white U.S. American engineer killed by the Contras while building a small hydroelectric dam in solidarity with the Sandinista revolution in a rural area near Matagalpa.[6] My father's attitude toward Linder reflected his mixed feelings toward white U.S. Americans as a group: he admired their good intentions and skills, even as he sometimes wondered about their common sense and naïveté.

My father saw white U.S. Americans as a distinct group, as fundamentally different people from regular Nicaraguans, a perspective most Nicaraguans I knew seemed to share. This perspective fostered in him and in many of my Nicaraguan relatives and friends a type of cultural ambivalence toward me and my siblings, one that was heightened when I moved to the United States in December 1983. It would fade in the following decades, as thousands of Nicaraguans moved back and forth between Nicaragua and the United States, blurring the supposedly rigid categories of national identity.

Although I grew up feeling Nicaraguan, and not much different from my peers, I was keenly aware of the "one of us/not one of us" mind-set that many Nicaraguans had and have toward "mixed" people like me. That it usually played itself out in predictable ways made things easier in practical terms. Thus it was not surprising to me that my academic and personal interest in feminism during the 1980s and 1990s was explained disapprovingly by many of my family members through the "not one of us" part of the "one of us/not one of us" dichotomy, whereas my interest in Nicaraguan history as a whole was explained by the fact that I was, after all, "one of us."

Life in the United States

A similar situation existed on the other side of my family, my white U.S. side. Although I was one of them by blood, I was, by definition (given the "one-drop rule" commonly implemented in this country), of a different culture and race. The most obvious manifestation of my "difference" was that I spoke English with an accent and that I was a recent "immigrant," even though I shared with them a European ancestry dating back to 1629 in what would become the United States.

Navigating racial politics in this country as the mixed-race child of a white woman is now commonplace, highlighted by the example of President Barack Obama.[7] But in 1983, when I moved to the United States with my mother and my siblings after my parents' divorce, it was a less common experience, although still complicated, as it is today. To make matters more complex, I belonged to two countries that were at war with each other.

To embrace an Anglo identity in the mid-1980s after everything I had lived through in Nicaragua was never an option. I retained my "one of us/not one of us" Nicaraguan identity instead, piling on additional identities: mixed race, U.S. Latina, and immigrant. The fluid nature of racial/ ethnic and national identity was obvious to me, even at the age of fifteen, as I attempted to navigate these waters in the least stressful way.

Revolutionary Contradictions

Before the Revolution thus arose out of the many contradictions I found myself facing early on in life. As a child, I watched my father's transformation into a fervent anti-Sandinista, while my mother, a non-Nicaraguan who had lived in Nicaragua for more than a decade at the time of the revolution, became an ardent supporter. I witnessed many political transformations such as these, which, however fascinating to a scholar, were deeply unsettling to a child. I harbored many questions over such things, until I was finally able to find answers for them on my own.

Among the many discrepancies I witnessed, some were more personal than others. I found it odd, for instance, that some of the "muchachos" hailed as heroes by the revolution were the same young men I'd had to avoid in the streets so as not to be fondled. I remember, for instance, having to cross the street every time I went past the local Sandinista People's Cultural Center (Centro Popular de Cultura) so as not to encounter the young men who would stand at the door, eager to harass the teenage girls who walked past them on the sidewalk.[8]

Concluding that the revolution was gendered and that "the new man" was sexist was not something I had to learn from a book. Indeed, given my experiences in Nicaragua, becoming a feminist in the mid-1980s was a decision that made sense to me.[9] My decision, like those of second-wave Nicaraguan feminists who remained in Nicaragua, grew in large part out of the contradictions within the revolution itself. The revolution's promise of equality, which contrasted sharply with the reality of continued gender inequality, helped turn many of us into feminists.

While a student at Oberlin College, I became not only a feminist, but also a student of Latin American history. As such, I was distressed by the portrayal of women in the well-intentioned, left-leaning books and articles published on Nicaragua in the 1980s. I felt a tremendous disconnect between the simplistic way many pro-Sandinista academics and political activists were portraying Nicaragua as a whole and the multifaceted reality I lived through with my family and friends. It seemed like the political and social complexities (obvious to most everybody now in retrospect) had been taken out of the picture for the sake of political convenience, as if somehow these complexities might negate the right of Nicaraguans to a leftist revolution, or the right to sometimes make the wrong choices. Placing the Sandinistas on such a moral high ground (again in retrospect) was a collective endeavor of Sandinista/U.S. and European leftist solidarity, one that set the stage for a terrible fall.

Timing

In many ways, then, this is the book I wished had been available two decades ago. That said, I do not think it could have been written during the revolution, before the Sandinistas were voted out of office in 1990, and before the advent of the Internet. Too many people were still unwilling to acknowledge they had been Somocistas, for fear of persecution. It was not until the defeat of the Sandinistas in 1990 and the return of the Liberals to power in the mid-1990s that the time seemed ripe for many to boast, once again, of their support for "El General Somoza." The Internet has also contributed to the creation of numerous cyber-Somocista communities, a topic I hope to address in future research.

The mid-1990s were the perfect years to begin my research project. Many of the Somocista women leaders of the 1960s and 1970s were still alive. If I had waited a few more years to interview them, it would have been too late; indeed, several of the high-level leaders I interviewed died in the late 1990s and early 2000s. On the other hand, one of the disadvantages of conducting my fieldwork when I did is that Somocista women and men who spoke to me insisted on anonymity. If I had interviewed them years later they might have agreed to go on the record without pseudonyms. This poses quite a significant problem, for it means that readers will not get the actual names of Somocista women leaders here. But, given the level of political polarization that plagued Nicaragua at the time, it was a compromise I felt forced to make. I am hopeful that, once this book circulates among Somocista women, and they realize that I have not used their words to vilify them, those who are still alive might allow me to use their real names in the Spanish version of the book.

Timing is crucial for a project such as this one. And the revisions I hope to make in the near future must happen relatively soon if I wish to continue engaging with those who were active in Somocista politics as adults before 1979. This brings up an important point regarding generations in Nicaragua.

Generational Differences

I am part of the last generation of Nicaraguans who lived through, and who remember living through, Somocismo. This often overlooked generation, in my view, is destined to play an important role in Nicaragua, for we are a bridge generation. We are the generation that (with a few exceptions) was too young to fight in the revolution[10] and too young to participate in the Literacy Crusade, but old enough (if you were a boy) to fight in the Contra war.

Many of the men of my generation would have finished high school, but were instead pulled out of school at sixteen to serve their mandatory two years in the revolutionary military service. More often than not, those who survived, full-blown men after their experiences on the battlefield, were too world weary to return to a classroom that treated them as children. And for those who wanted to play an active role as civilians in the revolution (those who chose not to escape the Contra war, as so many who could did), the FSLN's electoral defeat came way too soon, when they had barely turned twenty-one.

In short, my generation was old enough to make sense of what was going on, to sacrifice for the revolution like everyone else, but not old enough to participate in its decision-making processes. Nicaraguans of my generation are thus in a perfect position to take on research such as mine: many of us were in training for many years as careful observers (instead of active participants) of rapidly changing complex realities at the ground level. Those of us who were never part of the political elites—the vast majority of us—have a bottom-up perspective on both Somocismo and Sandinismo, and everything in between.

That many members of my generation went on to play prominent roles in Nicaraguan politics across the political spectrum does not contradict my point. When my generation is gone, most firsthand memories of Somocismo will also be gone. This might be a source of joy for those who wish to forget the suffering they endured under the Somozas. But for a historian who happens to be part of this generation, it is quite a monumental realization. That someone with my background would seek to address the history of Somocismo, then, is not at all unexpected.

Positionality

I am writing this preface on the eve of the thirtieth anniversary of the Sandinista revolution, at a time when the United States is considering the contributions a "wise Latina" like Supreme Court nominee Sonia Sotomayor might make to her country. As stated before, I believe that a person's cultural/ethnic, class, or gender background does not necessarily produce a particular result, precisely because identities are fluid and contextual. At the same time, I feel it is imperative to obtain diverse perspectives—including local ones—on a subject as important as a nation's history.[11] For this reason, I think that it is important for Nicaraguan authors (including those who are part of the ever-growing diaspora) to play a significant role in academic constructions of Nicaragua's past. I am adding my voice to that small but growing group of professional historians.

Privilege

To be able to sit and think and write is a privilege that most in the world are denied. That much is obvious. What I wish to briefly focus on here is how I used my class privileges to my advantage during fieldwork.

Whereas, in the United States, my appearance as a light-skinned Latina does not always grant me racial privileges due to other markers of identity, in Nicaragua, my light skin is an important component of a larger reality: I exude middle-classness. I inevitably used this to my advantage during fieldwork, particularly since I was often interviewing people who were situated in much higher class brackets than the one I grew up in. I could tell that my middle-class appearance put Somocista leaders at ease. Moreover, being middle class was useful in situations where my status as a young woman worked against me. The lesson I was putting into practice was one that I had learned as a child: class often trumps gender. My class background allowed me to better document Nicaraguan women's history. The irony of this is not lost on me.

Feminism and Partisan History

Readers deserve to know who wrote this book, why, and from what perspective. That information contextualizes the book. Nicaragua has been plagued by political polarization, and historians in Nicaragua have often reflected partisan points of view in their works. Thus it is possible to speak of Liberal historians, Conservative historians, Somocista historians, and Sandinista historians. So where does this book fit in?

The myth is that a professional degree, namely, a Ph.D., somehow shields the historian from true partisanship because we are, above all, committed to our sources and not to a political party or a specific political point of view. Though hardly anyone speaks of objectivity in the aftermath of the postmodern wave that hit academia in the 1990s, remnants of the "noble dream" of objectivity remain in the profession. My own position reflects the uncertainty that many historians feel. I proclaim that this book takes gender into consideration as a category of analysis (that I am writing from a feminist perspective), while at the same time noting that I am also faithful to the sources, no matter what. In other words, although the questions I originally asked might have reflected a feminist point of view, subsequent questions, as well as their answers, were dictated by the sources. But even that is misleading since my interpretation of the sources is itself a feminist interpretation.

In the end, I don't go as far as I could have in the continuum of feminist academic writing. I don't seek to be an advocate for the women I study, and I don't attempt to empower the women I interview, two of the original goals of feminist oral history and ethnography. I do, however, write the histories of first-wave feminists and Somocista women with varying degrees of empathy, a position that might anger many different sorts of people. Although empathy appears to have been ruled out as a necessary qualification for the U.S. Supreme Court, it is still allowed in the historical profession. Readers can judge for themselves whether it should have a place in the writing of Nicaraguan women's history.

July 2009
San Diego, California

ACKNOWLEDGMENTS

Before the Revolution was in the works for a very long time. So many people helped shape my thinking along the way that perhaps the best way I can thank them here is to do so chronologically.

I am particularly grateful to the lifelong friends (far too many to list individually) I made at the Colegio San José in Matagalpa between 1972 and 1983 against a backdrop of extreme political upheaval.

Among the many relatives who have supported me, inspired me, and challenged me over the years, I would like to thank Kathy Hoyt, Victoria Morales, Bayardo González, and Paula González. I also wish to thank María Helena de Rodríguez, Irma de González, Paula Hoyt, Mary Leonard, Fred Wegener, Lucy González Rodríguez, Bayardo González Rodríguez, the González Picado clan, and Sara Bathum. Bayardo González Vargas, Ben Rigberg, Charlotte and Paul Hoyt, Julio González Vargas, Carlos González Vargas, and Anibal Rodríguez all died before this project was completed. In different ways, they all impacted the final product.

For their friendship and support over the years, I wish to express my gratitude to Ruth Bearscove, Sister Mary Ellen Doyle, Marycruz Soto, Gaby Morales, Teresa Nuño, Vilma Olachea, Ninnette Luna, Orawon Chaila-pakul, Jenny Lindenaeur, Jennifer Guglielmo, Ximena Sosa-Buchholz, Suk Rhee, Dylan Dow, and Benny Andres. I wish to thank the many friends I made at Oberlin's Third World House and La Unión, far too many to mention individually. The grownups at Oberlin also deserve my appreci-ation, especially Willie Arroyo, Elisa Grajales, Tommy Woon, and Ehrai Adams.

I am profoundly indebted to my professors at Oberlin College and at the University of New Mexico (UNM): Kum-Kum Bhavnani, Chandra Mohanty, bell hooks, Cherrie Moraga, Ana Castillo, Margaret Randall, Angela Davis, Ana Cara, Steve Volk, Deena Gonzalez, Jane Slaughter, and Sandra Lauderdale Graham.

While at UNM, I had the extraordinary opportunity to work as Mar-garet Randall's assistant for the book *Sandino's Daughters Revisited: Fem-inism in Nicaragua*. Thank you, Margaret.

Working with Jeff Gould has been a highlight of my academic career. His insights on Nicaraguan history have made me a better scholar and— I hope—a better person.

Muriel Nazzari, Arlene Díaz, and Peter Guardino not only read my work and commented on my ideas; they also became my friends. I am deeply grateful for their mentorship and for their friendship. Also at Indiana University, I would like to thank Judith Allen, Jean Robinson, and Wendy Gamber.

I started to present my controversial research in Nicaragua in the mid-1990s. I am grateful for the enthusiastic welcome I received from Grupo Venancia in Matagalpa, El Colectivo de Mujeres in Matagalpa, and Fundación Mujer y Comunidad in Esteli. For their support, I would also like to thank the Fundación Xochitlquetzal in Managua and Matagalpa (especially Mary Bolt, Rosibel Blandón, and Hazel Fonseca), La Boletina, and Fundación Puntos de Encuentro (especially Amy Bank, Ana Criquillon, Julieta Bendaña, Vilma Castillo, Teresita Hernández, and Helena Ramos).

The scholars and staff at the Instituto de Historia de Nicaragua, in particular Margarita Vannini, Frances Kinloch Tijerino, Miguel Angel Herrera, Mario Rizo, and Maria Auxiliadora Estrada, also deserve my thanks, as do the staff at the Archivo Nacional, in particular Mauricio Flores and Ivania Paladino, a historian and a friend.

Over the years, I received suggestions, comments, and encouragement from many people. I am especially grateful to Betsy Kuznesof, Maxine Molyneaux, Florence Babb, Elizabeth Dore, Asunción Lavrin, Margaret Power, Ana Lau Jaiven, Marysa Navarro, Jennifer Bickham Mendez, Michel Gobat, Justin Wolfe, Cymene Howe, Paula Ford, Yolanda Marco, Nancy Appelbaum, Sandra McGee Deutsch, Lorraine Bayard de Volo, Pilar Bezanilla-Herr, Julie Cummings (Julia O'Hara), Marlene Medrano, Jesse Mendez, Eloisa Mendez, Francisco Barbosa, Erika Blum, Engel Ortega, Celina Gallardo, Diana Pritchard, Barbara Seitz de Martínez, Guillermo Martínez, Hector Carrillo, Jorge Fontdevila, Sharon Rogers, Marisol Acevedo, Debra Vekstein, Rosemary Boehmer de Selva, Patricia Elvir, and Saul Arana. My thanks also go to Claire Kinsley, Lisa Zimmerman, Turid Hagene, and Dean Kotlowski for their support, their encouragement, and, most of all, their friendship.

In Nicaragua, many people have encouraged me and taken an interest in my work. I am indebted to Silvia Torres, Vidaluz Meneses, Martha Cabrera, Sofía Montenegro, Dora María Tellez, Erick Blandón, María Teresa Blandón, Eddy Kühl Arauz, Carmen de Padilla, Sheyla Hirshon, Kitty Madden, Circles Robinson, Nadine Jubb, Gerardo Sevilla, Helen Dixon, Mariana Yonüsg Blanco, Luana Quattrini, and the late Josefina Arnesto.

I am grateful for the research and technical assistance I received from Arawí Hernandez, Rafael "Payo" Manzanares, and Lynda Leahy and for the copyediting that Jeff Lockridge provided. I am also indebted to the late Vilma Sevilla and her family and to the Ubeda and Paladino families. In the United States, I wish to thank the Fromens for candidly speaking to me about their family's past.

The people I interviewed are central to this book. Although most of my interviewees must remain anonymous, I wish to thank Margarita López Miranda, Jorge Eduardo Arellano, Azucena Ferrey, Tomás Borge, Miriam Argüello, and Rosita Mencías for graciously speaking with me, often in their homes.

I owe a great deal to my colleagues at San Diego State University. For their support and advice, I am grateful to Irene Lara, María Ibarra, Norma Iglesias, Norma Ojeda, Isidro Ortiz, Richard Griswold del Castillo, Leilani Grajeda-Higley, Kim Price, Betsy Colwill, Prisca Bermudez, Teddi Brock, Huma Ahmed-Ghosh, Esther Rothblum, Paula De Vos, and Anne Donadey. Special thanks go to Adelaida del Castillo.

For their financial assistance, I am grateful to Oberlin College, the University of New Mexico, Indiana University's History Department and Center for Latin American and Caribbean Studies, the Institute for the Study of World Politics, the American Association of University Women, the National Hispanic Scholarship Fund, and to the National Endowment for the Humanities, which granted me a Summer Stipend in 2004 specifically for this book.

I give special thanks to the friends and family members who took care of my children so that I could write. For peace of mind, I thank Ines Mast, Abigay Godínez, Raquel Rivera (Godínez), Ramón Rivera, Sandra Rivera, Judith Rivera, Ceci Rivera, Moises Rivera, Marie Gomes, Dora Ubeda, Paula González, Michael Zambelli, Kathy Hoyt, and, of course, Pina "Titi" Arellano.

I also want to thank Sandy Thatcher and the anonymous reviewers at Penn State University Press for their suggestions regarding the revision of the manuscript and for recommending it for publication.

Karen Kampwirth, Soili Buska, and Eugenia Rodríguez Sáenz helped keep this project alive. I couldn't have asked for better cheerleaders.

Four resilient women have kept me rooted over the years. My mother, Katherine Hoyt, my aunt, Victoria Morales, and Dora and Jeronima Ubeda are my role models and my inspiration. I dedicate this book to them.

Oscar Rivera's practicality, unflinching optimism, and commitment to my academic career have made *Before the Revolution* a reality. He has put many of his dreams on hold so that I could pursue some of mine. I thank him for that.

Finally, I want to mention my children, Raquel, Lucía, and Paulo. They don't yet know it, but I write for them.

Earlier versions of portions of this book have appeared in the following: "Del feminismo al Somocismo: Mujeres, sexualidad y política antes de la Revolución Sandinista," *Revista de Historia*, edición especial, no. 11–12 (1998); "'El diablo se la llevó': Política, sexualidad femenina y trabajo en Nicaragua, 1855–1979," in *Un siglo de luchas femeninas en América Latina*, ed. Eugenia Rodríguez (San José, Costa Rica: Editorial de la Universidad de Costa Rica, 2002); "Gender, Clientelistic Populism, and Memory: Somocista and Neo-Somocista Women's Narratives in Liberal Nicaragua," in *Gender and Populism in Latin America: Passionate Politics*, ed. Karen Kampwirth (University Park: The Pennsylvania State University Press, 2010); "Memorias de la dictadura: Narrativas de mujeres somocistas y neo-somocistas (1936–2000)," in *Mujeres, género e historia en América Central, 1700–2000*, ed. Eugenia Rodríguez (México, D.F.: UNIFEM, Oficina Regional de México, Centroamérica, Cuba y República Dominicana; South Woodstock, Vt.: Plumsock Mesoamerican Studies, 2002); "Mujeres somocistas: 'La pechuga' y el corazón de la dictadura nicaragüense, 1936–1979," in *Entre silencios y voces: Género e historia en América Central (1750–1990)*, ed. Eugenia Rodríguez (San José, Costa Rica: Centro Nacional para el Desarrollo de la Mujer y la Familia/Editorial de la Universidad de Costa Rica, 1997); "Nicaraguan Feminist Josefa Toledo de Aguerri (1866–1962): Her Life and Her Legacy," *Diálogos: Revista Electrónica de Historia* 5, no. 1 (2004); and "Somocista Women, Right-Wing Politics, and Feminism in Nicaragua, 1936–1979," in *Radical Women in Latin America: Left and Right*, ed. Victoria González and Karen Kampwirth (University Park: The Pennsylvania State University Press, 2001).

ABBREVIATIONS

AMNLAE	Asociación de Mujeres Nicaragüenses Luisa Amanda Espinoza (Luisa Amanda Espinoza Association of Nicaraguan Women)
AMPRONAC	Asociación de Mujeres Nicaragüenses ante la Problemática Nacional (Association of Nicaraguan Women Confronting the Nation's Problems)
AMROC	Asociación de Militares Retirados Obreros y Campesinos (Association of Retired Military Officers, Workers, and Peasants of Nicaragua)
ANMU	Asociación Nicaragüense de Mujeres Universitarias (Nicaraguan Association of University Women)
CIM	Comisión Interamericana de Mujeres (Inter-American Commission of Women)
FSLN	Frente Sandinista de Liberación Nacional (Sandinista National Liberation Front)
IACW	Inter-American Commission of Women (see CIM)
LIMDI y Cruzada	Liga Internacional de Mujeres Ibéricas e Hispanoamericanas y Cruzada de Mujeres Nicaragüenses (International League of Iberian and Hispanic American Women and Nicaraguan Women's Crusade)
NWP	National Woman's Party
PLC	Partido Liberal Constitucionalista (Constitutional Liberal Party)
PLI	Partido Liberal Independiente (Independent Liberal Party)
PLN	Partido Liberal Nacionalista (Nationalist Liberal Party)

UCA	Universidad Centroamericana (Central American University)
UMA	Unión de Mujeres Americanas (Union of American Women)
UMPL	Unión de Mujeres Profesionales Liberales (Association of Professional Liberal Women)
WILPF	Women's International League for Peace and Freedom

INTRODUCTION

In 1979, Nicaraguans overwhelmingly supported the overthrow of the repressive and corrupt Somoza family, who—backed by the United States—had been in power for forty-three years. Nicaraguans' support for the leftist Sandinista guerrillas who toppled the dictatorship, however, waned over the course of a prolonged counterrevolutionary war waged against the Sandinistas throughout the 1980s. In 1990, the U.S.–backed anti-Sandinista candidate, Violeta Barrios de Chamorro, won the presidential election. The Sandinistas, who had come to power through violent means, relinquished power peacefully after their defeat at the polls.

The Sandinista revolution lasted only eleven years. Nonetheless, it radically altered Nicaragua's political and cultural landscape. After 1979, revolutionaries proclaimed that Somocismo was dead, and everyone agreed that a new era of Nicaraguan political history had begun. Yet Somocismo proved to be more resilient than its enemies had thought, a fact that has complicated Nicaraguan politics enormously.

In a 2006 political survey of 490 Nicaraguans in the colonial city of Granada, 64 percent proclaimed that they would support an authoritarian government "if it resolved the country's economic problems."[1] And more than half (54 percent) believed that the Somocista years (1943–79) were the best Nicaragua had ever experienced.[2] These results were startling and unexpected, particularly for Sandinistas who had whole-heartedly believed that, indeed, Somocismo was truly dead. Somocistas found the results less surprising.

The authors of the Granada study concluded that, over the course of almost three decades since the Sandinista National Liberation Front (FSLN) ousted the right-wing dictator Anastasio Somoza Debayle, Somocismo had been "transformed into a positive historical point of reference" and that the undemocratic Somoza years had been "whitewashed" in the Nicaraguan imaginary.[3] They reasoned that economics factored into this shift. The study stressed the impact of financial difficulties on Nicaraguans' political choices, given the nation's status as the second poorest country in the Western Hemisphere, after only Haiti.[4] And it suggested that the economic development of the 1950s and 1960s, and the increase in the standard of living that accompanied it, looked good to many when compared to the war of the 1980s and the corruption, partisanship, and economic misery that have enveloped Nicaragua since 1990.[5]

It is important to note that those respondents who spoke favorably of the Somozas often began their statements with "I've heard that . . . ," "My parents say that . . . ," and "According to my mom. . . ."[6] In other words, many did not live through the Somoza years as adults but were none-theless molded by their elders' memories, which in turn were shaped by recent events. The study's authors urged readers not to become prisoners of this whitewashed Somocista past, forged in the depths of economic anguish. Instead, they suggested that Nicaraguans look past the bleak-ness of the present with renewed hope to the future.

I agree that the ongoing economic crisis in Nicaragua has helped to whitewash Somocismo. On the other hand, Somocismo is quite com-plex, and it is important not to dismiss or underestimate Nicaraguans' embrace of right-wing politics. *Before the Revolution* seeks to shed light on the Somoza years and on the decades that preceded them so that we may gain a more nuanced understanding of Nicaraguan history, one not nec-essarily based on the political and economic desperation of the present. It also seeks to provide historical contextualization for yet another finding of the Granada study, that, despite Nicaragua's high electoral participa-tion rates in presidential elections (higher than the world average since 1967; 73.5 percent in 2006), 58 percent of those surveyed who said they were not interested in politics were women.[7] This book thus offers a back-drop against which to understand contemporary women's participation (or supposed lack of participation) in politics.

The study contended that the relatively low level of interest in poli-tics on the part of contemporary Nicaraguans (both men and women) reflected their disillusionment with contemporary politics and political parties, a narrow definition of politics. Indeed, that 27 percent of all those surveyed said they were interested in politics, despite the extreme levels of political corruption seen in the last decades, offers a sign of hope for democratic forces in Nicaragua.[8]

The pages that follow document women's political participation in Nicaragua between 1821 and 1979. The twentieth century birthed four major women's movements in Nicaragua: first-wave feminism, a Somocista women's movement, a Sandinista women's movement, and second-wave feminism. My research documents the first two, the least studied and least understood of these movements. It also touches upon a fifth one, a rather small and perhaps short-lived nonfeminist Liberal women's movement that arose in the last decade of the twentieth century with a large contingent of neo-Somocistas in its ranks.

I contend that first-wave feminism developed in Nicaragua during the nineteenth century and was eventually co-opted by the Somoza dictatorship in the mid-twentieth century, when women obtained the right to vote. At that point, a nonfeminist Somocista women's movement flourished, giving the dictatorship badly needed credibility. Women's support for the Somoza regime helped keep the dictatorship in place. It also allowed thousands of women to become active participants in populist-clientelistic state-building efforts.

Before the Revolution addresses the goals, accomplishments, and motives of first-wave feminists and Somocistas. Before delving directly into the history of these two groups, however, let us review the events that led to the Sandinista revolution, a watershed moment in Nicaraguan history.

Historical Background

Midday on Sunday, February 26, 1978, in the town of Masaya, twenty-seven-year-old Faustina Castro Palacio was at home, breast-feeding her youngest child, when she heard a commotion outside.

> I heard bombs go off and saw that a group of people . . . two men and two women, took refuge in my house. . . . The National Guard came after them: . . . The road filled up with military vehicles of all types and two helicopters appeared. . . . There appeared to be about one hundred Guard members, firing without notice. . . . The National Guard machine-gunned the house, starting with the front door. . . . The gunfire lasted an hour and they stopped firing at my

house in order to fire at the house next-door. At that point I went out, like a madwoman, with my five kids hanging on to me, the oldest was eleven, and the youngest a year and a half. . . .

The Guard . . . forced me to go into the house next door to mine, on the left, while they followed about five meters behind. . . . In the entrance I saw a dead person lying on his stomach, and throughout the house I saw what appeared to be bundles of clothes drenched in blood. . . . Those bundles were the people who lived in the house. They had wrapped themselves in blankets to protect themselves. . . .

My eight-year-old son Isidro is still psychologically affected. . . . He has war psychosis, feeling terror every time he sees the National Guard. He has nightmares saying that he sees the Guard, hears gunfire, and sees blood. Sometimes he takes his clothes and rips them to shreds.[9]

Human rights abuses of this type, committed by the Somoza-controlled National Guard, were common in Nicaragua during the late 1970s, and they affected thousands of people in different ways. Witnessing what came to be known as the "Sabogales Massacre" radically changed Faustina Castro Palacio, an ardent Somoza supporter and member of the Somozas' Nationalist Liberal Party (PLN).[10] In her declaration before Nicaragua's Permanent Commission on Human Rights (CPDH), Castro Palacio noted,

I declare that I am a member of the Liberal Party and that I have worked at the electoral tables on behalf of Somocista Liberals. . . . If I could at this moment speak to General [Anastasio] Somoza [Debayle], I would tell him that I never expected my services to the government and the Liberal Party to be repaid in this way. Since he is in charge, I would ask of him, with tears in my eyes, like I have right now, that even if he puts me in jail, it is better for him to give up power because nobody wants him anymore [nadie lo quiere ya], and it is not fair that honest citizens be suffering. I do not say this out of hatred but because of what has been done to me. I felt so proud with a red flag in my hands during [pro-Somoza] rallies! A few weeks ago I had asked when elections were going to take place, for I was willing to give my vote to the Liberal Party and I had already registered to vote.[11]

Faustina Castro Palacio's story was corroborated by her tenant, twenty-one-year-old Norma Castillo de González: "[Faustina] is a . . . Liberal and

Somocista. . . . On that day when they did all those things to her, she said she regretted having been a Liberal and having voted all those years for [Somoza] . . . because the Guard did not take into account that she was a Somocista and a Liberal, because she wasn't just a Liberal, she was completely Somocista [*pura somocista*]."[12] When asked if Castro Palacio had a chance to tell the National Guard that she was a Somocista, Castillo de González responded: "No . . . but I think the Guard found out that she was very Liberal because [in her house] . . . she had posters of Somoza, mirrors with the President's photo, and she had many Somoza-related papers."[13]

Norma Castillo de González herself came from a Liberal family and, like her friend Faustina, could not understand why the regime was turning on its supporters: "Me, my family, my mother, my grandmother, my grandfather, my father all are very Liberal, because my entire family is Liberal and Somocista, and I don't know why the president is doing this. I don't know if he is the one who tells [the Guard to do these things], the one who gives the orders, or if it is the Guard that puts itself against us. . . . I ask the President to please not continue with this."[14] Unfortunately for Castillo de González, her nightmare had just begun on February 26. As a result of her declarations to the CPDH, Castillo was kidnapped on March 20. Although eventually released on May 8, she was tortured by her captors for information on anti-Somocistas in her neighborhood, information she did not have.[15]

Even National Guard members were outraged by the violence they were being asked to commit in an effort to keep the decades-old dictatorship in place. Carmen Rodríguez Prado, a twenty-one-year-old woman interviewed by Margaret Randall in 1979, recalled in *Sandino's Daughters* how she ended up joining the National Guard at age seventeen and how she eventually left to join the FSLN:

> There were eleven kids [in my family] and I was the next to last. . . .
> My father wasn't living with us anymore and I had to start helping support the family. . . . I was in my third year of high school . . . [and] every job I applied for, except the National Guard, required at least a high school degree . . . [so] I signed up. That was 1975. . . .
>
> I worked at the bureau of investigations. That was where they started ordering me to mistreat people. I couldn't do it. . . . After people were arrested, the women prisoners were brought to us. We were supposed to make them talk. They said beating was the only way.[16]

Eventually, Rodríguez Prado began talking to one of the Sandinista women in her custody, Comandante Mónica Baltodano:

She asked me a lot of questions: why was I in the National Guard? Did I like it? Was I aware of the atrocities being committed? I told her why I joined and that I hadn't realized what it would be like until I started working. . . . Mónica made me see the limitations of what I was doing. . . . Slowly I became aware that I had to do something else. I began to think seriously about joining the FSLN. . . .

Working for the Revolution within the Guard was very dangerous. . . . It was horrible in my family. My father backed Somoza, and one of my brothers was an officer in the Guard. Near the end they realized I was in the FSLN. [My brother] tried to pressure me [to leave the FSLN] but at least he didn't turn me in.

By 1978 . . . work inside the Guard was getting too dangerous. On May 15, 1978, I . . . joined the [Sandinista] insurrection.[17]

Like Faustina, Norma, and Carmen, thousands of Nicaraguan women stopped supporting the dictatorship in the late 1970s due to the atrocities committed by the National Guard. Some women, like Carmen, joined the armed struggle against the Somozas led by the Sandinista National Liberation Front. Others simply gave their tacit support to the leftist guerrillas.

Just how many women joined the armed struggle against the Somozas is hard to know. Margaret Randall and Helen Collinson have both argued that women made up 30 percent of the Sandinista guerrilla forces in the late 1970s.[18] Carlos Vilas, however, suggests that the figure was more modest, around 6 percent, and that most women who supported the Sandinistas did so in noncombatant roles that required them to carry messages, hide and move arms, and provide safe houses, food, medicines, and clandestine medical care.[19] Regardless of how many active female combatants there were, thousands of women were organized in the Association of Nicaraguan Women Confronting the Nation's Problems (AMPRONAC), a Sandinista women's organization created in 1977. According to Helen Collinson and colleagues, AMPRONAC had more than 8,000 members by 1979.[20]

Although the indiscriminate violence carried out by the National Guard made many Nicaraguans oppose the dictatorship, other factors also contributed to Anastasio Somoza Debayle's defeat in July 1979. Political and economic issues in particular led large segments of the population to seek new leaders, if not a revolution.

Nicaraguans of different social classes and different political persuasions came to support the overthrow of the Somoza dictatorship. For the elites, the Somoza family represented an important ally but also an unfair competitor. According to John Booth, the ambivalence of Nicaragua's upper classes toward the Somozas turned to opposition in the 1970s, when the dictatorship became "more a liability than an asset to most of the bourgeoisie. . . . The rift between the government and the private sector widened in 1977, when the regime removed certain business tax exemptions and imposed new business taxes."[21] Partly as a result of their economic disagreements with the regime, "one key group of Nicaraguan capitalists . . . established business interest links [that same year] with the FSLN."[22]

Different groups of the middle class opposed the Somozas, "more with each passing decade."[23] According to Booth, those who opposed the Somozas included "students from the 1930s on, the Independent Liberals from the 1940s on, the Social Christians in the 1950s and 1960s, and middle-sector unions [representing teachers, private-sector and government employees and health workers] in the troubled 1970s."[24] By contrast, opposition among the lower classes was "never unified."[25] Nonetheless, "the nationwide deterioration of economic conditions and the growing governmental repression in the 1970s turned many of the lower class against the regime by converting their economic grievances into more clearly defined antiregime positions and action."[26]

Karen Kampwirth summarizes the impact of Nicaragua's economic development on the poor from the 1950s to the 1970s:

> Starting in the mid-twentieth century, a series of socio-economic changes occurred as Nicaragua (like other countries in the region) became more tightly linked to the global economy. During the course of the Somoza regime, Nicaragua was characterized by a progressively more unequal distribution of resources as peasants were pushed off their land to make room for agro-export production. . . . Increased landlessness had the effect of putting downward pressure on wages, especially as the main cash crops—cotton and coffee—were not very labor intensive, except during the harvest. . . .
>
> While the supply of newly landless workers increased, the demand for workers remained largely fixed, leading to a fall in wages. To make things worse, food prices rose at the same time; as land was concentrated and converted to cash crop production, less land was utilized for food production.[27]

Two main responses to the increased landlessness in the countryside were migration to urban areas and women's entry into the labor force. Kampwirth argues that "since there were fewer economic opportunities for women than for men in the countryside, women made up a significant proportion of the hundreds of thousands who migrated to the cities during the second half of the twentieth century."[28] Women, in fact, made up a larger percentage of the urban population than men. In 1950, nearly 56 percent of urban residents were women. Thirty years later, more than 50 percent of urban residents were still women.[29]

Women participated in a shift toward urbanization that radically changed Nicaragua. Although the country's urban population was only 35 percent in 1950, by 1979, it had grown to 52 percent, with the largest concentration of urban dwellers located in Managua, the capital.[30] Carlos Vilas notes that "between 1950 and 1971 Managua almost quadrupled its population, going from less than 110,000 inhabitants to almost 400,000,"[31] while the population of the country as a whole doubled.

Once they arrived in the cities, women entered the labor force in large numbers. By the late 1970s, "women, who made up 30 percent of the economically active population in Managua, . . . constituted 70 percent of the service workers, 55 percent of the sellers and merchants, 37 percent of the office workers, [and] 24 percent of the artisans and operators."[32] As in the countryside, however, employment opportunities in urban areas were limited.[33] This was particularly true in Managua after the December 1972 earthquake "leveled about half the city, killed 10,000 and injured 20,000 people, destroyed over 40,000 homes and left over 160,000 people homeless."[34] Managua never fully recovered from the earthquake, which "left almost 52,000 people without work (57 percent of the city's economically active population) and forced the displacement of some 250,000—60 percent of the total population of Managua."[35] Unemployment would skyrocket a few years later, in the late 1970s, jumping from 13 percent in 1977 to 28 percent in 1979.[36]

The late 1970s witnessed not only an economic crisis in Nicaragua but a political one as well.[37] The Catholic hierarchy strongly criticized the human rights abuses committed by the Somozas' National Guard, the United States terminated all new U.S. aid to the dictatorship, and the FSLN grew in strength and adherents.[38] By late 1978, literally thousands of Nicaraguans took up arms against the Somozas, bringing about the triumph of the Sandinista revolution on July 19, 1979.[39]

A Revisionist Interpretation

The widespread support that both men and women gave to the overthrow of the Somozas' forty-three-year-old right-wing dictatorship led sympathetic scholars to maintain that women in Nicaragua first organized politically on the Left, and that their political awakening occurred recently, within the last twenty-five years of the twentieth century.[40] Anna Fernández Poncela, for instance, argues that "it was precisely through the anti-Somoza insurrection that women began to assert themselves most visibly in the history of the nation."[41] Scholars have also argued that feminist activism is a recent development in Nicaragua, a by-product even of the Sandinista revolution.[42]

I propose a radically different, revisionist version of Nicaraguan women's history. First, I claim that Nicaraguan feminism had roots in the postindependence period (1820s–1840s), although it did not start developing as a distinguishable movement with a coherent set of ideas until the second half of the nineteenth century. Second, I propose that the relationship between feminism and Liberalism from the mid-1800s through 1979—and particularly from the 1930s to the 1950s—is central to the history of Nicaraguan feminism. And, finally, I contend that women's support for the Somoza dictatorship helped maintain the regime in power between 1955 and 1979.

Nicaraguan women have been politically active for generations and, in fact, as early as 1837, had shown an interest in eliminating the "tyranny" of male domination. This interest grew into full-fledged campaigns for female suffrage and access to education for women in the 1880s. By the 1920s, a small, urban, predominantly middle-class group of Nicaraguan women began to call itself "feminist." Nicaragua boasted a vibrant feminist movement in the 1920s, 1930s, and 1940s. In the decades that followed, however, early twentieth-century feminism in Nicaragua was erased from the nation's historical memory. A new generation of women appropriated the goals of the feminist movement, creating a partisan, pro-Somoza, nonfeminist women's movement. By 1957, the year women first had the opportunity to vote, the Somozas took all the credit for women's suffrage, ignoring feminist contributions to that struggle.

Thousands of women voluntarily supported the Somozas and their right-wing Liberal Party between 1936 and 1979, but particularly between 1950 and 1979. These women self-identified as supporters of the Somozas and their Liberal Party. As a group, they were Catholic, middle- and working-class urban women who lived on the country's Pacific Coast and central highlands. The first generation of Somocista women to organize politically as a group was a generation of firsts: it included the nation's first woman attorney, first woman mayor, and first woman member of Congress. This group of women, born in the mid- to late 1920s, also included a large number of public school teachers. Many were unmarried.

Somocista women as a whole backed the Somoza family and its Liberal Party in exchange for suffrage and increased political, educational, and economic opportunities. Most came from Liberal families; they backed the Somozas' clientelistic system in part because they received goods, services, and, most important, jobs, in exchange for their votes and political support. Many were also attracted to the Somozas' populist leadership style, their anti-Communism, their economic policies, and the Liberal Party's long-standing position in favor of women's secular education and women's suffrage, a position very much at odds with the Conservative anti-Somocista tradition but typical among Liberals elsewhere in Latin America.[43]

Somocista women, however, were never a homogeneous group, not even politically, and they were certainly not naive. Most did not support every action the Somozas took. And they supported the Somozas' patron-clientelistic system only so long as they considered its benefits to be a fair exchange for that support. In the late 1970s, once they felt the system was falling apart, some Somocista women became Sandinista supporters.

Although Somocista women worked hard to secure increased access to employment, education, and public office for women, they were not feminists. Their primary concern was the well-being of their male-dominated party. Women's issues always took second place, as they did among Sandinista women before 1990. Both groups shared a lack of organizational autonomy within their parties.[44] Both were originally mobilized from above, within women's sections of their parties. Somocistas were organized in the Women's Wing (Ala Femenina) of the Nationalist Liberal Party from the 1950s through 1979. Sandinistas were organized in AMPRONAC, in the late 1970s, and then in the Luisa Amanda Espinoza Association of Nicaraguan Women (AMNLAE), in the 1980s and 1990s.

To compare Somocista with Sandinista women is heresy in many Sandinista and pro-Sandinista circles. FSLN members and sympathizers find it hard to admit similarities between themselves and the supporters of the bloody dictatorship they so bitterly opposed. Just as controversial is my contention that maternalism (the exaltation of motherhood promoted as policy by many right-wing governments), which played a crucial role in anti-Somocista (and later Sandinista) women's mobilization, played a relatively minor one in Somocista women's activism.

The jailing, disappearance, and assassination of thousands of young people by the Somozas' National Guard forced anti-Somocista women to organize as mothers and to adopt a maternalist discourse rarely seen among Somocista activists.[45] Surprisingly perhaps, the Somozas—unlike other right-wing regimes—did not emphasize motherhood as the only

appropriate role for women.[46] Nonetheless, Somocista women did sometimes mobilize as mothers, especially in their fight against the Sandinista
guerrillas (a fight they labeled "a war against Communism"), suggesting
that maternalism acquired greater importance in the context of war or
when there is a possibility of war. Another instance where maternalism
prevailed within Somocismo was in the discourse of individual women
looking for jobs or economic assistance within the clientelistic system.
It was precisely to fulfill their roles as female heads of households that
many working-class women (a group I call "maternal breadwinners")
supported the dictatorship, hoping to advance economically in exchange
for their pro-Somoza votes.

Unlike in Chile under right-wing general Augusto Pinochet, where
state-sponsored maternalism fueled right-wing women's activism in
Mothers' Centers,[47] in Nicaragua, maternalism did not become an integral part of state policy until the 1980s, when, in response to the Contra
war, women throughout the country were encouraged to organize in Sandinista Mothers' committees as either mothers of combatants or mothers of heroes and martyrs.[48] The Committee of Mothers of Heroes and
Martyrs brought together women whose children had died in the struggle against Anastasio Somoza Debayle and in the Contra war financed by
the United States. The committees' purpose was to organize women
politically and offer them state assistance in the form of loans, homes,
and medical attention. Roser Solà and María Pau Trayner wrote in 1986,

> The most important aspect of the mothers' movement is the chan-
> neling of maternal potential in defense of the Revolution. Attention
> and assistance of any kind given to a mother who lost a child in the
> struggle is of vital importance to make sure that the enemies of the
> revolution do not take advantage of her pain. To convince all those
> mothers of fallen sons who are isolated or resentful of the necessity
> of joining a group to better confront their problems is also urgent
> and necessary. In this way, the death of the son is situated in the
> true revolutionary context: that of giving one's life for the complete
> liberty of one's people. In this way, the mothers also feel inclined to
> participate in the revolutionary tasks.[49]

Given the high percentage of female heads of households in Nicaragua
(23 percent in 1977 and 25 percent in 1985),[50] it should come as no surprise that a large number of mothers of Sandinista heroes and martyrs
were single mothers.[51] Most important, many of them depended or would
depend financially on their children once they reached their fifties,[52] a

relatively old age in Nicaragua, considering average life expectancy for women was fifty-seven years in the late 1970s and sixty in the early 1980s.[53] It was not uncommon for women to have lost several children in battle, making them especially vulnerable in the difficult economic times of the late 1970s and the 1980s.[54]

Carlos Vilas has made the connection between the status of these women as heads of households and their eventual dependence on the state for assistance in his study of petitions for pensions and subsidies presented by the relatives of Sandinista heroes and martyrs in the early 1980s. Vilas examined the backgrounds of those men and women who died during the late 1970s in the struggle against the Somozas and concluded that "more than half of the participants (54 percent) were children born out of wedlock [and] almost half (47 percent) were raised and lived during their formative years (first 12 years) in families with a single head of household—the mother in the majority of cases. [Moreover,] the head of household . . . had to spend the greater part of the day outside the home, for occupational reasons."[55]

Women's roles as breadwinners and their reliance on their grown children for financial support in their old age motivated many women to join groups such as the Mothers of Heroes and Martyrs in the aftermath of their children's deaths. It is my contention that, like the Sandinistas, the Somozas also benefited from single mothers' economic vulnerability. Both regimes were able to obtain the support of female heads of households who were in desperate economic situations. The Sandinistas achieved this in part by financially rewarding middle-aged and elderly mothers who had lost children to the revolutionary cause.[56] The Somozas did so by offering relatively young single mothers—and working-age urban women in general—limited employment opportunities, especially after 1950.

In 1950, women made up 14 percent of the nation's economically active population. That proportion would rise to nearly 29 percent in 1977.[57] The increase in women's employment outside the home was related both to the rise in rural landlessness and urbanization mentioned earlier and to the liberal, populist, patron-clientelistic modern state the Somozas forged while in power.

Historian Knut Walter has noted that Nicaragua was "a late starter" when it came to state formation and that

> the Somocista regime laid the foundations of the modern Nicaraguan state by implementing a number of important changes in the Nicaraguan political system. In the first place, it neutralized or co-opted the old caudillo leadership based on regional interest

groups and replaced it with a broad coalition of agricultural entre-
preneurs, government bureaucrats, and party and labor organizations favorable to the regime. In the second place, it strengthened
and specialized the state's institutional framework as a result of the
growing complexity of Nicaraguan society and the need to resolve
the issues (social, financial, and legal) that accompanied export-
oriented growth. And finally, it used coercion in moments of political crisis during which the basic contradictions and tensions
within the state became evident, although the regime did aspire to
a level of legitimacy that would allow it to function without constantly having to bring its coercive power into play.[58]

Women's employment was crucial in the provision of social services to
the Nicaraguan population and in the expansion of the welfare system.
Women constituted a low-paid workforce considered especially appropriate for social service tasks. Thus the Somozas offered women state
employment as teachers, nurses, secretaries, receptionists, telegraph and
telephone operators, bank tellers, social workers, day care workers, dieti-
tians, laboratory technicians, pharmacists, judges, attorneys, cooks, and
cleaning personnel in public buildings.

In twentieth-century Latin America, according to Maxine Molyneux,
women "were not excluded from the liberal [state-building] project";
indeed, "as time progressed, they became a more visible part of it."[59] Most
important, perhaps, the formation of modern states "as envisioned by
Latin American elites, was itself premised on the selective incorporation
of women into public life."[60] Nicaragua under the Somozas resembled
other Liberal twentieth-century Latin American states whose "populist
governments sought to establish a more extensive system of welfare,
albeit one that was only selectively inclusive and that reproduced the
clientelistic structure of corporatist favoritism."[61] These states, Molyneux
goes on to say, "sought to mobilize women, and they made direct appeals
to women [both] as political subjects" and as "client-citizens."[62]

Women's dual standing as political and economic "clients" and as
political "citizens" is crucial to our understanding of the Somocista
state and Somocista politics in general. To explain how this dual identity
worked, it is important to heed Javier Auyero's advice and go beyond
the "prefabricated and stigmatizing images of the exchange of votes for
favors. Clientelism must be approached through its least known and least
spectacular side: the everyday dealings of political brokers, the practices
and perspectives of so-called clients, and the problem-solving network
that links 'clients,' brokers, and political patrons."[63]

Although Auyero's research focuses on contemporary Argentina, his insights apply to the Somoza dictatorship as well. Auyero argues that "information hoarding and resource control" are two "equally important practices in the functioning of clientelistic networks." Moreover, he contends that "engaged participation in . . . problem-solving networks reinforces sociopolitical identities as much as it provides goods and favors."[64] As both voters and state employees, urban, working- and middle-class women were able to participate in Somocista client networks at all but the highest levels, which were usually reserved for men of the Somoza family. Hoarding information and controlling resources, Somocista women, like Somocista men, helped forge a Somocista populist sociopolitical identity.

Jeffrey L. Gould argues that Anastasio Somoza García's "consolidation of power can only be comprehended in light of the support of broad sectors of the working classes" and that workers expressed a "contradictory acceptance and simultaneous rejection of the dominant exploitative system."[65] Similar dynamics were at play in women's support for the Somozas, especially in the years after women's suffrage was won (1955–79). Most Somocista women did not support the regime unconditionally and most were willing to play by certain rules but not by others. This conditional support for the dynasty helps explain why Faustina Castro, a longtime Somocista, could change her mind so quickly about the Somozas after witnessing the massacre of her neighbors at the hands of the National Guard.

The belief that "the Somozas were good to those who were good to them"[66] summarizes many Somocistas' understanding of the regime. Women, like men, understood the Somozas' "goodness" to be the opportunity to work, vote, and participate in a clientelistic network that offered them information and resources. As corruption and unemployment increased within the last Somoza administration, resources became less available and the importance of women's and men's citizenship and work diminished, leading some Somocistas to support the Sandinistas. The increased militarization of politics and the increased importance of the National Guard in society also had an impact on the nature of Somocista patron-client relations, leading to the alienation of many Nicaraguans from Somocismo.

Although women's participation in formal economic sectors was curtailed when Nicaragua's economy collapsed in the late 1970s, the Somozas had nonetheless succeeded in mobilizing women across different economic sectors, some of which grew even during hard economic times. In addition to targeting women teachers, professionals, and service sector workers, the Somozas made an effort to mobilize the largely female market sellers and prostitutes as well. Members of these two groups would support the regime over the long term.

The figure of the prostitute came to symbolize the moral corruption of the dictatorship for those on the Left. Brothels were among the first buildings to be destroyed during the Sandinista revolution in 1979, and dozens of prostitutes were jailed, to be eventually "rehabilitated" by the Sandinista state.[67] The political mobilization of these "women of ill repute" and the Somozas' institutionalization of prostitution for the economic gain of their National Guard led anti-Somocistas in Nicaragua to equate all Somocista women's activism with prostitution.[68] Three additional factors caused the Somoza period to be remembered—even today—as one of extreme sexual disorder, in which the Somozas' female supporters are supposed to have been particularly corrupt. State-sponsored sexual violence against anti-Somocista women and the personal role men of the Somoza family played in the sexual torture of their victims outraged Sandinistas and Conservatives alike.[69] Some Conservatives were also outraged by the Somozas' incorporation of urban women into the labor force.

Pedro Joaquín Chamorro, the vocal opposition leader assassinated by the Somozas in 1978, described the Somoza period as "the total inversion of the moral values of Nicaraguan life: prostitutes against mothers, alcohol against civic duty, blackmail against honesty, lowlifes against citizenry."[70] The mothers would triumph against prostitutes after the defeat of the Somozas in 1979. But what about the right-wing political culture that so many Nicaraguan women had embraced under the dictatorship? Did Somocismo simply disappear in 1979? Not at all, as the 2006 political survey of Granada made clear. Ingrained right-wing clientelistic identities and traditions among Nicaraguan women can explain why so many of them voted against the Sandinistas in 1990, why so many voted in favor of a right-wing populist Liberal candidate in 1996, why so many voted for the Liberal Party again in 2001, and why the dictatorship lasted so long in the first place. It can explain, as well, both the eventual disillusionment with the neoliberal policies implemented in Nicaragua after 1990 and Sandinista leader Daniel Ortega's return to power in January 2007.

The examination of sexual politics under the dictatorship is also crucial to our understanding of recent political developments in Nicaragua. That the Somoza period is still characterized as one of sexual disorder is a political victory for both the FSLN and the Conservative Party, for it means that the official Somocista portrayal of the regime as orderly did not prevail. Ironically, however, the image of sexual disorder was popularized precisely because it reinforced already-established societal restrictions against women in public life, restrictions upheld by a significant sector of anti-Somocistas, including most Conservatives. Heir to the Conservative Party's tradition extolling women's maternal and domestic roles in society, Violeta Barrios de Chamorro justified her participation in politics, as she would her presidency (1990–96), by proclaiming herself to be "the Mother of the Nicaraguans."[71] Indeed, "doña Violeta" set about rectifying not only the gender policies of the Sandinistas but also those of the Liberal Somocistas which did not coincide with Conservative views on women.

The links between dictatorship and prostitution had a profound effect on the FSLN leaders, who wasted no time in banning prostitution in the first few months of their rule. As Helen Collinson and colleagues note, "for the Sandinistas, prostitution epitomized all the wrongs of the Somoza regime."[72] The FSLN fashioned its policies on gender in response to the Somozas' corruption: the revolutionary "New Man" was not to engage in the sexual degradation of women, a characteristic of Somocista masculinity. Against this backdrop, it is not surprising that, when former Sandinista president Daniel Ortega stood accused of rape and sexual abuse by his stepdaughter, Zoilamérica Narváez, in the late 1990s, many FSLN supporters found what Narváez claimed Ortega did unimaginable—sexual abuse had taken place under the Somozas; it was not supposed to occur under the Sandinistas.

Although Narváez's accusations might lead some to see similarities between the Somoza dictatorship and the Sandinista revolution, they should not obscure the important and very real differences between the experiences of Somocista and Sandinista women. Somocista women had to defend a regime that systematically oppressed women through state-sponsored prostitution rings and the rape of female prisoners. Sandinista women did not. And although both were treated as "mujeres públicas" (loose women or prostitutes) by their enemies for assuming public political and economic roles in society, the mobilization of Sandinista women and their struggle for autonomy from the FSLN eventually led to the emergence of a second wave of feminism in Nicaragua. By contrast, the mobilization of Somocista women and their acceptance of their dependent status effectively co-opted Nicaragua's first wave of feminism and delayed the reemergence of feminism until the early 1990s.

Methodology

When I began this research project in 1994, I was interested in documenting the history of early twentieth-century feminism in Nicaragua.

Thus I gathered as much information as I could on Josefa Toledo de Aguerri (1866–1962), Nicaragua's most important suffragist, and her generation of feminists. My search led me to interview Toledo de Aguerri's former students, assistants, and friends, as well as to visit her grave and the few monuments erected in her memory.

My search for Nicaragua's forgotten feminism also led me to the study of Somocista women, for I soon came to realize that I could not understand early feminism in Nicaragua without understanding the women's movement that eclipsed it, and vice versa. Moreover, I came to believe that Somocista women's lives shed light on the experiences of the generations of Nicaraguans who followed them.

The history of first-wave feminists in Nicaragua is thus intrinsically linked to the history of Somocista women. Indeed, without this link, we cannot explain the demise of first-wave feminism, and the Somocista women's movement seems to appear out of thin air. Moreover, it is by addressing the shift from feminism to Somocismo that we appreciate the continuities and discontinuities in twentieth-century Nicaraguan women's history. The formation of a Somocista women's movement and the displacement of feminists also add credence to Knut Walter's arguments about the formation of the modern Nicaraguan state. Women were part of the "broad coalition . . . favorable to the regime" that the Somozas used to replace the "old caudillo leadership based on regional interest groups."[73] Just as important, women's support for the regime allowed it "to function without constantly having to bring its coercive power into play."[74]

Like many other Nicaraguans, I was more familiar with individual Somocista women's lives than with the trajectory of Nicaraguan feminism before 1979. This familiarity, in my case, bred curiosity and the knowledge that female Somocistas were a complex and contradictory group of women, who deserved to be studied in their own right. I soon decided that they would be a central focus of my research.

I conducted more than fifty interviews with Somocistas and anti-Somocistas between 1994 and 2009. Most interviews took place between 1997 and 1998 and lasted between fifteen minutes and two hours. A handful, however, lasted between six and twenty hours and took place over the course of days or even years.

In my search for informants, I attended three major Liberal political events: a Liberal Party rally in Matagalpa in 1996, a Liberal Women's assembly in Managua in 1998, and the 1998 Liberal Party Convention in Managua. At these events, I interviewed many women and some men. The rest of my informants I contacted through the snowball method: one informant led me to the next and so on. Some informants I located through friends, the Internet, or the telephone book. Others were acquaintances and family members, an unavoidable situation in a small country. I was surprised to find that one informant, an elderly Somocista woman I had never met or heard of before, was a distant relative. When I called her to request an interview, she asked my full name, my father's name, and my town of origin. With this information, she was able to figure out that we were related, and she agreed to the interview. I, however, did not know that we were until I showed up at her door and she greeted me with great affection.

Many of my informants wanted to know my father's name, my hometown in Nicaragua, and my family's political affiliation before they agreed to be interviewed.[75] I told whoever asked that my father had been a long-time member of the Conservative Party and that, like most Nicaraguan families, mine included both Somocistas and non-Somocistas. Hardly anyone wanted to know what my own political persuasion was, but I assured everyone I spoke to that my intent was not to write a partisan history. I assume that my gender, my middle-class appearance, my short stature, my academic credentials, the fact that I was only ten years old in 1979, and the many years I have spent outside Nicaragua put most informants at ease. I cannot help but think that many of the people I contacted agreed to be interviewed because they were curious about my unusual research project. Others simply appreciated a chance to talk to someone who was interested in their lives. Some former Somocista leaders, on the other hand, seemed to relish the attention and being taken seriously again.

Of course, not everyone I contacted agreed to be interviewed. Some Somocistas were clearly afraid or suspicious of me, or both. One man, for instance, asked to see inside my bag as he wondered out loud whether I had a gun there. Others, such as the members of the Alemán administration I attempted to talk to in 1998, when Arnoldo Alemán (1997–2002) was still in power, were too busy to bother with an interview. Given the sensitive nature of the issue, they might have also not wanted to talk about their Somocista pasts.

In searching for Somocista female informants, I looked for "women who had had a long trajectory within the Liberal Party." With this euphemistic language, I hoped to avoid insulting or alienating potential informants. I also wanted to avoid recent converts to Liberalism. What I hoped to do was to interview women who self-identified as Somocistas during the dictatorship and who continued to do so in the post-Sandinista period. This, in the end, was not hard to do; I was able to interview a total of two dozen Somocista women of varied class and regional backgrounds.

For obvious reasons, most of the women I interviewed were older than fifty. Many, in fact, were in their late sixties, seventies, and eighties. The interviews with members of this older generation are crucial to documenting the transition from feminism to the Somocista women's movement. They are also important to our understanding of the Ala Femenina and women's political mobilization as a whole under the Somozas. Many of their stories and points of view are already lost to future generations: several of the women I interviewed have died in recent years.

I also interviewed many Liberal women who were not Somocistas, some Conservative women, some Christian Democratic women, and some Sandinista women. The Liberal, non-Somocista tradition in Nicaragua is often overlooked by academics interested in women's history. Nonetheless, it is crucial to understanding Nicaraguan women's political activism. Women like Angélica Balladares, who were born in the 1880s and came of age politically within Liberalism before the Somozas took power, did not become Somocistas. To the contrary, they became critics of the regime.[76] This non-Somocista legacy is proudly claimed by many contemporary Liberal women.

Over the course of the late 1990s, I was able to present my findings to groups in three different Nicaraguan cities: Managua, Esteli, and Matagalpa. These public presentations gave me an opportunity to hear the responses of my mostly Sandinista audiences to my research conclusions. As I note in the preface, these responses were initially negative because of the subject matter of my research. Nonetheless, I was eventually able to establish a dialogue with many anti-Somocistas and to incorporate at least some of their concerns into this project. I value our exchange of views greatly and feel it contributed significantly to my thinking on the writing of history.

I interviewed about a dozen men for this project, half of whom were Somocistas and half, anti-Somocistas. I also spoke to dozens of men and women informally about my research results, eliciting many comments. Unfortunately, I was able to conduct only one interview with a woman who practiced prostitution during the Somoza period, and none with male clients. This is clearly a gap in my study, one I hope to fill through future research. Of the handful of Liberal market women I interviewed, most who were active in politics in the late 1990s and early 2000s had not been active during the Somoza period. Most of the female Liberal market activists I encountered were in their thirties, forties, and early fifties. I searched for some in their sixties and seventies but did not find any. This, I presume, is a result of Nicaraguan workingwomen's short life expectancy, although elderly working-class women might be found at home taking care of their grandchildren.

As noted in the preface, to protect my informants from harm, I promised them I would neither reveal their identity nor any information that would make them easily identifiable. For some informants, anonymity was not an issue because they were public figures and what they told me was not of a sensitive or controversial nature. This was the case, for instance, with interviews of FSLN Comandante Tomás Borge and Conservative politician Miriam Argüello, as well as with interviews of a few non-Somocistas who simply gave me factual information.

Organization

Before the Revolution is divided into six chapters. Chapter 1, "Feminism Before Somoza," deals with the history of feminism before the Somoza family's rise to power in the 1930s. Chapter 2, "From Feminism to Partisan Suffragist Politics," documents the transition, in the 1940s and 1950s, from nonpartisan feminism to a one-issue women's movement dominated by committed Liberal and Conservative Party members. Chapter 3, "The Aftermath of Women's Suffrage," addresses the question of what happened after women won the vote in 1955, first portraying the electoral system that developed under the dictatorship and then discussing in detail the Ala Femenina, the Women's Wing of the Nationalist Liberal Party, and the role it played in the formation of Somocista populist clientelism. Chapter 4, "Somocista Women's Lives," tells Somocista women's stories in their own words. Chapter 5, "The Activism and Legacy of Nicolasa Sevilla," tells the story of an alleged prostitute and madam who became the founder and the only female leader of the Somocista Popular Fronts, a clientelistic network of working-class people who engaged in violence against the populace. Chapter 6, "Sex and Somocismo," deals with sexual politics, prostitution, and maternalism under the dictatorship.

The book does not address in great detail the atrocities committed by the Somozas and their supporters; it does not deal extensively with religious issues or racial differences, nor does it cover the history of women on Nicaragua's Atlantic Coast, who won the right to vote in 1894.[77] Indeed, to my knowledge, no one has studied the history of women on the Atlantic Coast before 1979 in depth.

Instead, my book tells how nonpartisan feminism got erased from history in the 1950s; how the first generation of university-educated women of a small, poor country ended up supporting one of the most abhorrent dictatorships in twentieth-century Latin America; and how a handful of working-class alleged prostitutes got to be highly visible in a right-wing, nonmaternalistic regime. In doing so, it tries to show how all of these issues are related and why all of this matters to the formation of the modern Nicaraguan state and twentieth-century political identities and culture.

Before the Revolution is only one of a growing number of nonpartisan (neither Somocista nor Sandinista) histories of Nicaragua being written by Nicaraguans. My contribution is unique because I am writing about a recent and controversial period without having lived through it either as an adult or even as a teenager. I can only hope that my lack of first-hand experience is made up for by my relative nonpartisanship—and that my book helps to establish a dialogue on Somocismo not only between Somocistas and anti-Somocistas but also across generations.

ONE

FEMINISM BEFORE SOMOZA

In 1940, teacher Josefa Toledo de Aguerri, a self-proclaimed feminist, suffragist, and advocate of women's education, published a series of essays entitled "Feminism and Education." In one of them, she wrote, "One of feminism's characteristics is to consider it possible for woman to find in her own self 'her means and end,' to be able to live independently of man, if she so desires, and earn her own living."[1] She concluded the piece by noting: "The world will march toward justice . . . when each woman is able to express her mind's vigor, [and] her impulse for action."[2] Toledo de Aguerri adopted the term "feminism" in the early 1920s, although it was being used earlier in the century in Nicaragua and other parts of Latin America.[3] The concern with women's subordinate status in society was not new in Nicaragua, however. Indeed, Toledo de Aguerri began her campaign for women's and girls' educational rights in the 1880s. And she was part of a movement that could trace its origins back to the 1820s and the early days of Nicaraguan independence.

This chapter provides a broad picture of the struggle for women's rights in Nicaragua in the nineteenth and early twentieth centuries, when three key developments in the history of first-wave feminism took place that would facilitate the formation of the Somocista women's movement in the mid-twentieth century. First, there emerged a tenuous and ambiguous relationship between feminists and Liberals. Second, the feminist move-ment became consolidated under the leadership of one woman, Josefa Toledo de Aguerri. And, third, despite that leader's broad vision, women's suffrage became the one issue that gained prominence within feminism in the first decades of the twentieth century.

The chapter is divided into six sections. The first defines the terms "feminism" and "feminist" as used in the book. The second covers Josefa Toledo de Aguerri's contributions to nineteenth- and early twentieth-century feminism. The third deals with feminism's early years (1820s–1880s). The fourth discusses the role Liberal ideology played in the strug-gle for women's political and civil rights during the nineteenth and early twentieth centuries. The fifth deals with women's rights during Nica-ragua's Liberal Revolution (1893–1909) and traces the beginnings of the women's suffrage movement. And the sixth section documents the course of women's rights and autonomous feminism in the years after the Liberal Revolution ended, but before the Somozas came to power.[4] Among the feminist organizations of this period we find the Nicaraguan Feminist League, the International League of Iberian and Hispanic Amer-ican Women and Nicaraguan Women's Crusade (LIMDI y Cruzada), the First Pan-American Women's Education League, the Inter-American Commission of Women (IACW), and the Workingwomen's Cultural Center.[5]

Defining Terms

By "feminism," I mean the support for women's rights in civil and polit-ical arenas, accompanied by a personal stand against male domination in other areas of life. I call "feminist" all those who gave such support and took such a stand before the early 1920s (when Toledo de Aguerri adopted the terms). Thereafter, however, I call "feminist" only those who subscribed to feminism as defined and who also *regarded themselves* as feminists.

I have borrowed the use of "feminist" for the nineteenth century from June E. Hahner's work on Brazil. Hahner argues that "while [historians] generally seek to avoid the anachronistic use of terms, 'feminist' is nev-ertheless a useful adjective for describing over time . . . [the] opponents of gender inequality."[6] I find that using "feminist" in the Nicaraguan case allows us to make a link between nineteenth- and twentieth-century efforts to end gender inequality. If this link is not highlighted, early twentieth-century feminism appears to grow out of nowhere.

I have also heeded historian Nancy F. Cott's cautionary advice against using the term "feminism" too broadly. I agree with Cott's argument that feminism is a quite specific movement and that "expanding [the term 'feminism'] to cover every worthy or new endeavor women take up equates the term with 'what women did' and renders it meaningless."[7] Moreover, feminism has to do with women's consciousness, making it particularly important to value self-labeling.[8] For these reasons, I believe that, once the use of "feminism" became widespread in Nicaragua in the early twentieth century, and women could choose to call themselves "feminists," those who chose not to were simply not feminists, but something else. This is not to say, of course, that reformers who did not call themselves "feminist" were necessarily less important than feminists, only that most nonfeminist reformers did not give gender issues top priority, an essential characteristic of feminists as I understand the term.[9]

Inevitably, according to these criteria, the number of people who qualify as feminists in Nicaragua's history is rather small. However, it is my contention that these mostly urban, literate, upper- and middle-class women—and men—have played an important role in Nicaragua's past and that their influence has been considerable. Josefa Toledo de Aguerri's accomplishments and limitations exemplify in many ways feminism's legacy in Nicaragua.

Josefa Toledo de Aguerri's Contributions to Nineteenth- and Early Twentieth-Century Feminism

Although Toledo de Aguerri was certainly not the only feminist in Nicaragua during the late nineteenth and early twentieth centuries, her vision and her activism in particular are vital to understanding the history of first-wave feminism there. The reasons for this are quite simple. Her life spanned almost a century, a key century for women's rights in her country. No other Nicaraguan feminist participated in both the nineteenth-century struggles to secure secular secondary education for girls and the mid-twentieth-century campaigns for women's suffrage.

Equally notable was the extent of Toledo de Aguerri's feminist involvement. She dedicated her entire adult life to implementing her feminist vision. She was involved in a myriad of national and international feminist organizations, many of which she established herself; she founded Nicaragua's first feminist journals; and, in her speeches, writings, and activism, she addressed an extraordinarily wide array of issues from a feminist perspective

Ironically, Toledo de Aguerri's strengths—her longevity, her extensive involvement, and her long-standing leadership—became not only her weaknesses but also those of the feminist movement. In the late nineteenth and early twentieth centuries, she did not just lead Nicaraguan feminists; she was considered their "benevolent dictator."[10] Indeed, her firm hold on the movement and her top-down leadership style would make it difficult for a new generation of feminist leaders to emerge.

Instead of becoming full-fledged feminists, many of Toledo de Aguerri's female pupils went on to become *suffragists* in the 1940s and 1950s. Dozens of these women would later become the leaders of the Somocista women's movement. Like their teacher, these women would adopt a hierarchical leadership style. Unlike their teacher, however, the former students would hone their style through their participation in the Somoza dictatorship.

Although a full account of Toledo de Aguerri's life and legacy is beyond the scope of this book, it is important to note that only after her life is placed in its proper historical context can scholars gain a full picture of Nicaragua's feminist history. That said, let us turn now to a brief overview of the rise of feminism in the nineteenth century.

Feminism's Early Years, 1820s–1880s

Pro-independence elites in Nicaragua drew a connection between republicanism and women's emancipation. An 1837 editorial published in the official (government-approved) newspaper *Aurora de Nicaragua* stated that "during three centuries of slavery and tyranny . . . the fair sex was submerged in ignorance, causing notable damage to society; and if that conduct was indispensable for upholding an oppressive regime, it is no longer necessary now that we are ruled by a republican system."[11]

Early on in the postindependence period, some elite Nicaraguans—among them the *Aurora* journalist Gregorio Juárez, "one of the most enlightened men of the time"—felt something had inevitably changed for the better in the "dawn" of independence.[12] A handful of individual women of the wealthy classes were able to take advantage of the greater acceptance of women's expanded societal roles. In 1824, for example, Manuel Antonio de la Cerda (1780–1828), Nicaragua's soon-to-be head of state, named his daughter Juana Ubalda his private secretary, a position traditionally held by a male.[13]

Despite the actions of men like Juárez and de la Cerda who took it upon themselves to publish declarations in favor of women's education and name women to nontraditional posts, independence did not bring about fundamental changes in the relationship between men and women in Nicaragua, or elsewhere in Latin America for that matter.[14] Teresa Cobo del Arco argues that "between 1821 and 1893 Nicaraguan society experienced great transformations; nonetheless, these did not significantly alter the colonial legacy in terms of gender relations."[15] In a distinct departure from colonial times, however, women, their education, and their place in society came to be subjects of an escalating public discussion.

Although the discussion took place initially among elite male intellectuals and politicians who published and read newspapers like the *Aurora*, women continually expanded both the boundaries and the practical implications of that discussion. In 1852, for example, Josefa Vega attempted, albeit unsuccessfully, to enroll at Nicaragua's University of Granada. Undeterred, she appealed directly to the national government and was eventually granted permission to conduct "minor" studies in philosophy at the university. The executive resolution that settled her case ordered that other women's requests be treated in the same fashion.[16] Although women were by no means granted full or equal access to a university education, they had won at least a small victory.

Like Juana Ubalda, Josefa Vega had the social standing necessary to pursue an uncommon enterprise for a woman. Like Ubalda, Vega also had the support of a father who was a politician.[17] What made Vega unique, however, was her maternal grandmother. According to the historian Alejandro Barberena Pérez, Josefa Chamorro was "an untiring warrior" in the struggle for Central American independence: "No other nineteenth-century woman distinguished herself as much in the fight against the Spanish. Her properties were at the disposal of the pro-independence forces, and were confiscated by Spain. . . . Her home in Granada was the focus of the movement, and the Spanish considered her to be a primary conspirator."[18] In 1812, Josefa Chamorro was even jailed, for "feeding several revolutionary caudillos, allowing them to hold meetings in her home, and for hiding gunpowder and ammunition" used in battle that same year.[19] Eventually, however, Chamorro was freed and became, as a result of an inheritance, "the biggest capitalist in Granada."[20]

Undoubtedly, Josefa Vega's class background and family ties enabled her to become the first female student at the University of Granada. Nonetheless, her struggle had repercussions outside her social class. From the mid-1800s onward, many of Vega's peers rallied around the call for increased educational opportunities for girls and women. This call for greater public secular education at the primary, secondary, and normal (teacher-training) levels would characterize Nicaraguan feminism from the mid- to late nineteenth century.

Increased education for a few led both to increased educational demands for the many and to explicit feminist organizing by students and teachers alike. Scholars have noted that, throughout Latin America, the first generations of secular "female school-teachers [like Toledo de Aguerri] . . . formed the first women's groups to articulate . . . a feminist critique of society."[21]

Liberalism and the Struggle for Women's Political and Civil Rights

Despite the rise of Liberal advocacy for the education of women in the early nineteenth century, the political chaos and anarchy that prevailed in Nicaragua between 1821 and 1856 made it hard to consolidate Liberalism and to enact many of the changes Liberals proposed on women's and girls' behalf.[22] Arguments over women's education would continue into the last decades of the century, when women's political roles and women's suffrage emerged as subjects of bitter debate. These debates became especially heated in the 1870s and 1880s and onward, as Liberalism became stronger and more defined in Nicaragua, and as it came to challenge the Conservative, Catholic traditions that had prevailed in the post–William Walker period (1857–93). It was no coincidence, perhaps, that feminist demands multiplied between the 1890s and 1910, for it was then that Nicaragua's Liberal Revolution took place under the leadership of General José Santos Zelaya.

Liberal parties ruled the nation from 1893 to 1909 and from 1929 to 1979. According to philosopher Donald C. Hodges, Nicaraguan Liberals, at least in principle, "believed in constitutional government, the rule of law, and government by the consent of the governed through a freely elected legislative body. They believed that People had certain natural and inalienable rights, of which the most important was freedom from the exercise of arbitrary and unlimited authority. They believed in the right to property; they were modernizers and defenders of capitalism; they opposed government interference in the economy; and they supported the separation of church and state. Many were anticlerical, and some . . . were also ardent nationalists."[23]

Pointing out the gap between theory and practice, historian Ciro F. S. Cardoso notes that "for the general populace . . . the great contradiction of Central American Liberalism was between the proclamations of equality for all citizens and the actual social situation."[24] Liberal elites, he notes, felt "profound contempt for the Indian and peasant masses, which they distrusted."[25]

On the other hand, in Nicaragua, the attitude nineteenth- and early twentieth-century elite Liberal men had toward women as a group was, on the whole, paternalistic rather than contemptuous. Although also somewhat distrustful of women, Liberals generally felt responsible for protecting "the fair sex," and improving women's situation in society. Elite men of most other political persuasions felt similarly.[26] Disagreements arose not over whether Nicaraguan women's status should be improved, but over what kind of improvements should be made.

Liberals wanted women to be "enlightened" members of an ever-changing, secular society.[27] Nineteenth- and even early twentieth-century Conservatives, however, wanted women to continue receiving a religious education, as they had during the colonial period, and to follow Catholic doctrine regarding marriage, divorce, and procreation.[28] They believed women's lot, like men's, was enriched by religiosity, tradition, and stability.[29] Indeed, the Conservative Party's slogan in the 1910s was "God, Order, and Justice."[30] According to historian Knut Walter, the position taken by attorney Carlos Cuadra Pasos in the 1930s was typical among Conservatives:

> In general, Cuadra Pasos thought that the Liberal reforms had destroyed the old patrician order, that ancestral bond between the *caudillo*/landowner and the people, and replaced it with a relationship between a nouveau-riche bourgeoisie and salaried workers. The generous, charitable relationship between the upper and lower classes had given way to a "plutocratic" attitude on the part of the employers toward their employees. In sum, the mass of the people no longer expressed respect for the upper class, while the upper class held neither respect nor compassion for the people.
>
> Cuadra Pasos's position was one of looking back with nostalgia on a past that presumably was crumbling in the face of secular and urban forces. At most, the role of the Conservative Party was that of keeping alive that nostalgia and pressing to limit or contain change in Nicaraguan society.[31]

With regard to women, as late as 1926, Conservatives in Granada proclaimed that "the great woman is the modest woman consecrated to the religious and social duties of the sphere of life in which she finds herself . . . the daughter who lives in obedience . . . the wife who guards in her heart the severe words pronounced by the [priest] . . . living only for the being with whom she shares her fortune [*las dichas*] . . . [and] being . . . his guiding angel . . . the saintly widow who consecrates all her thoughts . . . to the Creator . . . the solitary nun who prays day and night and mortifies her body for the failings of humanity."[32]

During the late nineteenth and early twentieth centuries, the elite men of the Liberal and Conservative Parties—most of whom did not take into account what women themselves had to say about their status—disagreed profoundly not only on the issues of civil marriage and divorce, both of which were institutionalized in the 1890s under Liberal general José Santos Zelaya's presidency (1893–1909), but also on the issue of women's political rights. Although not all Liberals supported women's suffrage, many did, especially the most radical. One of Nicaragua's most prominent Liberal intellectuals, in fact, was among the first scholars to write an entire book supporting women's political rights. Modesto Armijo titled his 1912 Juris Doctorate thesis *The Political Rights of Woman*. It constituted a defense of feminism in Nicaragua:

> Antifeminists are wrong. The objective is not to masculinize the female, nor to feminize the male; it is to give each sex the place deserved by each. . . . And it is not fair to say that woman's participation in public things will distract her from her obligations in the home. Is a farmer distracted from cultivating the land, a business man from his affairs, a doctor from his patients, etc., by having to go a few times a year to manifest his will at the voting booth?
>
> What feminism does not accept is that in the name of a supposed superiority, man be turned into a master and woman into a slave.[33]

What writings like Armijo's suggest is that in Nicaragua, as in Mexico, there were divisions not only between Liberals and Conservatives but also between moderate and radical Liberals.[34]

Although it is not my intention either to romanticize Liberalism or to exaggerate its importance in the struggle for women's rights, I disagree with Teresa Cobo del Arco's conclusion that "between 1821 and 1893 there were no substantial differences between Conservatives and Liberals, both of which saw the family as the fundamental basis of society, although the latter were in favor of civil marriages and divorce."[35] The radical aspects of Liberalism paved the way for feminism in Nicaragua, whereas a similar progressive tradition did not exist among Conservatives. And although some aspects of Catholicism were arguably more beneficial to women than some secular Liberal laws,[36] Catholic progressive thought would not fuel a radical political movement in Nicaragua until the 1960s. Moreover, the Conservative Party did not have any formal ties to Liberation Theology, the radical Christian movement that arose throughout Latin America in the 1960s and 1970s.

What, then, led Cobo del Arco to conclude that Liberals and Conservatives were essentially of one mind when it came to women's rights? At first glance, her sources show almost no difference between the Liberal and Conservative discourse on women. Thus she cites Conservative journalist Enrique Guzmán (1843–1911): "When free love [civil marriage and divorce] was legalized in Nicaragua . . . no one thought there existed two women capable of rebelling against Church laws. And now . . . you can see, in [the space of six months] we have had 385 insurgents in skirts." And again, when Guzmán goes on to ask: "How can women have the same rights as men if they are substantially dissimilar beings [*seres sustancialmente desemejantes*]?"[37] Cobo del Arco then cites the Liberal attorney José Madríz (1867–1911), who served as Nicaragua's president in 1909–10, and who appears to write in a similar vein: "The idea of a woman citizen who presides over an electoral directory, who harangues a political club, or disputes a candidate's triumph at the polls while her children cry abandoned at home, is greatly inferior to that of the prudent woman, who consecrates herself with total abnegation to the care of her family."[38]

Despite the similarities, we can detect a difference between Guzmán's and Madríz's positions if we look at other remarks by Madríz, whom Cobo del Arco quotes as saying: "By advocating woman's liberty I do not propose to make her equal to men in all things, much less in the social functions she carries out. Woman must reign in her home."[39] Madríz considered himself to be "advocating woman's liberty," however limited this liberty might have been, whereas the Conservative Guzmán was reacting with revulsion to the perceived effects of the new divorce and marriage laws upon women's behavior.

Still, Cobo del Arco is correct in noting that women's roles as mothers and wives were promoted by both Liberals and Conservatives. Maternalist sentiment would also infuse nineteenth- and early twentieth-century feminism, albeit with some radical nuances. Josefa Toledo de Aguerri, for example, wanted women to be good wives and mothers but nonetheless also believed they had the right to choose other options in life: "Woman . . . must be educated so she can perform well in whatever place she occupies [*cualquier lugar que le corresponda*], giving her freedom to choose what is in accord with her individual characteristics."[40]

Women's Rights, 1880s–Early 1910s

During the early 1880s, a group of intellectual writers in the Liberal city of León strongly criticized the discriminatory treatment women suffered in society.[41] These writers presented papers on the history of women's oppression at meetings held in their literary club and later published the essays in their newspaper, *El Ateneo*. In one such essay, published in 1881, J. Dolores Espinosa deplored the subjugation of women in ancient times:

> Before Christ, Plato was the only one who, guided by a great emotion, proclaimed woman's liberty. . . . But he proclaimed her free only among the privileged classes, and then he himself demeaned her by snatching away from her the virtuous title of mother.
>
> Oh, the history of humanity presents us such a long chain of woman's suffering!
>
> And how sad it is to confess that man is the one who has given woman all her pains and humiliations.[42]

In that same issue of *El Ateneo*, another passionate author, R. Contreras, described the plight of women in greater detail:

> In modern society I see only one throne, the throne of a male humanity. In vain I search for the place where a female humanity should be seated: the spot is empty. . . . We have seen woman go through different degrees of brutal force without liberating herself completely from it: she went from the cruel oppression of the savage to isolation, from isolation to corruption, from corruption to the cloister, from the cloister to the home, from the home to society, from society to public life. . . . Yet does this mean that redemption has been consummated? I open the Civil Code and I read: woman cannot enter into legal agreements without permission from her husband . . . woman cannot testify in court unless she does so on her own behalf . . . woman cannot be a legal guardian of strangers. . . .
>
> I then open the Constitutional Code and I read: only male Nicaraguan citizens can exercise political rights. . . .
>
> Sor Juana Inés de la Cruz was right: accept women as you have made them or make them as you want them to be. . . .
>
> If woman is intelligent and sensitive, what else does she need? All she needs is for us to lose some of our greed. History is incomplete. . . .

Lift woman up, gentlemen, and in doing so, you will lift your-selves up![43]

Twelve years later, Francisco Montenegro would do more than write articles in support of women's suffrage. Taking advantage of the reforms being implemented in Nicaragua under Zelaya's Liberal Revolution, Montenegro made an unsuccessful yet "vigorous" push for women's enfranchisement during the Constitutional Assembly of 1893.[44] Although Montenegro's campaign failed and Nicaraguan women had to wait another sixty-two years before they could vote, feminists would win two small vic-tories in the upcoming years. First, the Nationalist Liberal Party (PLN), the main Liberal party in the country, promised to endorse women's suffrage: "It is only just that woman be given access to the ballot box and to every public post; the Nationalist Liberal Party will support this idea so that it is put into practice."[45] Second, the PLN also decided to admit as members all women over the age of twenty-one who formally requested membership.[46]

In its program, the Nationalist Liberal Party explained the reasoning behind its commitment to women's political rights: "In the world's cur-rent state of civilization, the civil and political rights of both sexes are rec-ognized in principle. . . . Therefore, it is not fair that, while obeying blind traditions and prejudices, [the Nicaraguan woman] continues to be com-pletely removed from public affairs, condemned to suffer all the ill-fated consequences of men's mistakes and ambitions."[47]

Feminists also made other gains during this period. Women's civil rights were expanded in 1908, allowing married women to personally administer their own estates and to claim inheritances.[48] Furthermore, new legislation allowed women to attend college without first having to petition the government.[49] Equally important, it was during Zelaya's pres-idency that civil marriage and divorce were first allowed in Nicaragua, as part of the formal separation of church and state. Additionally, state-funded secular primary education for boys and girls became obligatory.[50]

The turn of the century was also marked by an increase in the number of individual women who took on important roles in nontraditional fields. For example, the writer Julia de Rivera Castro edited the Liberal newspaper La Tarde in 1896, although only its June and July issues, perhaps because of the strong criticism she was subjected to in the Conservative news-paper El Tiempo.[51] The Chinandega poet Rosa Umaña Espinoza (1872–1924) also made herself heard during this Liberal era. She published her first books of poetry, Recuerdos y esperanzas and Ayes del alma, in 1906 and 1909, respectively.[52] According to folklorist David Whisnant, "her poetry centered on the pain and abuse of attachments to men . . . and especially on the dishonest pretense that a double standard imposed on women."[53] In one of her poems, Whisnant notes, "virgins sell their virtue at the foot of the altar; other poems dare to address abortion and infanticide."[54] Umaña would publish a third book of poems, *Luz del ocaso*, in 1916.[55]

The years between 1880 and 1910 were particularly rich ones for feminism in Nicaragua. They were marked both by the beginning of the movement for women's suffrage and by the gaining of important women's rights in the civil arena. Unfortunately, however, the links between feminism and Liberalism in this era are only starting to be explored. For example, the history of civil marriage and divorce—two of Zelaya's main achievements—remains to be written.

Women's Rights and Autonomous Feminism
After Zelaya and Before Somoza

Despite the support Liberals as a group gave to the struggle for women's political rights, individual Liberal men had mixed feelings about women's participation in politics. Max Jerez, for instance, writer for the Liberal León newspaper *El 93* (named after the year Zelaya came to power), explained in a 1916 editorial that, even though his newspaper supported female suffrage, he and his colleagues did not think it appropriate for women to participate in political rallies or clubs *until* they were indeed able to vote:

> Without a law [which gives the Nicaraguan woman political rights], we do not understand her need to organize in clubs and attend the meetings held in the public plazas. If she had the right to vote, all those feminine organizations would be fine. . . .
>
> As long as she does not have political rights, as long as she is not a citizen, the Nicaraguan woman must not jump into the arena where the parties struggle.[56]

Most important perhaps, Max Jerez felt that women's participation in politics was unnecessary: "The men who form the great Liberal Party do not need the healthy example of woman to be patriots; nor does Liberalism need the collectivity of women to be respected."[57]

The mixed messages expressed by Liberals like Jerez contributed to the delay of the franchise for women, who, as he notes, were widely organized in clubs and prosuffrage female associations. Nevertheless, these ambivalent Liberals did not completely succeed in their efforts to prevent women (both feminist and nonfeminist) from participating in formal politics. In 1917, a group of Liberals "criticized their leaders for preventing women from voting in party elections."[58] Most likely encouraged by the support received by men such as these, women slowly began to be directly involved in politics. Although women could not yet officially vote in national elections, in 1921, suffragist María Cristina Zapata (1898–1970) was elected as Chinandega's delegate to the Nationalist Liberal Party Convention.[59]

In addition to participating—albeit minimally—in the PLN, women were part of the state's bureaucratic apparatus. When Toledo de Aguerri became general director of public instruction (education) in 1924, she was part of the first group of Nicaraguan women to officially enter the world of government. Before her, in 1922, poet María Selva Escoto de Ibarra, known also as "Aura Rostand" and the sister of poet Salomon de la Selva, had been the first Nicaraguan woman to be named consul to the United States.[60] And, in 1924, the feminist Juanita Molina de Fromen (1893–1934), Toledo de Aguerri's friend, was named "vice minister of education"—"the first cabinet post ever offered to a woman in a Latin American country at that time," according to Molina's husband, Gunnar Fromen,[61]—a post she declined. The appointment was significant in two other respects: it was a unique example of Conservative support for women's rights, and it was made by a Conservative who called himself a "feminist," President Bartolome Martínez.[62]

Also during this period, Toledo de Aguerri founded Nicaragua's first feminist journals: *Revista femenina ilustrada* in 1918, which she edited for more than a decade, and *Mujer nicaragüense* in 1929. Feminist journals and organizations flourished during the 1920s and 1930s, many of them influenced directly by the feminist activism taking place in other Latin American countries, the United States, and Europe.

During the interwar period, Josefa Toledo de Aguerri organized middle-class women into philanthropic women's clubs modeled after those in the United States. These Clubs de Señoras de la Capital, according to Nicaraguan teacher Edelberto Torres (1898–1994), "were able to take bourgeois women away from . . . bridge . . . [and redirect their attention toward] making human life more valuable."[63] Toledo de Aguerri was also involved in the Pan American Roundtable (Mesa Redonda Panamericana), an organization founded in Texas in 1915, and one that many Nicaraguan suffragists would join. The goal of this organization was "to provide mutual knowledge, understanding, and friendship among the peoples of the Western Hemisphere."[64]

Nicaraguan feminists had personal contacts with foreign feminists and traveled widely. Toledo de Aguerri visited feminists in Cuba and the United States in 1920, meeting personally with the suffragist Amelia Maiben de Ostolaza in Havana.[65] Toledo de Aguerri also had contacts with Spanish feminists, who urged her, in 1933, to form a Nicaraguan chapter of the International League of Iberian and Hispanic American Women (LIMDI y Cruzada).[66] Founded by the Mexican feminist Elena Arizmendi, LIMDI sponsored public lectures on women's history, cultural events, and social projects. In Managua, it created the Working-women's Cultural Center in 1936.[67]

International ties generally served to legitimize and strengthen the work of Nicaragua's feminist organizations. In 1918, for example, Toledo de Aguerri's position as president of the Nicaraguan chapter of the Union of Pan-American Women (Unión de Mujeres Panamericanas) helped her to gather statistics and speak authoritatively on a pressing problem that was a national embarrassment—Nicaragua's extremely high infant mortality rate.[68] Her participation in an international organization widely publicized the extent and severity of the problem, thus increasing the chances for a solution.

Two Nicaraguan women would attend the April 20, 1922, meeting of the Panamerican Conference on women that took place in Baltimore: Juanita Molina and María Clotilde Vega. Vega was the official delegate from Nicaragua and Molina was the secretary of the Nicaraguan delegation. The meeting was sponsored by the League of Women Voters in the United States; its topic was the overall well-being of women and children.[69]

Another organization directed by Toledo de Aguerri was the Unión de Mujeres Americanas (UMA), founded originally in 1935 in New York; the Nicaraguan chapter was created in 1939. Similar to the Clubs de Señoras, UMA fostered middle-class women's cultural expression and sponsored literary contests, among its other activities.[70] Unlike other, more militant and socialist-influenced women's associations of the 1930s and 1940s, UMA was able to survive the Somoza years and still exists in the twenty-first century. Not surprisingly, its president in the late 1990s was one of Toledo de Aguerri's former students."[71]

Knowing which women were involved in twentieth-century associations is crucial to understanding the history of women in Nicaragua. Names are potential gold mines, for they allow us to piece together the class, occupational, political, and regional backgrounds of female activists. Moreover, they enable us to understand the links between family, class, and politics in Nicaragua. The latter subject has been addressed by Carlos Vilas, who argues that "social class exists above all as a network of

families in a particular region and as interrelated lineage structures. . . .
The extended family, with its far-reaching system of loyalties and interests, is a typical actor in stages prior to urban, industrial capitalism, and
one of the foundations of Nicaragua's social structure and political system until today."[72] Thus a study examining the ties between members
of women's organizations and Nicaragua's ruling families (the Gurdián,
Icaza, Vijil, Terán, Cuadra, Chamorro, Cardenal, Lacayo, and Pellas families, among others) would add significantly to our understanding of
the relationship between lineage, feminism, and Somocista politics in
Nicaragua.[73]

Another highly active suffragist during the 1920s and early 1930s, particularly in the international arena, was Juanita Molina de Fromen (fig. 1).
A brilliant young woman, Molina held bachelor's and master's degrees
from Columbia University and completed over half the coursework
toward a doctorate there. Fully bilingual, she taught at Hunter College for
a few years before working with the New York City public school system
until her untimely death in 1934.[74] Appointed by Liberal President José
María Moncada (1929–32), Molina de Fromen served as educational
adviser to the Nicaraguan government from March through August 1930.[75]

Moncada had also named her the official Nicaraguan delegate to the
meeting of the Inter-American Commission of Women (IACW or CIM
in Spanish) that took place in Havana in February 1930.[76] The commission had been created two years earlier at the Sixth International Conference of American States, which also took place in Havana.[77] The
IACW, which "operated as an autonomous body" within the Organization of American States (OAS) from 1928 to 1938,[78] emphasized building
bridges between Latin American feminists and coalitions between U.S.
and Latin American feminists; it described itself as "the first governmental organization in the world to be founded for the express purpose of
working for the rights of women."[79]

Many of the members of the IACW were also members of the
Women's International League for Peace and Freedom (WILPF), originally founded in 1915. The league had taken a strong stance against the
U.S. occupation of Nicaragua during the 1920s.[80] There was a WILPF
chapter in Nicaragua, although little is known about its members.

Like many others, Juanita Molina de Fromen had opposed the presence
of U.S. Marines in Nicaragua. Nonetheless, she maintained a friendship
with presidents Moncada (1929–32) and Juan Bautista Sacasa (1933–
36).[81] Both Moncada and Sacasa were elected in U.S.–supervised elections. It was under Sacasa, who took office in January 1933 as the Marines
were leaving Nicaragua, that Anastasio Somoza García, the head of the

National Guard left in place by the Marines, killed the nationalist patriot Augusto C. Sandino, from whom the Sandinista National Liberation Front took its name.

Juanita had hoped to attend the Montevideo conference of the IACW in November 1933 but was unable to do so for lack of funding.[82] Nonetheless, she and her husband, Gunnar, carefully prepared the documentation on the status of women in Nicaragua to be presented at the conference. Juanita and Gunnar would work closely with Doris Stevens, chair of the IACW, and the National Woman's Party, headquartered in Washington, D.C., until Juanita's death in 1934. In the early 1930s, Molina de Fromen was also in contact with U.S. suffragist Alice Paul, as was another Nicaraguan suffragist, María A. Gámez, daughter of the famous historian José Dolores Gámez Guzmán (1851–1918). María Gámez also corresponded with Stevens, who was well aware of Gámez's feminist activism in Nicaragua.

The history of Nicaragua's independent feminist organizations during this period and of its women's organizations in general still needs to be documented. Hardly anything is known, for example, about the Nicaraguan Feminist League or the Nicaraguan chapter of WILPF. We do know, however, that women's activism in Nicaragua during the early twentieth century caught the attention of foreign visitors. During his 1926 stay in Central America, U.S. traveler Wallace Thompson noted that, throughout the area, there had been an effort "to organize the women and to move to secure them broader legal rights and in connection with this, even the vote."[83]

Conclusion

In the nineteenth century, Nicaraguan Liberals, influenced by the rhetoric of the Enlightenment, sought to grant women limited rights. As a result, nineteenth- and early twentieth-century feminists—women like Josefa Toledo de Aguerri and Juanita Molina de Fromen—felt an affinity for Liberalism. That affinity however, would not translate into feminists' unconditional support of the Nationalist Liberal Party. To the contrary, feminists greatly valued the independent nature of women's mobilization. The turn toward partisanship in the 1940s and 1950s described in chapter 2 would signal the demise of first-wave feminism as well as its erasure from Nicaraguan popular memory.

T W O

FROM FEMINISM TO PARTISAN SUFFRAGIST POLITICS

Turning to the period from the 1930s to the 1950s, this chapter examines suffragist efforts, the divisions within the suffragist movement, and the eventual dominance of partisan politics in the larger Nicaraguan women's movement. In addition to covering the last political battles of Josefa Toledo de Aguerri, Juanita Molina de Fromen, and María Gámez, the chapter documents the activism of Nicaragua's second generation of suffragists, focusing on the discourse used by three separate—yet often overlapping—groups of women: the Central Women's Committee (Comité Central Femenino), Conservative suffragists, and Liberal suffragists.

The Central Women's Committee was made up of nonpartisan feminists as well as women from the Liberal and Conservative Parties who came together to push for the vote and for feminist legal changes such as rape law reform. Conservative suffragists were also organized in the Women's Propaganda Committee within the Conservative Party, which sought to bring down the Somoza regime through women's votes. Liberal suffragists, on the other hand, sought to maintain the Somozas in power through participation in the Ala Femenina, the Women's Wing of the Nationalist Liberal Party, thus rewarding the party that had a long-standing promise to grant them the vote.

The Struggle for Suffrage in the 1930s:
Josefa Toledo de Aguerri's Last Public Battle

Female suffrage captured Nicaraguans' attention in a way no other issue did. In the twentieth century, it was as divisive a topic as it had been in the nineteenth. Feminists, of course, were the ones most interested in obtaining the vote for women. And Liberals listened to and applauded feminists' calls for suffrage when the Liberal Party returned to power under the presidency of José María Moncada (1929–32).

Juanita Molina de Fromen and her husband, attorney and suffragist Gunnar Fromen, considered Liberal President Moncada a friend, and they had high hopes for the passage of a constitutional amendment granting women suffrage during his administration. "Great news from Nicaragua!" Molina de Fromen would write in her March 21, 1930, letter to Alice Paul, a leading U.S. suffragist and founder of the National Woman's Party:

> On the 19th, Mr. Fromen and I were received by . . . General . . . Moncada . . . and were informed . . . that he has submitted to the Chamber of Deputies and the Senate here a proposal to amend the Constitution . . . to the effect that the VOTE BE GRANTED TO ALL WOMEN WHO CAN READ AND WRITE.
>
> . . . President Moncada is a man of unusual foresight and greatly interested in the welfare of the Nicaraguan women, realizing that this amendment to the Constitution, if passed by Congress, will mean the regeneration of our women since new ambitions and possibilities will enter into their lives.[1]

Molina de Fromen wanted Paul and other feminist leaders in the United States to write letters of support to Moncada "and also to the Presidents of the Senate and the Chamber of Deputies, asking them to pass the said amendment."[2] Unfortunately, we do not know whether Paul and others did so, nor the details of President Moncada's efforts on behalf of women's suffrage. What we do know, of course, is that these efforts failed.

Molina de Fromen returned to the United States in August 1930 and continued to be active in Nicaraguan feminist politics from New York for four more years, until her death at the age of forty-one. Other feminists continued to be active in Nicaragua, trying to obtain suffrage in time for the November 1932 presidential elections.

According to the *New York Times*, Clark Howell Woodward, the U.S. admiral in charge of supervising the November 1932 presidential and congressional elections in Nicaragua "in a letter . . . to Señora María A. Gomez, a feminist leader in Managua, announced that while he was in sympathy with her proposal that women [be] permitted to vote he could not accede to her request that they be allowed to do so in the November elections. He advised Señora Gomez to present the project of permitting women's suffrage to the next Congress."[3]

María Gámez was not to be stopped by Woodward's refusal to intervene in Nicaraguan politics on behalf of suffragists. Feminists had the support of Deputy Ildefonso Palma Martínez, who had already introduced his "Bill in favor of the vote for women in Nicaragua" in Congress in late June 1932, a few months before Woodward's announcement. The proposed law stated that "the right to vote belongs to Nicaraguans, men and women twenty-one years old or older; those who are eighteen can also vote, if they are married or know how to read and write."[4] Had it been adopted, the law would have granted women the vote as early as 1933, too late for the 1932 U.S.–supervised elections, but in time for the municipal elections soon after that and the presidential elections in the mid-1930s.[5]

Given the political climate, Gámez was not very optimistic about the suffrage bill's chances in 1932, even though it had the support of quite a few deputies.[6] When indeed it failed to pass, Gámez and Palma Martínez simply waited a few months and tried again in 1933, under the new president.

One of the politicians supporting female suffrage during this period was Rodolfo Espinosa R., who in an August 1932 speech had commented that "nothing would be more just . . . than to see the Nicaraguan woman deciding with her vote the national destinies in the 1936 election."[7] Espinosa would go on to become vice president under Juan Bautista Sacasa and would again express his support for women's suffrage in December 1933.

In early January 1933, soon after Liberal President Sacasa had taken office, Ildefonso Palma Martínez presented his bill to Congress for a second time.[8] It was defeated in the Chamber of Deputies by a vote of twenty to three.[9] Possibly in response to the defeat, in 1933, Angélica Balladares de Argüello, president of the Nicaraguan Feminist League, published a pamphlet in support of women's suffrage: *Feminist Decalogue, i.e., Ideals and Work Programs That the Nicaraguan Feminist League Seeks to Realize*.[10] The league continued to work for women's suffrage throughout the 1930s, albeit to no avail.

Electoral politics in Nicaragua during this period were complicated by the U.S. occupation, which lasted until January 1933. In María Gámez's June 17, 1932, letter to Doris Stevens, she was already critical of the U.S.

Marines' position on suffrage—limiting the vote, as before, to "males over twenty-one, or over eighteen if married or able to read and write."[11] She confided to Stevens that the electoral law drafted by Army Brigadier General Frank McCoy in preparation for the 1928 election was inherently flawed. Gámez argued there was nothing in Nicaragua's constitution that prohibited women from voting; that McCoy chose to ignore this was, in Gámez's words, "inexcusable in an American, given the degree of culture North Americans have regarding women's rights."[12] María Gámez's criticism of McCoy as someone who should have known better, given women's right to vote in the United States and the supposed U.S. support for women's rights abroad, was literally lost in translation. Doris Stevens read a watered-down version that stated simply that McCoy's actions were "inexcusable for a man of North America in connection with the rights of women."[13]

The electoral law Gámez refers to was one that the U.S. Marines had "pushed the Nicaraguan congress to pass" in advance of the U.S.–supervised presidential election of November 1928.[14] According to Carleton Beals, a U.S. American journalist writing in Nicaragua at the time, McCoy had the "unlimited support of all the powers that be in the United States." "The McCoy Law," as it came to be called in Nicaragua, "became a sort of Holy Bible in which no one could dot the i's or cross the t's. This man became Moses on Nicaragua's Mount Sinai with his Ten Commandments. His law had to be passed even if Hell froze over. Nothing that might happen in Nicaragua could make him change his program even one iota."[15] McCoy could have encouraged women to vote in Nicaragua in 1928 but, like Woodward in 1932, was unwilling to do so. The U.S. refusal to support women's suffrage in Nicaraguan elections thus had a concrete and detrimental effect on women's rights.

In contrast to the occupation of Nicaragua, according to Ellen DuBois and Lauren Derby, U.S. occupation of the Dominican Republic from 1916 to 1924 "brought a model of modern womanhood that was emancipatory for many women even though it was a foreign imposition."[16] DuBois and Derby link the presence of the U.S. Marines there to industrialization and urbanization, and, in turn, to a key characteristic of "the modern woman"—her entry into the workforce. The same could not be said for Nicaragua.

It is true that many associated "modern" Nicaraguan womanhood with U.S. imperialism and sought to prevent women (for the most part, elite women since they were the ones who could most afford it) from smoking, playing sports, and wearing makeup.[17] On the other hand, as Michel Gobat notes, "the transformation of elite femininity troubled [primarily] a small . . . group of oligarchs."[18] Moreover, many in Nicaragua (feminists as well as nonfeminists) seemed well aware of the contradictions in both "modernity" and U.S. military intervention, as evidenced in Gámez's criticism of McCoy. Indeed, unlike women in the Dominican Republic, Nicaraguan women would not enter the workforce in large numbers until years after the U.S. occupation, and this would be associated not with U.S. intervention but with Somocismo, a key point I address in chapter 6.

María Gámez's correspondence with Doris Stevens both reveals a great deal about feminist politics in Nicaragua under U.S. occupation and demonstrates the importance of international ties for first-wave feminist identity. It is here that we learn crucial details about individual Nicaraguan feminists. For instance, despite strong support from elite male politicians, Gámez claimed she stood alone as a feminist: "I may be the only one in Nicaragua," she wrote Stevens in her June 17, 1932, letter, "but you can count on me in everything that deals with the rights of women and making them effective."[19] Future research may tell us more about Gámez's relationship with Josefa Toledo de Aguerri and Juanita Molina de Fromen and whether all three felt equally isolated. Alternatively, we might learn that saying she might be Nicaragua's "only" feminist was only an attempt to enhance Gámez's status in the eyes of foreign feminists.

We do know that Gámez and Toledo de Aguerri were friends and that Toledo considered both Gámez and María Cristina Zapata to be feminists of conviction. Indeed, Toledo de Aguerri noted in her writings that Gámez and Zapata had become increasingly engaged with feminist politics after 1919.[20] Gámez herself acknowledged her long-standing involvement in feminism when she wrote to Stevens that she had been a feminist for many years "without having obtained any satisfactory results."[21] Gámez had also been a contributor to Toledo's *Revista Femenina Ilustrada* as early as 1920, the same year Toledo wrote an editorial entitled "What Is Feminism?"[22] Where, then, was Toledo de Aguerri in 1932, when Gámez wrote she might be the only feminist in Nicaragua? Could perhaps Toledo, then sixty-six, have temporarily retreated from politics in the aftermath of her daughter's 1930 death from tuberculosis, while she sought to raise her granddaughter as her own?[23]

Juanita Molina de Fromen tried to deal with complicated illnesses and raising a family in the early 1930s before finally committing suicide in 1934. Unfortunately, we do not know whether she and María Gámez (who died within ten years of Molina) were friends. We do know, however, that Molina de Fromen was largely unaware of the history of feminism in Nicaragua, writing in her March 21, 1930 letter to Alice Paul that

President Moncada's actions of behalf of women's suffrage took place even though "the women of Nicaragua have not even asked for the right to vote."[24] Future research may reveal exactly how and where Molina became a feminist, if not in Nicaragua under the tutelage of Toledo de Aguerri.

Despite defeats in 1930, 1932, and 1933, the mid-1930s were a particularly hopeful period for feminists. In 1936, the newly installed Somoza administration seemed particularly receptive to feminist concerns. Anastasio Somoza García's wife, Salvadora Debayle de Somoza (fig. 2), belonged to many women's organizations. She and her family were also personally acquainted with Josefa Toledo de Aguerri, the most famous feminist of the period. The first lady's father, the medical doctor Luis H. Debayle (1865–1938; fig. 3), had shared a strong friendship with Toledo de Aguerri based on their mutual devotion to the arts and their service to the poor.[25] Perhaps due to this long-standing friendship, feminists received encouragement from the extended Somoza family even before Somoza García's ascent to power. In October 1933, Nicaragua's acting ambassador to the United States, medical doctor Luis Manuel Debayle (the son of Luis H. Debayle), gave a speech to a group of National Woman's Party (NWP) members at their headquarters in Washington, D.C.[26] This was the same organization that Juanita Molina de Fromen was involved with; she had, in fact, also given a speech to the NWP around the same time.[27]

Luis Manuel Debayle, Anastasio Somoza García's brother-in-law, was familiar with the feminist arguments for women's suffrage in his country. He summarized them as follows: "The Feminists in Nicaragua claim that, inasmuch as the Constitution does not mention sex as a qualification or hindrance to citizenship and its prerogatives, the custom that has excluded women from the vote and, in general, from the right to hold office, has no fundamental basis."[28]

Perhaps as a public relations ploy, or perhaps because he genuinely believed in the feminists' proposal, Debayle praised the work of both the National Woman's Party and the Inter-American Commission of Women, calling it "splendid." He went on to say: "The country that has not given its women the opportunities afforded to its men advances very slowly towards the goal of the perfect state, and the hope of every nation lies in its recognition of this fact." Debayle also stated that, in Nicaragua in 1933, "all professions are open to women except that of the law. We have our women pharmacists, teachers and doctors upon whom we look with pride, and we find more and more girls each year seeking education as a weapon for facing life rather than, as formerly, waiting for marriage to solve their problems."[29]

Statements like these confirm what Juanita Molina de Fromen and María Gámez had claimed, namely, that some individuals in the Nicaraguan government were aware of feminists' demands and open to their suggestions in the early 1930s. Most important, the awareness and openness continued throughout the decade. Luis Manuel Debayle, for instance, continued his involvement with the National Woman's Party throughout the 1930s.[30]

In 1937, a few years after Debayle's speech, Toledo de Aguerri was the keynote speaker at a cultural event organized in honor of Salvadora Debayle de Somoza. Since doña Salvadorita, as the first lady was called, was the honorary president of LIMDI y Cruzada, one of the many feminist organizations Toledo participated in, the keynote address was appropriately about feminism.[31]

In her presentation, Toledo de Aguerri carefully explained LIMDI y Cruzada's feminist objectives:

> 1st—To create schools . . . [including] technical schools, so that women can support themselves, [and] literacy schools for peasant women, who make up the majority of the country.
>
> 2nd—The social and political liberation of woman. Practical schooling in the social and political duties of citizenship, for without a voice and a vote [women] cannot offer their social and political cooperation.
>
> 3rd—National autonomy. We inherited from our ancestors a Nation [Patria] we must conserve and defend.
>
> 4th—[To foster] Intellectual Culture through conferences on the Sciences, the Arts, and Literature, to give woman a greater understanding, so as to demand from her greater responsibility.[32]

Two years later, in 1939, Somoza García drafted a new and controversial constitution. Its most radical article proclaimed that the Nicaraguan state had no official religion. In retaliation, the Catholic Church excommunicated several members of Congress including Guillermo Sevilla Sacasa, a main supporter of the new article and Somoza's future son-in-law.[33] Believing the climate was ripe for feminist change, Toledo de Aguerri was involved in presenting yet another petition to Nicaragua's Constitutional Assembly on February 23, 1939, urging the Somoza government to make good on its promise, and to grant women suffrage: The Nicaraguan woman "hopes with confidence that the President of the Republic, General A. Somoza, will fulfill the promise he made in his Governing Program [Programa de Gobierno]. He understands that one must govern with the acquiescence of the entire country, not only with a certain part of it."[34]

In this suffrage drive, feminists used different tactics from those they had used in the 1893 campaign, knowing the highest levels of government were well aware of their goals and thinking they had considerable support within the seemingly radical Somocista regime. If, during the nineteenth century, men tended to speak for women, this certainly was not the case in 1939. In the "Feminist Petition to the Constitutional [Assembly] Demanding Woman's Rights as Citizen of the Republic," drafted by Toledo de Aguerri, women spoke quite forcefully on their own behalf:

> In the name of justice and reason we, a group of Nicaraguan women, have come as representatives of the country's women, to ask that you faithfully interpret our way of thinking and feeling with regards to our rights as citizens of the Republic. . . .
> We ask that the Nicaraguan woman [have] the right to:
> a.—"the same political treatment as man."
> b.—"the enjoyment of equality in civil matters."
> c.—"the widest opportunities and protection in the workplace," and
> d.—"the greatest protection as mothers."
>
> THESE DEMANDS ARE MADE BY
> the poor woman . . . the middle-class woman . . . the intellectual and wealthy woman.[35]

Many independent feminist groups and organizations were involved in preparing this petition and Toledo de Aguerri belonged to almost all of them. Among the organizations were LIMDI y Cruzada, the Nicaraguan chapter of the Women's International League for Peace and Freedom (WILPF), the First Pan-American Women's Education League, the Inter-American Commission of Women, a group of teachers, and the Working-women's Cultural Center.[36]

This women's rights campaign was so important that the *New York Times* reported even its planning stage in 1938.[37] It was after the campaign's failed attempt at winning the vote for women in 1939 that Josefa Toledo de Aguerri started to be displaced by a new generation of women's rights activists who identified themselves primarily as suffragists. This second generation of suffragists included many of Toledo's former students. Unlike their teacher, however, the former pupils tended to be fiercely partisan. This characteristic would radically change the face of women's activism, facilitating the emergence of the Somocista women's movement in the 1950s.

The Defeat of Women's Suffrage in the 1930s

On the one hand, the U.S. occupation of Nicaragua worked to postpone securing the vote for women in the late 1920s and early 1930s. Unable to defeat Augusto Sandino's army, and concerned both about antiwar sentiment back in the United States and about holding a smooth election in Nicaragua given the devastating effects of the ongoing guerrilla war, the Depression, and the 1931 Managua earthquake, the U.S. Marines were more interested in ending their occupation than in enabling Nicaraguan women to vote.

On the other hand, the conflict between secular Liberalism and Catholicism also had a negative effect on efforts to achieve women's suffrage. The Catholic Church actively organized women during the 1930s and 1940s in groups such as the Young Catholic Workers (Juventud Obrera Católica).[38] Since the Church was allied with the Conservative Party, Liberals feared that the majority of women, if given a chance, would vote for Conservative candidates. That was exactly the rationale Guillermo Sevilla Sacasa (fig. 4), an anticlerical Liberal delegate to the Constitutional Assembly, gave for his antisuffrage vote in 1939. Although he conceded that feminists had a long history of independent activism, he believed that most women would be manipulated by their confessors into voting against their own interests. As Sevilla Sacasa explained to the assembly,

> The feminist current is felt everywhere. It races, throbs . . . throughout the Universe. . . . As I . . . contemplate the panorama offered by the Nicaraguan population . . . I see that a group of brave women rises proudly above the general feminine mass. . . . Any one of these women is . . . worth more than a hundred men . . . and could exercise suffrage better . . . than most men. . . .
> [B]ut unfortunately . . . the Nicaraguan woman, in general terms . . . is not fit [capacitada] to vote. . . . She is not fit precisely because our woman lacks philosophical and religious independence. . . . [O]ur woman becomes transformed and loses all independence when she kneels before a priest in the Confession booth, or when she . . . listens to the words of a Bishop. . . . A Minister of the Church . . . can do what he wants at that moment with our woman.[39]

According to journalist Ignacio Briones, Sevilla Sacasa was so opposed to giving women the vote that he ordered his fellow delegates to ignore feminist protests outside Congress. Briones claims that, expecting feminists to continue their protests, Somocista Liberals, in league with "Conservative accomplices" of the regime, formed groups "of fanatics that were in charge of ridiculing and even insulting the women suffragists. In that infamous task, they arrived at the sidewalk in front of the Escuela Normal de Señoritas [the school Toledo de Aguerri administered] with posters asking the young women if they would rather have been born men. And they branded them 'dykes' [marimachas]."[40]

Whether most Nicaraguan women would have voted for Conservative candidates had they been able to vote in 1939 is impossible to tell, although it appears that the Conservative Party believed exactly that and thus had supported this particular campaign for the vote.[41] What is clear is that Liberals believed they had nothing to win by giving women the vote at the time, even though the Liberal Party had just ratified support for female suffrage in January of that same year during their convention in León.[42]

The example of Mexico, where large numbers of proclerical women were organized in the Feminine Idealist Party (Partido Idealista Femenino), might have given Nicaraguan Liberals pause. There Liberals were convinced that giving women the vote would mean a return to a Catholic state.[43] Finally, even though socialists and Communists played no prominent role in Nicaragua during the 1920s and 1930s, given the propensity of some Nicaraguan Liberals to believe that women could be easily manipulated by male politicians, the ties some feminists had to socialism might have made them uncomfortable and uneasy about female suffrage.[44]

Nicaraguan suffragists themselves had something to say about the role that Catholicism played in their political decisions. Attorney Amelia Borge de Sotomayor confirms in her 1953 Juris Doctorate thesis that the Catholic Church did attempt to exert strong political pressure on women and that, indeed, Conservatives were interested in the female vote because they knew the clergy held a great deal of power over some women.[45] But Borge felt that Liberals and Conservatives had underestimated Nicaraguan women's ability to think for themselves. To prove her point, she describes events that took place in the city of León in early 1953.

The Spanish Dominican priest Felipe Muñoz, a newcomer in León, found out that a chapter of the Pan American Roundtable existed in the city and decided to go after its members in his sermons. According to Borge de Sotomayor, Muñoz called members "Masons and doubters . . . threatened them with excommunication . . . and warned them that those who belonged to the Roundtable could not join the associations of his church, La Merced." Borge recounts that roundtable members were angry and wanted to respond publicly in the press, but they decided instead to remain silent. At that point, three members out of fifty-four decided to leave the organization. Borge de Sotomayor contends that, because so few women had heeded Muñoz's call, the Church decided to heighten its offensive: it proclaimed that there had been a Mason-sponsored attempt to assassinate Muñoz. In light of the accusation, two more members left the roundtable.[46]

Frustrated with these meager results, Muñoz decided to send each individual roundtable member a note, personally signed by him, that stated: "If in 48 hours of reading this note you do not formally renounce membership in the Roundtable, you will be left out of the association of Our Lady of Mercy and will be deprived of its spiritual benefits."[47]

After receiving the personalized notes, most of the remaining members were outraged and decided to reply to Muñoz at once. Borge de Sotomayor remembers that they did so respectfully but decisively. Their responses, which emphasized "the Pan-American ideal," put an end to the conflict. Although a total of ten women did terminate their membership in the Pan American Roundtable, according to Borge, two of them did so only in order to maintain "peace in the home," while five of them later sought to return to the organization.[48]

With this example, Borge de Sotomayor illustrated her point that "the Nicaraguan woman has won the battle [for suffrage], she simply needs to have her triumph be officially recognized."[49] In other words, Nicaraguan women had proven that they were not at the mercy of the Catholic Church and that they could think for themselves. Borge felt it was time for the Liberal Party to acknowledge that.

Constitutional Reforms

As María Gámez stated in 1932, and as Luis Manuel Debayle acknowledged in 1933, Nicaragua's early constitutions did not explicitly exclude women from voting. Presumably, there was no need to legally bar women from doing so, given the lack of support for female suffrage in the early nineteenth century. The 1826 Constitution simply noted: "Citizens are those natural or naturalized Nicaraguans who are married or over eighteen years of age, who have employment [oficio] or a profession to subsist from."[50] The 1838 Constitution added property as a requirement for citizenship, but made no mention of gender. The 1858 Constitution changed the marriage requirement to that of parenthood and added "good conduct" to the list of prerequisites, but still did not restrict women from voting. Neither did the 1893 Constitution, which instead stressed citizens' ability to read and write and marriage over parenthood and good conduct.[51] It was not until 1939 that the Constitution made reference to women in order to exclude them: "In terms of the active vote for woman, the law will determine when she can exercise suffrage; the votes of at least three-fourths of the members of the Legislative [Branch] are needed to dictate dispositions on this matter."[52] The 1948 Constitution was practically identical to the one drafted in 1939; changes were not made until 1950. The 1950 Constitution stated: "Citizens are those male and female Nicaraguans over the age of twenty-one and those over eighteen who can read and write or are married, and those under eighteen who have academic degrees."[53]

According to the 1950 Constitution, women could "be elected or named to public office, except for the cases explicitly noted in the Constitution"; they were prevented from voting by the following exclusionary clause, almost identical to the one in the 1939 Constitution: "Woman will exercise active suffrage according to the law drafted on the matter, [upon receiving] the votes of two-thirds of the totality of each Legislative Body [Cámara]."[54] Finally, on April 20, 1955, the constitutional reform making women's suffrage a reality became law.[55]

The Struggle for Suffrage in the 1940s and 1950s: A New Generation Takes Over

Little is known about the closed-door negotiations between Liberals and Conservatives that led women to obtain the right to vote in 1955, under Anastasio Somoza García's administration. We do know, however, that in 1944 the Liberal Party once again declared its support for women's suffrage.[56] Then, in 1945, Deputy Roberto González, a Liberal who had distanced himself from the Somozas, "presented a bill in the Chamber of Deputies to grant women [the] equal right with men to vote in national and local elections."[57] Somocista Liberals defeated the bill, arguing once again that it was not yet the right moment to grant women the vote and that women's dignity could be placed in jeopardy if they were able to vote. In fact, Liberals argued, they were voting against women's suffrage as a sign of "respect toward women and the home."[58]

Although the 1945 bill was defeated and two of Nicaragua's most important feminists, Juanita Molina de Fromen and María Gámez, had died,[59] women's suffrage continued to be brought up as an issue in legislative sessions.[60] It would be brought up again in the 1948 and 1950 constitutional debates, with positive results only in the latter debate. According to the *New York Times,* the 1950 Constitution was "criticized by leading Nicaraguan women inasmuch as suffrage rights would not be exercised until [the elections of] 1964. Some women [petitioned] Congress for reconsideration of the article and immediate suffrage."[61]

Attorney Joaquina Vega presented before Congress the "Exposition in Favor of the Vote for the Nicaraguan Woman" in 1950. On behalf of the Central Women's Committee and the Nicaraguan Feminist League, Vega demanded that the Nicaraguan government follow through on the public commitment it had made to granting women the vote:

> [Nicaragua] is internationally committed [to the vote]. Article 55 of the United Nations' Letter signed by Nicaragua's Representative in San Francisco obligates [the country] not to discriminate on the basis of sex in human activities.
>
> The Ninth Conference of American States celebrated in Bogotá imposes on Nicaragua, as a signing nation of that Treaty, the obligation to make legal reform, granting civil and political rights to Woman.[62]

One new characteristic in the suffragists' 1950 demands was a link they made between suffrage and reforms in the penal code regarding rape, a response to the wave of sexual violence against girls that had recently received a great deal of attention in the local press.[63] As things stood until 1992, under Nicaraguan law, rape was a private matter and could only be prosecuted if a victim, guardian, or eyewitness formally reported the crime to the police. Moreover, the law encouraged survivors to resolve rape cases privately and marry their rapists. This became a common solution to the rape of single women and girls by their boyfriends or acquaintances. Another option was for the victim to accept payment from her rapist.[64] What follows is the argument feminists made for suffrage as a means to change the rape laws:

> [The Nicaraguan w]oman needs the active vote, not only to participate in presidential elections in which even a man's vote, under certain circumstances, is sometimes a myth, but also to be able to participate in the National Congress . . . to be able to make her voice heard and request, on her own, laws to protect her dignity. On a daily basis, the newspapers reflect the crimes that are committed

against her, allowed by her physical weakness . . . the crime that should be a public crime cannot be prosecuted automatically [*de oficio*]. Instead, its punishment is left to private vengeance, as in barbaric times. The illogical consequence is that in some cases the victim's parents, perhaps due to poverty or to low morals, extend their hands to accept a disgusting payment and the crime is punished thus.[65]

Women's petitions did not bring about a change in the rape laws or immediate suffrage in 1950, but two small victories were won. First, the Conservative Party decided to publicly support women's suffrage at the time.[66] And, second, "a resolution was approved that would permit Congress, by a two-thirds majority vote, to extend the franchise to women when it saw fit."[67] This resolution replaced the previous one, which required that women wait until the 1964 elections to vote. With bipartisan support, suffrage was only five years away.

Although feminists had only recently expressed strong concern over the existing rape laws, they had stressed the moralizing potential of giving women the vote as early as the 1930s. María Gámez, for instance, felt that women needed to have a greater input in Nicaragua's political life because men had "lost all notion of democracy,"[68] and were dedicated to "the vice of liquor."[69] In fact, the bill presented by Deputy Ildefonso Palma Martínez to Congress in 1933, a bill presumably drafted (at least in part) by Gámez herself, stated the following: "We should give women the opportunity to intervene in everything man has managed for over a century without great benefit to the Republic; perhaps her interference will be of more benefit and will bring us some severe lessons in moral politics."[70] In a note sent to Doris Stevens with a copy of the bill, Gámez added, "I repeat that these countries will not be able to advance much in their material and moral progress without the moralizing influence of woman."[71] The moral potential of the vote would be one that some suffragists would look forward to for decades to come.

The New Suffragists

Although we know little about what Anastasio Somoza García and Emiliano Chamorro Vargas said in the private talks that led to the 1950 "Pact of the Generals" and the constitutional reforms that paved the way for suffrage in 1955, we do know that nonpartisan feminists of Josefa Toledo de Aguerri's generation were not the only suffragists. Even as the nonpartisan Central Women's Committee presented its 1950 Pro-Vote Exposition to Congress, Liberal and Conservative women, some of them members of the committee, actively lobbied their parties to grant them immediate suffrage in 1950, instead of waiting until 1964, the date originally proposed by the government. Although feminists, Liberal suffragists, and Conservative suffragists all had women's suffrage as their goal, each group's discourse differed slightly from the others', as did its rationale for suffrage.

Conservative women organized the Women's Propaganda Committee within the Conservative Party in 1950. The committee president was Ninfa Aburto, the vice president Margarita Cole Zavala, the secretary Clementina Vivas, the assistant secretary Socorro Mojíca, the treasurer Mariana Gámez de Estrada, the assistant treasurer Rosa Gutiérrez, and the representatives (*vocales*): Nelly Sequeira, Haydée de Chamorro, Carmen Martínez, Clarisa Martínez, and Zoila Torrentez.[72] Vice President Margarita Cole Zavala noted in a speech before Conservative women that she agreed with General Chamorro that

> today's woman is not destined to the home and the needle, we are active soldiers to fight side by side with our men. [We are] women soldiers of the homeland [*patria*] and the time to fight has arrived. We must fight for our rights, raise the spirits of the men, so that it will not be said that we women are only words and more words. If we are able to vote we must make sure our men vote for Emiliano Chamorro Benard [a Granada businessman and inexperienced politician chosen as the Conservative presidential candidate in 1950— not to be confused with General Emiliano Chamorro Vargas], for Liberal men and women say that during Conservative rule only illiteracy existed, but that was not the case. Today it is. . . . If you are poor and you are able to obtain a scholarship for your child they will take it away from you a few days later with the objective of balancing the Public Education budget.
>
> We must show our men . . . that we know more than how to be mothers, wives, sisters, and daughters. We also know how to represent our homeland, which is oppressed today and yearns to be free. . . .
>
> Let us fight, women, without fear of blows and being slapped [by our enemies]. . . . I have already received [blows] and many of us will receive them. Do not be afraid of the cold steel of the rifles. I have already had one against my chest when we fought to end Somoza's extended stay in power [*continuismo*].[73]

Cole Zavala believed the vote would help women defeat Somoza García: "Women are the decisive factor in many of the actions taken by men. Woman made possible the fall of the tyrant Jorge Ubico, and in another period, she helped bring down the other tyrant Maximiliano Hernández Martínez in El Salvador. All Nicaraguans have been suffering for seventeen years under Somoza . . . while [he] enjoys and exploits Nicaragua as his private hacienda."[74]

Cole Zavala also believed the vote would bring honesty to politics: "We women have been denied the vote because we cannot be bought like merchandise. . . . Our votes cannot be bought. We will vote honestly for Nicaragua. The time has arrived; we women must march on Managua and conquer our liberties by any means possible."[75] Saturnina Guillén, a Conservative journalist who signed the feminist petition for suffrage presented by attorney Joaquina Vega in 1950, was as adamant as Margarita Cole Zavala in her support for the vote, and she, too, believed women would bring morals to politics:

It was only four months ago that Señor General Anastasio Somoza García [fig. 5], among the thousand promises he made, publicly recognized the Nicaraguan woman's right to vote. We thought he would respect the treaties signed with the United Nations. . . .

Why can't [the Nicaraguan] woman vote when she scores more points than many voting men in morality, honesty . . . and culture? Why is there fear regarding women's suffrage?

No one will believe in the sincerity of the legislators when they state that "a period of preparation is necessary in order to establish a level of culture [among women voters]." Why do they not have these doubts about men? Is it not sad and shameful that they speak this way, those who receive the votes of men who are barely able to scribble their names on paper . . . ?

Now, I ask myself, who needs preparation [to vote]? who will be prepared . . . ? In what school will we take that class . . . ?

We will conquer the vote because the time has come and we will obtain it in spite of the stumbling blocks put in our path. And the day we throw our weight on the electoral scale, on that day worthy and honest men will achieve power. They will build a free homeland.[76]

Guillén was also critical of the lack of support for women's suffrage exhibited by both parties: "We need to hear in the parliamentary discussions the voice of General Emiliano Chamorro defending our rights . . .

we also want to know if the government will comply with its sacred international obligations and not allow the Nicaraguan woman to be scorned."[77]

Conservative women as a group sought to achieve two concrete objectives through the vote: to bring down the Somoza regime and to infuse morality into politics. Rosa Gutiérrez, a Conservative leader, noted in a 1950 speech imbued with maternalist rhetoric that Conservative women "continue the political struggle against the dictatorship to save their husbands, children, siblings and parents."[78] Saturnina Guillén, like Cole Zavala, stressed that, with the vote, "the feminine element would be a bulwark of administrative honesty. Bars and gambling houses, which have enriched only a few, and perverted minors, would disappear."[79]

The high hopes Conservative women had for women's suffrage disappeared over the years as they saw women's votes help legitimize the regime and make it easier for the Somozas to engage in behavior many of them deemed immoral. By 1966, the relatively docile Women's Conservative Front had replaced the militantly radical Women's Propaganda Committee.[80] Not until 1977, with the creation of AMPRONAC (Association of Nicaraguan Women Confronting the Nation's Problems), would some Conservative women become part of a more radical women's organization. Conservative women's political choices were indeed limited throughout most of the dictatorship since the Conservative Party often collaborated and would share power with the Somozas' Nationalist Liberal Party before the revolution of 1979.[81]

Predictably, Somocista Liberal suffragists had an opposite view of the vote from the one held by Conservative women. The only commonality the two groups shared was their fierce commitment to partisan politics. Liberal suffragists wanted to be able to vote for Luis Somoza Debayle, a man who was highly supportive of his party's female members (figs. 6 and 7). One Liberal woman noted in a 1957 speech: "All Nicaraguan women should vote for Luis Somoza Debayle, standard-bearer for the humble, peace of mind for the poor, hope for the meek and mild hearted. We only wish . . . the good of the homeland and the happiness of the people. The entire Nicaraguan past is filled with General Somoza. His son Luis will fill the future."[82] This type of rhetoric was echoed in Liberal rallies throughout Nicaragua.

Also present in Liberal women's speeches was the subject of justice, interpreted as the ability to vote for the Somozas. Matilde Haydée Díaz wrote in 1957: "We are going to vote for the first time! We are going to exercise for the first time the female vote in the free elections of 1957 . . . ! A star that shines permanently in the consciousness of men guides us: Justice."[83] Generally lacking from Liberal suffragist discourse was the emphasis on morality present in the Conservative and feminist discourse.

Although nonpartisan feminists shared with Conservative women a belief that the female vote would bring morals to politics, they also saw themselves as a third force in politics, one that would bring about feminist legislative change to empower women. The 1950 Pro-Vote Exposition stated: "It is sad to see our realities face to face; our traditions need a substantial reform in which the law elevates and backs Woman, given the lack of Moral respect that no longer exists. It is only with the exercise of the Vote that we will bring this into effect because it will be our right in action, which we will possess to oppose the State."[84]

Feminists also used the language of justice in lobbying for the vote, but were careful not to mention the overthrow of the Somoza government as an explicit objective: "The female Vote cannot be postponed for all women in the different positions they find themselves in because all [of them] struggle as much as men . . . in life's travails. The female Vote will let us structure a purified democracy and a humanist social justice . . . destroying selfishness ensures the harmonizing of contradictory interests and [leads us] toward an equilibrium organized without discrimination."[85]

Given their partisan differences, it is no surprise that suffragists were divided over tactics and personalities in the 1950s. According to *La Prensa* reporters, a heated argument took place in public between suffragists María Teresa Sánchez (1918–1994; a Liberal poet who would later become an anti-Somocista), Margarita Cole Zavala (a Conservative), and Joaquina Vega (a Liberal) in 1950.[86] Sánchez and Cole Zavala wanted General Emiliano Chamorro to be the one to read the suffragists' proposal before the assembly; Vega had another delegate in mind for the task.[87] María Teresa Sánchez accused Vega of being "absolutist" in her governing style and her five-year-long tenure as president of the Central Women's Committee. Vega responded by saying that Sánchez had not been a consistent member of the feminist organization, whereas she herself was simply interested in obtaining the vote.[88] If, however, she had become an obstacle in the path toward that objective, Vega was willing to resign her post.[89] Suffragists were eventually able to work out their differences to present a united front before Congress, but to no avail. Suffrage was still seven years away, and the suffragist movement would disband once the vote was obtained.

There appears to have been an additional conflict among those women who supported the vote, one that Liberal attorney Amelia Borge de Sotomayor refers to in her 1953 thesis. Although she would eventually become a key figure in the pro-Somoza Ala Femenina, two years before women gained the vote, Borge de Sotomayor believed that women needed to organize and join the Women's Party (Partido Femenino) in order to truly reach "absolute human rights." Moreover, she wrote, "I do not believe in the ladies' commissions that are at the Congress to witness the debates over the female suffrage bill, when we all know, including the deputies presenting the bill, that [the vote] will not be obtained until women, becoming interested in the subject and seriously organizing ourselves, demonstrate that we are worthy of the exercise that we demand."[90]

Suffragists were inevitably divided over what tactics to use to achieve the vote. On the one hand, there was the question of what type of suffragist organization was better suited for the task: independent or partisan. On the other hand, there was the question of what type of support to go after: male politicians', women's, or nonelite men's. The second question was one that feminists had debated at least since the early 1930s. In their correspondence, María Gámez and Doris Stevens considered it, with Stevens suggesting that Nicaraguan feminists follow the U.S. model and try to gain the support of male politicians. Nicaraguan feminists tried all sorts of tactics, with mixed results in the short term.

According to Francisco Obando Somarriba, an independent Liberal and a critic of the Somoza regime, part of the problem during the 1950 Constitutional Assembly was that none of the delegates wanted to present the feminist proposal for suffrage before the assembly. In the end, Alcibíades Enríquez agreed to read the suffragists' exposition, which was greeted with much ridicule by his colleagues. Josefa Toledo de Aguerri was present in the assembly that day, and upon hearing the delegates' reaction to the petition for suffrage, supposedly left the room in tears.[91]

Before concluding this chapter, let us briefly consider the views of others who have a different understanding of the events I just described. Historian Antonio Esgueva, for one, argues that it was the Conservatives, and not the Liberals, who wanted to grant women suffrage in the twentieth century. In a rather brief 1997 article, Esgueva writes,

> From the year 1938 onward, the Conservatives brought to the negotiating table a concern for female suffrage, a subject that did not please Somoza—according to Dr. Alvarez Montalbán—because the feminine element would be controlled from the Confession booth by the priests, who were Conservatives by tradition. . . .
>
> In the Pact of the Generals [signed in 1950 by Anastasio Somoza García and the Conservative caudillo Emiliano Chamorro], the

Conservatives once again went to battle demanding that "the ability of woman to elect and be elected" be among the basic principles of the Constitution to be promulgated that same year.[92]

Unfortunately, Esgueva does not develop his argument any further, making it difficult to incorporate into the history of women's suffrage in Nicaragua.

In 2008, Teresa Cobo del Arco also put forth the idea that twentieth-century Conservatives were often more interested in giving the vote to women than the Liberals. Specifically, she noted that, in 1950, Somocista Liberals were the ones who defeated the suffrage bill, making Conservative caudillo Emiliano Chamorro declare that the Conservative Party would have to take over the cause of women's suffrage.[93] Cobo del Arco further noted that, in 1953, it was a Conservative deputy, Juan Munguía Novoa, who introduced a bill in Congress to make women's suffrage a reality. Somocista Liberals once again defeated the bill, arguing that the time was still not ripe for Nicaraguan women to become full citizens, although they would soon change their minds.[94]

Cobo del Arco suggests that the Liberal failure to grant women the vote before 1955 contradicts the propaganda put forth by the Somozas from the 1950s on, namely, that the Liberal Party never swayed in its support for women's suffrage. She is right to draw attention to the Somozas' rewriting of history: they co-opted Nicaraguan feminism and, in the process, took all credit for women's suffrage, a credit they did not deserve—a point I first made over a decade ago, in 1996.[95]

The argument that Liberals were divided over women's suffrage for almost a century is also one I first made many years ago and one that I continue to make in this book. Indeed, I have always argued that the mixed feelings Liberals as a group had about women in politics delayed women's suffrage. Moreover, I have also held that women themselves played an important role in the process of co-opting Nicaraguan feminism and erasing first-wave feminism from Nicaragua's collective memory, a point Cobo del Arco echoes.

Undoubtedly, Liberals were concerned over the role the clergy would play in women's political choices, a concern that delayed women's enfranchisement. This point is neither new nor controversial. I have made it myself and documented it in detail.

Where I disagree with Esgueva and Cobo del Arco is in their assessment of what motivated Conservative politicians to support women's suffrage. In my opinion, the motive of these elite Conservative men was practical, not ideological: their belief that women would overwhelmingly

vote for Conservative candidates. In the case of Liberal suffrage supporters, however, their motive was both practical and ideological.

That women's suffrage took as long as it did to become a reality in
Nicaragua is not surprising to me. What historians, including myself,
have been unable to uncover, however, are the exact reasons why (beyond
the embarrassment of international pressure) Anastasio Somoza García
finally decided to enact women's suffrage in 1955, rather than wait until
1964. This question has yet to be answered in the growing field of Somocista studies.

Journalist Ignacio Briones adds an interesting perspective to this discussion. He argues that Fascist Conservative intellectuals who collaborated with the Somozas in the 1930s played a role in Liberals' delayed
support for women's suffrage. Briones writes that "these intellectuals
provided political support for Somoza [García] and in their minds there
was no possibility of recognizing a single right for women. They all said
that voting was an offense to feminine virtues."[96] This is certainly a topic
that deserves further attention, for it might help explain the internal
dynamics of the Liberal Party in relation to women's right to vote.

Conclusion

The vote mattered not only to nonpartisan feminists but also to women
of different political persuasions. Moreover, *when* the vote was won, *how*
it was won, *who* fought to win it, and *what* happened after it was won matter in the history of feminism in Nicaragua. When suffragists embraced
partisan politics, the stage was set for the demise of first-wave feminism
and the emergence of a Somocista women's movement.

Nonpartisan feminists' hopes of opposing the state with women's
votes were dashed in the aftermath of women's suffrage. A collaborative
relationship with the state would quickly dominate the women's movement. Ironically, the struggle for suffrage provided Liberal women an
arena in which to learn some of the skills they would use between 1955
and 1979 to mobilize women on behalf of the Somoza regime.

T H R E E

THE AFTERMATH OF WOMEN'S SUFFRAGE

Although the Somozas maintained themselves in power through a dictatorship, they held periodic elections, which had great symbolic value for Somocistas despite their fraudulent nature. These elections were especially important for the women supporters of the regime, who first cast their votes in a national election on February 2, 1957, four months after Anastasio Somoza García was assassinated by the revolutionary poet Rigoberto López Pérez.

Not many Nicaraguans voted in 1957, but Liberal women did so in large numbers (fig. 8), helping to elect Somoza García's eldest son, Luis Somoza Debayle.[1] The *New York Times* reported that the turnout for electoral registration, held in November 1956, was "very heavy, with women voters registering for the first time in Nicaraguan history."[2] These Somocista women were mobilized by the Women's Wing (Ala Femenina) of the Nationalist Liberal Party (PLN), a women's organization that differed radically from feminist groups in structure and goals. Unlike the independent feminist organizations Josefa Toledo de Aguerri belonged to, the Ala Femenina was directly subordinated to the hierarchy of the male-dominated PLN, a party over which Ala members did not have much control. Moreover, the Ala's primary focus was the well-being of the party; women's issues (however loosely defined) always took second place.

Co-founded in 1955 by Olga Núñez de Saballos (1920–1971), Nicaragua's first woman attorney, the Ala Femenina played a central role in upholding the dictatorship and erasing feminism from the Nicaraguan imagination. The Ala helped garner women's votes for the Somozas from the late 1950s throughout the mid-1970s. It focused primarily on the presidential elections of 1957, 1963, 1967, and 1974, giving the regime a credibility it sorely lacked. It also helped the Liberal Party establish a new way of dealing with women as political actors in society (figs. 9 and 10).

Created to deal with women's suffrage, a new factor in party politics, the Ala was designed to meet the needs of both the Liberal Party and Nicaragua's first numerically significant generation of university-educated Liberal women. On the one hand, it displaced previously independent (mostly feminist) women's organizations, allowing the party to exercise direct control over Liberal women, who were now potential voters. On the other hand, it opened up for Liberal women a sanctioned—albeit limited—political space in which to maneuver and become involved in electoral politics as voters. Significantly, the PLN popularized the creation of "women's wings" within other male-dominated parties in Nicaragua as well. The pattern—common elsewhere in the world—became well established during the dictatorship and continues to this day.[3]

Over time, the Ala served to link women's political and economic participation in Somocismo. It came to include both working- and middle-class urban women, most of whom were recruited at their workplaces. The Ala became an exclusively female populist clientelistic network in which some women participated with pride and others with chagrin. The percentage of women who joined under duress is hard to know; nonetheless, in anti-Somocistas' recollections, it was quite high.

Most Nicaraguans today do not know that women's suffrage was enacted in 1955 or that women were finally allowed to vote in 1957. This is not surprising: for all those who opposed the dictatorship—Conservatives, anti-Somoza Liberals, and Sandinistas alike—the fraudulent elections were simply not newsworthy. The Conservative anti-Somoza newspaper La Prensa, for example, hardly mentioned women's suffrage at all in 1955. This silence, of course, has to be understood in the context of extreme repression and censorship of the press, which made it difficult to report on controversial topics.

This chapter documents some of the problems that evolved in the aftermath of women's suffrage. It deals extensively with how the Somozas manipulated elections and intimidated the population into voting for them. It traces the way in which Somocista Liberalism eclipsed feminist struggles for women's rights, making feminism invisible to future generations.

And it deals directly with the most important organization in the Somocista women's movement, the Ala Femenina, focusing on the Ala's organizational structure, electoral work, and role in creating a Somocista populism through a nationwide client-broker-patron network of women.

The Importance of Voting for Somoza

Elections under the Somozas served as both commemorative events and rituals intended to calm "anxiety about change or political events, eliminate citizen indifference toward official concerns, promote exemplary patterns of citizen behavior, and stress citizen duties over rights."[4] Through language and ceremony, they helped establish authority and legitimated the Somozas' "right to rule."[5]

William Beezley, Cheryl Martin, and William French argue that "successful rulers throughout history have understood that their dominion rests on much more than force alone. Persuasion, charisma, habit, and presentations of virtue serve as familiar techniques and exhibitions of authority. In particular, those in power have grasped the crucial importance of public ritual in symbolizing and constantly recreating hegemony. . . . [C]eremonies . . . may . . . mask social divisions by seeming to unite disparate groups in shared ritual, and provide opportunities for popular revelry that may defuse the potentially disruptive impulses of subordinate groups."[6]

Elections brought together Somocista men and women of different social classes in celebration. For Somocistas, voting for the Nationalist Liberal Party was the ultimate expression of citizenship in a country without an electoral tradition or a tradition of popular democracy. Moreover, voting reinforced the Somozas' clientelistic version of citizenship, one that required Nicaraguans to "reiterate and reaffirm" the regime's hegemony on a regular basis.[7] I find Mary Kay Vaughan's interpretation of hegemony quite useful in my analysis of the Somoza dictatorship:

> Hegemony, in Gramscian terms, means rule by consensus. Coercion may precede consensus and continue to be an aspect of state power, but hegemony rests on moral and intellectual persuasion. It embraces an ensemble of symbols, images, and visions of the past and the future that take hold among social subjects to shape identity, memory, loyalty, and meaning, and to energize action. These ideological elements cannot simply be disseminated from the top by elites commanding institutions such as schools, clubs, and political

parties. Rather, the hegemonic discourse emanating from the . . . state . . . result[s] from the interactive processes involving multiple social groups and interweaving a multiplicity of discourses.[8]

Vaughan's conclusions regarding patriotic festivals in Mexico are also relevant to the study of Somocista elections. She highlights the festivals' mobilizing character, arguing that the patriotic festival must be seen as "a channel for articulating hegemony" rather than merely as a way for the state to impose itself on the population.[9] And, indeed, in their role as "channels for articulating hegemony," Somocista elections served to mobilize the population and strengthen Somocista populist culture.

The Intricacies of Voting in a Dictatorship

Voting under the Somozas also affected the relationships between individual men and women. When, for instance, thirty-three-year-old Mercedes Rivera voted for the first time in 1957, her lover, Ignacio Moncada, cracked her skull with a spike (*perno*). Rivera in turn denounced Moncada to the police.[10]

Cases like Rivera's, however, were rare. One of the most common reactions to the 1957 election was confusion, among men and women alike. One woman wrote to *La Prensa*:

> Dear Director,
> I registered . . . in the proper precinct and electoral table. I had no special reason not to do it, and I was told that registering to vote was obligatory, although voting itself would not be.
> But now I hear different opinions. Some say that all those who registered are obligated to deposit their votes in the ballot boxes; others say we are not required to do so. Some say that we must choose between one of the two registered parties, the Liberal [Party] and the so-called Nicaraguan Conservative Party. Others say that a citizen who has another candidate in mind can write in the name of that candidate on the ballot. Yet others maintain that there is no such obligation to vote.
> In short, Director, there is some confusion and one doesn't know for sure what to do to remain within the law, without forcing one's feelings one way or another. If I were a Liberal, I would not have a problem; but the fact is that I am a Conservative and some names on the green ballot [the Conservative Party's color] I cannot accept.[11]

Although the letter's author appears to express a genuine and justifiable confusion, she also appears to be using her position as a newcomer in electoral politics to criticize the Somozas' Conservative allies. This case represented a new development in Nicaraguan history. Suffrage allowed women to critique the political system from within.

In the end, not everyone who registered to vote actually cast a ballot on election day. Indeed, according to *La Prensa,* "in Granada precincts where 600 had registered to vote, only 120 or 100 citizens voted." Not surprisingly, most of those who voted did so for the Somozas.[12]

There were many irregularities in the 1957 election and they would persist up until 1979. These irregularities were no accident, however; they were deliberate electoral practices designed to ensure that the elections would always favor Somocista candidates.

One popular electoral practice during the dictatorship was to disregard the legal voting age. This worked especially well when an entire family went to the polls together. Dora Ubeda, for instance, a mestiza resident of a rural area in northern Nicaragua, recalls that she voted alongside her older siblings in the 1957 election, although she was only thirteen at the time.[13]

Another practice by Somocistas was to restrict access to the polls. Nemesio Hernández, an elderly member of the Matazano indigenous community of Matagalpa, recalls that, throughout the dictatorship, only the male workers of the coffee plantation where he worked were taken to the polls. Political parties did not organize the rural women of his area.[14]

A third electoral practice had to do with the public nature of the votes being cast. Although voting was officially secret by 1974, poll workers tended to be members of the Liberal Party, and they knew everyone's political persuasion. Somocistas thought this was perfectly fair. A precinct director explained in a 1974 article in *Novedades,* the Somozas' newspaper, how he knew who voted and how each person voted:

> I just read in the newspaper *La Prensa* . . . an account by William Ramírez in which he affirms that the votes cast last Sunday were not secret, which the writer deduces from a report I gave to a congenial Costa Rican female reporter on how many votes had been deposited in some precincts under my charge and how many of those votes were favorable to the PLN candidates. . . . I will explain to you how easy it was for me to know how many of the citizens who entered the precinct to vote cast their votes for the PLN. As you know, our Party in its magnificent organization has, as the first authority, a precinct club for each electoral precinct. Each club is

made up of five members each, all of them neighbors of the respective precinct. These members are assisted by five activists, and for the registration of voters and the election five additional activists are added. There are thus fifteen people in each precinct who know perfectly the residents of the precinct's jurisdiction.

In this way, and since the precincts under my charge are located in Las Brisas [a middle-class residential neighborhood in Managua], where each block is known by a letter, and each block is divided into homes that are perfectly numbered [a rarity in much of Nicaragua], I had my precinct clubs, assisted by their respective activists, conduct a complete and exact census of all the Liberal citizens in capacity of voting who lived in the five precincts in my care.

After each Sunday of voter registration a comparison was made between the lists made public by the Directories and the census, and I was able to verify that almost one hundred percent of those who claimed they were Liberals in the census had registered to vote.

On election day, I gave instructions so that members and activists of the precinct clubs would be present on the sidewalk in front of each electoral table with a copy of the census. They were to write down every Liberal who went in to vote, and every person who came out from voting and wasn't in the census.

In this way, it was very easy to know at any point how many citizens who had voted had done so most probably for the Liberal Party and how many perhaps had voted for the Conservative Party. I must tell you that once the count was made and the final electoral results were known, the number I had of Liberal voters was exact and the number of Conservative voters was wrong by a small margin. This I attribute to [the following:] some who did not appear in the census as Liberals (very few by the way) annulled their votes.[15]

Although, at least in theory, this precinct director was in favor of secret voting, some Somocistas were openly against it. Writing to Luis Somoza in 1962, Isidro Sequeira opposed the secret ballot for those who could not read or write: "I write to you in order to let you know what I think and that is that we should not accept the secret vote until there are no illiterates in Nicaragua because in the countryside is where they most exist and they are not aware of all the damage that the Conservative Party has done to Nicaragua. . . . [An alternative option] is for the secret vote to be only for those who know how to read and write and not for those who cannot sign their names."[16]

Yet another practice that tarnished elections under the Somozas was the pressure Somocistas exerted on Conservative voters to formally renounce their political affiliation. Letters of renunciation were common. One such letter read: "I, Nicolas Artola Zamora, legally an adult, married, a farmer, a resident of . . . in the Department of Managua, Nicaragua, by this means declare: That I have been a member of the Nationalist Conservative Party of Nicaragua; but I renounce my affiliation to that party and instead affiliate myself to the Nationalist Liberal Party for whose ideals I will fight with all my energies."[17]

A second letter stated:

> We, Eduardo Presentación Reyes Robles, single, a farmer, José Angel García Díaz, married, a farmer, Felix Pedro Mena Alemán and José Cupertino Mena Alemán, married, carpenters, legally adults, and from this neighborhood, hereby
>
> DECLARE
>
> That our political ideas have been CONSERVATIVE, and we have been members of the Conservative Party, but recognizing that the Nationalist Liberal Party, presided by the Supreme Chief [Jefe] . . . Anastasio Somoza García [has] great merits of quality, and stands for Progress, Peace, Work, and Liberty for citizens, from now on we RENOUNCE the party we have belonged to and with free will, solemnly PROMISE . . . to support the candidacy of General SOMOZA GARCIA . . . and cooperate in every way with the prosperity of our country [and] with the patriotic ideas brought to term by Nicaragua's Superman, Gen. Somoza.[18]

Two of the men whose names were affixed to the second letter were illiterate and could not sign their renunciation, evidence that Isidro Sequeira's concern over the political manipulation of illiterate citizens was well founded. But, at least in this case, it was the Liberal Party, and not the Conservative Party, that took advantage of the situation.

There were many other irregularities in Somocista elections. One had to do with the imposition of outside candidates on local communities, as happened in El Realejo, according to a letter sent to Anastasio Somoza Debayle in 1972:

> We wish to make you aware of the sad way in which Srta. Irma Guerrero Chavarría [a local Somocista *caudilla;* fig. 11] is treating us. She has cared little for the rights of a town, the stability of the Liberal Party in power and the prestige and good name of our

Nationalist Liberal Party's supreme chief [*jefe*] and abolished all the Liberals of historic Realejo who were to participate in the next February election. She put as mayoral candidate of this town an unknown woman named María Eugenia Romero, who lives in Corinto, and has not lived a single day in El Realejo, which violates Article 23 of the Organic Law of Municipalities.[19]

Members of the Liberal Party also complained that the same people kept running as local candidates, creating monopolies of power and dividing local Liberals. This was the case of La Concepción according to a letter sent to Luis Somoza in 1958, which noted:

> Five men, led by Sr. José María López M. have had their way against the general opinion. One of their worst mistakes has been to maintain, over many years, Sr. Rubén Gómez at the front of almost all public posts, among which we can name the following . . : Mayor, Substitute Mayor, Mayoral Secretary, Secretary to the Judge . . . Charities Treasurer, etc.; but said civil servant far from occupying that precious authority for the well-being . . . of the town has taken refuge in it to commit the most disastrous arbitrary actions, to the point where he maintains this humble town in the most desperate terror and fear.[20]

The most objectionable of all the electoral practices that took place under the Somozas are also the most well known: censorship of the press, the purchase of votes, the outright theft of elections, and violence against citizens. A standard practice under the Somozas, censorship was heightened in the months leading up to elections, as was the case in 1957, when the government censored the independent press.[21] Over all, the attacks against the non-Somocista media were vicious and inexcusable. Although the buying of votes is hard to document, the exchange of food and liquor in return for attending Liberal political rallies is not. According to party records, in 1958, one rally alone in the Department of Boaco cost 15,000 córdobas, a sum that included 2,000 córdobas designated specifically for liquor in the budget submitted by the organizers:

Transportation costs to bring party
members from the municipalities and
districts: C$1,000.00

Food for the party members who attend: C$6,000.00

Funds used by leaders . . . to bring people: C$2,000.00

Propaganda, fixing of streets, meeting place,
decorations, etc.:   C$1,000.00

Total: C$10,000.00

Note: We have not included the cost of liquor . . , which we nonetheless consider a necessity, to distribute *after* the rally. The cost is cal-
culated to be an additional *two thousand córdobas*. We have also not
included the cost of . . . the banquet or lunch or reception, etc. for
Delegates or prominent people who will be attending from other
departments, which we estimate will amount to an additional
C$3,000.00.

Summary:

Costs of the rally: C$10,000.00

Additional costs specified in the note: C$5,000.00
_____

Total: C$15,000.00[22]

The theft of elections was also a common practice under the dictatorship, although it was not always necessary, given the high rates of absten-
tion in Somocista elections. In the 1974 elections, the manipulation of
votes was especially obvious. According to Somocista statistics, of a total
population of 1,895,177 Nicaraguans, 1,152,268, or 60.8 percent of the
population, registered to vote. Of these, 799,992 actually voted: 733,662
voted for the Liberal Party and 66,330 voted against the Somozas. Political scientist George Bowdler notes that, according to the official record,
the number of registered voters exceeded the number of Nicaraguans
over the age of eighteen by 240,000.[23]

Violence against the population was also a trademark of the dictatorship. The act that merited perhaps the greatest condemnation was the
assassination of the anti-Somocista journalist Pedro Joaquín Chamorro
in 1978. But, surprisingly, Somocistas directed their violence or threats of
violence not only against Sandinista guerrillas, Sandinista supporters, and
anti-Somocistas like Chamorro. Somocista Liberals were also their targets.
In 1971, Iván Hernández, a political coordinator for the PLN wrote the following complaint in a telegram to president Anastasio Somoza Debayle:

I wish to inform you with all my respect that on Saturday the 13th of this month, the Political Coordinators Sra. Carmen Lara de Borgen [fig. 12] and Sr. Oscar Reyes Zelaya, with pistol in hand, struck terror among a number of residents of the Reparto José Somoza, Open Number 1 [a neighborhood of Managua], along with people who according to them were members of the office of National Security, to force them to register as members of the Liberal Social Action Movement. I inform you of this so that these coordinators [will] be punished, for all they do is create a division within . . . our glorious party.[24]

Liberal on Liberal violence of this type was the result of local power struggles within Somocismo. The threats of violence made by Lara de Borgen and Reyes Zelaya demonstrate one of the ways that particular versions of Somocismo were created and maintained. Carmen Lara de Borgen, a well-known political broker within the Somozas' patron-client system, actually ended up forming her own organization, one that focused on helping poor women through charity.[25]

The Ala Femenina and the Emergence of a Somocista Women's Movement

It is only against this backdrop of electoral fraud, political intimidation, and violence (in which women participated extensively) that we can understand the emergence of a Somocista women's movement and the role the Liberal Party's Ala Femenina played in Somocista politics. Although the Ala Femenina was not the only Liberal women's organization in Nicaragua between 1936 and 1979, it rose to prominence quite quickly, becoming the most visible and most powerful women's organization under the dictatorship. The Ala was the only Liberal women's group to dedicate itself exclusively to the political well-being of the party, the only mass Somocista women's organization, and the only association that organized women at their workplaces and in their neighborhoods. Moreover, it was the only women's organization to last more than twenty years and boast a membership of 6,000.[26]

Other organizations, such as the Association of Professional Liberal Women (UMPL; founded in 1969), had different agendas to follow; their goals tended to be professional, educational, charitable, or social in nature. According to its founder and former president, by 1979, UMPL had 2,000 members, 1,500 of them active, primarily licensed teachers and nurses but also attorneys, pharmacists, and medical doctors. Among their other activities, UMPL members gave out free medicine to poor peasants and provided free legal services for incarcerated women on behalf of the Liberal Party.[27]

Another popular organization in the postsuffrage period, founded in Managua in 1954, the Nicaraguan Association of University Women (ANMU) eventually affiliated with the International Federation of University Women (founded in 1919). Although ANMU was apolitical according to its statutes, its members tended to be Somocista women; in 1968, they included the following Ala leaders: attorney Esperanza Centeno Sequeira, Ofelia Padilla de Mesa, and attorney Amelia Borge de Sotomayor. Sequeira and Padilla were founding members of the organization. Like most other women's organizations of the period, membership was restricted. To join the ANMU, a woman needed not only to be college educated but also to have the support of two members. Moreover, former ANMU presidents remained highly involved in the organization as members of an advising council.[28]

Whereas organizations like the UMPL and ANMU attracted professional women who wanted to network and be involved in charitable and professional work, the Ala attracted middle- and working-class women more interested in participating in political activities such as voting and campaign rallies. The Ala was for women who wanted to be explicitly involved in political work. On the other hand, many women found themselves having to join the Ala in order to obtain or retain a job.

The Ala's Origins

As noted in chapter 2, some Ala leaders had been suffragist activists in the 1940s and early 1950s. Ala Femenina founders also had ties to Somocista youth groups. In fact, the Ala was originally called the "Ala Femenina de Juventud Liberal Nicaragüense."[29] According to Marta García (pseudonym), one of the younger founders of the Ala, some female members of the Juventud Liberal Nicaragüense (Nicaraguan Liberal Youth) had become too old for that organization. The creation of a partisan women's organization in 1954 was meant in part to resolve that problem.[30]

Indeed, women actively participated in Somocista youth groups and their leadership. This ensured that women would be represented at every level and that the groups would address women's issues. For instance, in a radio show sponsored by Juventud Liberal, women were given an opportunity to express their views in a segment entitled "The Nicaraguan Woman Speaks."[31]

Many of the women who participated in Juventud Liberal went on to participate in the Ala Femenina.[32] The experience they gained and the contacts they made in Juventud Liberal served them well in the years to come. On the other hand, the formation of the Ala met with the disapproval of Josefa Toledo de Aguerri for bringing partisan politics into the women's movement and with criticism from some Liberals for bringing women's issues into Liberal politics.

Alejandra Flores (pseudonym), Toledo de Aguerri's former student and a former Ala member critical of the association in the 1990s, told me that her teacher was disappointed with Olga Núñez de Saballos for making the Ala a partisan organization and that was why Toledo did not participate in it.[33] Another former Ala member and former student of hers, Maritza Zeledón (pseudonym), noted that Toledo de Aguerri's mid-twentieth-century feminist organizations included only a few women, most of whom were older. Because of the generation gap, it made sense to Zeledón that Toledo and her cohort were not directly involved in the Ala.[34] The conclusion of two other founding Ala members was similar. They saw Toledo de Aguerri as a role model, but felt she was too old to have been heavily involved in the suffragist movement of the 1950s. In their view, her age also prevented her from collaborating with the Ala.[35] Ironically, at the time I interviewed these former Ala members, they were almost as old as Toledo de Aguerri was in the 1950s, yet they did not consider their age an obstacle to their participation in politics.

In any case, it appears that an ambivalent relationship existed between Toledo de Aguerri and the members of the Ala. This ambivalence seemed evident in the September 1955 issue of the Ala magazine. The magazine included a two-page article by Toledo, "General Thoughts on Patriotism" (Divagaciones sobre patriotismo), an appropriate topic since the magazine was honoring Nicaraguan independence. Though, at first glance, Toledo de Aguerri's (presumably commissioned) article might have proven a desire to participate in the Ala, a closer look demonstrates that this was not the case. Indeed, the article was not commissioned; it was a reprint of a piece published in 1927, one with no commentary on contemporary events.[36]

Even at the beginning, Toledo de Aguerri appears to have had limited involvement in Ala events. In late September 1955, a group of predominantly Ala women gathered together to form the Nicaraguan chapter of the Central American Women's Athenaeum (Ateneo Femenino Centroamericano). Although this was exactly the sort of organization that Toledo de Aguerri liked to join, she did not attend the event, due to illness, according to the Ala magazine. It is also possible, however, that she simply wanted to avoid the company of Ala members, given the political disagreements she had with them.[37] On the other hand, that she was invited at all means that Toledo de Aguerri was not completely out of the Ala picture yet, even though she was already eighty-nine years old.

The relationship between Ala members and Toledo de Aguerri was certainly complicated. At certain points, Ala members embraced "doña Chepita" as a foremother, while at other points, they simply ignored the woman who had taught a great number of them their ABCs. Throughout the 1950s, even when she was embraced as a role model, Ala members placed Toledo de Aguerri's achievements in the distant past, even though she was still very much alive. Thus, in a 1955 *Ala Femenina* magazine article, Gladys Bonilla Muñoz wrote:

> Nicaragua, beautiful land of great lakes and volcanoes, as she has been called by poets, has on many occasions been chosen by destiny to be the birthing place of great genius; thus we have Rubén Darío, who revolutionized the Spanish language and a great woman, unadorned . . . like a violet, doña Josefa Toledo de Aguerri, guide and propeller of the nation's feminism, who has encouraged her compañeras in struggle.
>
> Her only goal has been to prepare woman, improve her social and economic standing. It is because of this that today's and tomorrow's youth owes recognition and admiration . . . to this dedicated lady [*señora*].
>
> Worthy ladies cooperated with her in that age, they had in common intelligence and the burning flame of feminism. Thus we have writers like doña María A. Gamez and María Cristina Zapata. . . . These prestigious ladies deserve the name of "Pioneers of National Feminism."[38]

Since the term "feminism" had negative as well as positive connotations throughout the twentieth century, it does not seem at all unreasonable that some Ala members wanted to distance themselves from Toledo de Aguerri and her generation of feminists. This became especially true in the 1960s and 1970s, when the term "feminism" came to be associated with radical cultural expressions of the feminist movement in the United States, like the burning of bras. Politics, however, was the main reason why Ala women played down their ties to doña Chepita. They wanted to prove that their interest in women's issues took nothing away from their primary commitment to the Liberal Party. According to my Somocista informants, this commitment was perfectly understood by Luis Somoza, but not by everyone else. Marta García claims that, to damage the Ala's reputation, other Liberal women accused its members of being feminists (i.e., lesbians and heterosexual women who hated men): "We had many enemies. One woman said to us, 'This [Somocismo] is not [supposed to be] about feminism. It is about Liberalism.'" Accusations such as this one made it hard for her to identify with an abstract international feminist label. In her defense, García offered her own definition of feminism, which ironically was very similar to the one Toledo de Aguerri used: "We felt very feminist: we were defenders of [the Nicaraguan] woman and wanted her to be integrated [into politics and society]."[39]

The connection individual Ala members had to feminism varied widely. The founding members of the Ala, according to the September 1955 *Ala Femenina* magazine, included, among others, Olga Núñez de Saballos, Mary Coco Maltez de Callejas, Esperanza Centeno Sequeira, Lucrecia Noguera Carazo, Amelia Borge de Sotomayor, Zaida Fernandez de Ruiz, Gloria Zeledón, Clementina Arcia, Evelina Mayorga, Ofelia Padilla, and Gladys Bonilla Muñoz. Within this group, those who had witnessed the struggle for suffrage and had perhaps participated in it appear to have had a uniquely complicated relationship with feminism. Amelia Borge de Sotomayor, in particular, appears to have had a long-standing commitment to both Somocismo and her own right-wing version of feminism.

In her 1953 Juris Doctorate thesis, Borge had offered a fairly standard definition of feminism: "the movement that tends to achieve the just improvement of woman's condition in a society."[40] Her commitment to this ideal lasted from the early 1950s, when she wrote her thesis, through the mid-1970s. In 1955, she gave a lecture on the history of feminism at the Liberal Party Headquarters (Casa del Partido Liberal).[41] In 1975, she was chosen as one of the official Nicaraguan delegates to the World Conference on Women held in Mexico City during International Women's Year.[42] A year later, she continued to work on women's rights and attended the Hemispheric Conference for Women held in August 1976 in Miami, Florida.[43] She then served a two-year term as vice president of the Inter-American Commission of Women (IACW) from 1976 through 1978.[44]

We do not know whether Borge de Sotomayor, whom I was unable to interview, still called herself a "feminist" after the mid-1950s, nor whether she was an active suffragist before 1953, nor how she understood the relationship between her commitment to women's rights and her support for the Somozas. What we do know is that she came from a Liberal military family. She suffered from ill health and died a few years ago.

Another Ala leader who appears to have had a complicated political path is Olga Núñez de Saballos. In 1945, she became Nicaragua's first woman lawyer. Like those of attorneys Amelia Borge de Sotomayor in 1953 and Modesto Armijo in 1912, her Juris Doctorate thesis was on the topic of women's rights. In the 1957 elections, Núñez won a victory for all Somocista women when she was elected Nicaragua's first woman deputy in Congress, a position she held until her death from a heart attack in 1971, at the age of fifty-one. She also held a wide variety of other governmental positions. From 1950 through 1956, before being elected to Congress, she served as vice minister of education, the post offered to Juanita Molina de Fromen decades earlier. Like Molina and Borge, she was also active in the Inter-American Commission of Women. And like Molina, Núñez also studied in the United States. She studied English at Bucknell University, obtained a master's degree in international relations from American University, and took additional courses at Johns Hopkins University.

Núñez's curriculum vitae paints a picture of exemplary Liberal womanhood, the sort of picture that was promoted by friends and relatives after her death. Journalist Ignacio Briones, however, presents information that complicates that portrayal. He claims that, in 1957, two years after the founding of the Ala Femenina, Núñez de Saballos wrote a letter to Luis Somoza Debayle "in which she noted the dangers to the nation's peace and to the permanency of Liberalism in power if he became president. The Constitutionalist movement [a Liberal movement opposed to Anastasio Somoza Debayle] was born out of that letter." According to Briones: "Olga stated in her letter that 'the democratization of the PLN depended on having no more Somozas become President.' For these words, she was accused of being a 'Communist.' Some of her colleagues, among them Lucrecia Noguera Carazo, were also accused of being Communists."[45] If what Briones contends is true, then indeed the history of the Ala Femenina is more complex than what my research has revealed. This possibility is worth pursuing in depth at a later time. Given that what Briones contends was not mentioned by any of my informants, however, I will assume for now that it might not have taken place quite in the manner he says it did.

The Ala and Somocista Populism:
Building a Nationwide Client-Broker-Patron Network

Unlike other Managua-based political organizations, the Ala Femenina had representatives on Nicaragua's Pacific and Atlantic Coasts. Friendships between Ala members in the country's different provinces (*departamentos*) cut across regional divides, fostering solidarity among Somocista women. By building an urban, state-sponsored nationwide network of women, the Ala helped forge important—yet hierarchical—links between the various geographical regions in Nicaragua.

In part, the Ala's success was due to its member recruitment tactics and organizational structure. Its inner-circle members tended to be middle-class professionals handpicked by the organization's leaders. Former Ala member Antonia Rodríguez (pseudonym), for instance, recalls that Olga Núñez de Saballos, an Ala co-founder, personally invited her to attend Ala meetings. Rodríguez, a professional, was recruited in the mid-1960s, soon after she arrived in Managua from her hometown in central Nicaragua. To be invited to join such a prestigious organization was an honor for Rodríguez, who had tired of the limits that her small town placed on professional middle-class women.[46] Ala membership gave her the respect she sought as a woman, a professional, and a Liberal.

In the Ala Femenina, Rodríguez found a ready-made set of friends, mentors, and colleagues. Through the Ala, she was able to insert herself into a clientelistic system as a broker. The connections she made in the organization have lasted her a lifetime, helping her (and her friends, relatives, and "clients") obtain employment and other material benefits. The Ala helped Rodríguez adjust to life in the capital, incorporating her directly into the center of Liberal political life; through it, Rodríguez came to be personally acquainted with dozens of high-level female and male politicians who could help her and her clients out in times of need. Like other Ala members, Rodríguez attended, co-planned, and co-organized Ala meetings and pro-Somoza rallies. Rodríguez provided the Managua Ala office with her insider's knowledge of central Nicaraguan politics, thus helping the organization devise campaign strategies appropriate for the region.[47]

Through personal communication and frequent interaction between friends, the Ala forged a nationwide grassroots network of Somocista women. Because the interdependence among those members who participated voluntarily ultimately rested on friendship, shared experiences as professionals or workingwomen, a shared commitment to the Nationalist Liberal Party, and membership in a patron-client system, Ala solidarity remained high throughout most of its existence. Central to the Ala's success, however, was its organizational structure, its firmly established pyramid of command, which fostered efficiency and helped boost its members' morale.

At the highest level of the pyramid were the president of the republic and the Nationalist Liberal Party chair. The second level was made up of the Ala's National Board of Directors (Directiva Nacional), which comprised a president, vice president, secretary, treasurer, and representatives (*vocales*) from the different provinces.[48] Directly below the National Board of Directors were the Ala regional chapters in each of Nicaragua's sixteen provinces; and, below them, the 134 county-level (*municipio*) Ala affiliates. Finally, at the bottom of the pyramid were the Liberal Women Committees in electoral districts (*cantones*) throughout the nation.[49]

Although elections were held within the Ala, the highest posts of the National Board tended to be for life. For most of the organization's existence, attorney Olga Núñez de Saballos served as president, teacher Mary Coco Maltez de Callejas (fig. 13) as vice president, journalist Lucrecia Noguera Carazo as secretary, and attorney Esperanza Centeno Sequeira as treasurer. The Ala also had a permanent legal counselor, attorney Amelia Borge de Sotomayor.[50] After Núñez de Saballos died unexpectedly from a heart attack in 1971, rivalries rocked the Ala, according to some of my informants. One Ala leader told me that after thinking it over, she decided not to contest Mary Coco Maltez de Callejas's position as leader in the aftermath of Núñez's death: "I was not going to become Mary Coco's rival." In the end, my informant kept working with the Ala and remained friends with Maltez.

In the 1960s, the Ala received funds from the Liberal Party through Pablo Renner, the party chair. "We never managed money," Marta García told me. "The party gave us the money we needed but we had to ask for it." Since Ala members were volunteers, the money was used to buy food—mainly sandwiches and drinks—for working-class people attending the pro-Somoza rallies, although sometimes it was given as an inducement to attend. T-shirts, buttons, banners, and bandanas were also commonly given out.[51] Surprisingly, the Ala's National Board did not have its own office; members tended to gather at Núñez de Saballos's home, at the Military Casino, or at the Liberal Party's headquarters.[52] Moreover, since most Ala leaders did not know how to drive, they had to hire drivers and borrow vehicles from family members, friends, or the Liberal Party in order to attend rallies and other political events.[53]

Like the Somoza regime, the Ala was hierarchical, undemocratic, and authoritarian. And also like the Somoza regime, the Ala leadership was accused of imposing official candidates on local communities and bribing voters.[54] Through their participation in the Ala, women learned the ins and outs of hierarchical, rather than democratic, politics. Although Ala leaders incorporated working-class women as well as women from regions outside the capital into their pyramid of command, only urban middle-class professional members participated in national decision making. In short, the Ala reinforced a class hierarchy among women both within its own structure and within society at large. It stressed the importance of local identities for its own gain, even as it helped bolster the political and bureaucratic primacy of the capital.

The Ala network helped create a clientelistic Somocista populism. Unlike others interpreting the regime, historian Jeffrey L. Gould contends that "the Somozas [up until the 1960s] created a populist political style that combined an anti-oligarchic discourse with appeals to the working masses. . . . Workers and peasants largely accepted the Somozas' variant of populism and its corresponding rules of the game, but, at the same time, they shaped and transformed Somocista populism."[55]

Building on Gould's analysis, my research leads me to postulate that the Somozas made a strong appeal for support to Nicaragua's women. They backed women's suffrage, women's political participation within Liberalism, and women's participation in the labor force in exchange for women's political support. Moreover, they attempted to control the rules of the game through co-optation and appropriation.

Like workers, however, Liberal women as a group were also able to "shape and transform" Somocismo and make it their own, especially after suffrage was obtained in 1955. They did so through their participation in clientelistic networks, which constituted the basis for the Somocista populism created by urban women after 1955. The Ala was very useful in incorporating middle- and working-class women into a client-broker-patron network. Poor women became the clients of middle-class Ala women, who in turn functioned as brokers for the regime. How this process worked can be seen clearly in a letter written to Luis Somoza in 1957 by Sandy Johnson (pseudonym), a politically astute Ala leader from Bluefields:

> Greeting you cordially, I direct this letter to you with the objective of suggesting the political convenience of giving each one of our female constituents . . . a blanket, an object that lasts a while as will the memory [of the gift]. . . .
>
>   I am aware that you sent, in your name, provisions for poor families, which will be given away after the election. I want the blankets only for the women in my charge . . . with them we will hold a rally with great political effect.[56]

At this point, I should discuss in greater depth what I mean by "populism" and what I see as the relationship between urban women, populism, and clientelism under Somocismo. Borrowing from Alan Knight,

I define "populism" as a political style that "implies a close bond between political leaders and led."[57] Although I do not believe populism is necessarily an urban phenomenon, rural women were largely excluded from participating in the versions of Somocista populism that I studied.

With regard to urban women organized *as* women, two distinct populist periods can be discerned: before the vote, when women in feminist organizations were able to play an independent role in politics; and after the vote, when feminists were replaced by the Ala, and Liberal women helped create a semi-institutionalized populism. Here again, I am borrowing from Knight, who argues that "populism . . . has a limited shelf life; and, over time, tends either to lose momentum and fail or, in a few cases, to undergo 'routinisation,' whereby the initial populist surge is eventually diverted into more durable, institutional (and 'mediated') channels."[58] The Ala was a "durable, institutional, and mediated channel" that came into existence as Somocista populism fluctuated and changed in the mid-1950s.

I do not see the reliance on clientelism as a diversion from or a corruption of populism, nor do I see populism and clientelism either as inherently evil systems of mass manipulation or as uncomplicated systems that necessarily meet the needs of "the people."[59] What I am arguing is that, through clientelism, Somocista women who worked outside the home were able to forge a Somocista identity that was both political and economic, based on the Liberal ideals of freedom and unity. Indeed, through clientelism, Somocista women such as Sandy Johnson gained an unprecedented amount of power and leverage within the dictatorship. Rocío Cruz (pseudonym), a market vendor in her late thirties, summarized that Liberal legacy during an interview I conducted with her in 2000. Cruz inherited her Liberalism from her mother and their workplace, the Mercado Oriental in Managua, which at the turn of the century boasted more than 20,000 female vendors: "I was practically born in the market. My mother brought me here six days after I was born. . . . Liberalism for me is freedom, unity. There is a sisterhood [*hermandad*] that I myself have experienced. We are always united [*estamos unidas siempre*]. Freedom [means that] we say what we feel."[60]

Somocista working-class women took the right to say what they felt and to state their economic needs directly to the Somozas seriously. They used their long-standing participation in Somocismo, most often demonstrated by a leadership position in their local Ala committee, to request a hearing with the highest power in the land, someone who in turn would meet some of their material needs. In a January 1957 letter to Luis Somoza, Clara Benavides (pseudonym), a working-class vendor and local Ala leader in Managua, followed this proven formula by stating:

On the 17th of this month I made a solemn proclamation in your honor for the period 1957–1963 without any help . . . only with that of my female companions in struggle. . . . With . . . this I wish to . . . let you know that I have three small children who are badly dressed and malnourished. I am [also] in debt, owing eight months[' rent] on the house where we have acted on behalf of your struggle. I beg you, if it is not possible for you to help us out with cash, that you do it by allowing me to purchase . . . 500 liters of liquor [*aguardiente*] in order to be able to solve my situation and that of my children.[61]

Accessibility was the cornerstone of the Somozas'—particularly Luis Somoza's—populist style of leadership. As hard as it may be to believe, Luis Somoza and his assistants appear to have read and responded to the thousands of letters he received in the 1950s. Clara Benavides's letter, like many others found in the Somozas' files located today in Nicaragua's National Archive, has Luis Somoza's comments and initials on the margins. The comments indicate to Somoza's assistants the response he wished to send to Benavides "thanks for appreciated cooperation during campaign and tell her that she'll be remembered, etc. L.A.S. [Luis Anastasio Somoza]"

The Somocista bureaucratic apparatus was quite efficient. The response sent to Benavides was written the day after she wrote Somoza her letter. We know this because a copy of the telegram sent by the Office of the Presidency was attached to Benavides's original letter and filed with other correspondence between Benavides and Luis Somoza. The exchange between Benavides and Somoza is ultimately important because it exemplifies both the populist and the clientelistic nature of Somocismo and the give-and-take required to make the system work.

Middle-class Somocista women were also heard by Luis Somoza. Marta García, an Ala co-founder, described him in glowing terms: "Luis believed in women's intellectual capacity and demonstrated that to us. He was a very intelligent man. He had an extraordinary memory. He remembered peoples' names. He was very charismatic. He knew how to listen. . . . His assistants were humble men. He was a humanist. He was a pragmatist, a just man. He listened to me."[62]

Intimate Reciprocity

I argue that Somocista women (and here I mean women who voluntarily supported the Somozas and who called themselves "Somocistas," *not*

women who opposed the dictatorship or who were ambivalent or con-
flicted about it) understood citizenship under the Somozas not so much
in terms of rights and responsibilities as in terms of reciprocity, which
was, in their eyes, the basis for Somocista populist clientelism. To under-
line the personal and paternalistic way these women experienced the
inherent inequality of the clientelistic relationship, I use the term "intimate reciprocity" to characterize what they (and possibly some men)
expected of Somocismo. (A separate issue has to do with the differences
between men's and women's participation in clientelistic citizenship, a
comparison beyond the scope of this book.)

Others have used "intimate reciprocity" to mean something a bit
different. Ara Wilson, for instance, uses the term in her study of women
sex workers in contemporary Thailand to name "intimate commercial
exchanges."[63] Although, in the case of Somocista women, the clientelistic
exchanges did not usually involve sex, they were very personal in nature,
often born out of extreme economic desperation. Asking the Somozas for
material or moral support was a last (legal) resort for many women. After
that, there were often only limited options left: theft, prostitution—or both.

Appropriating Feminism

As Anastasio "Tachito" Somoza Debayle (the third and last Somoza to
become president) campaigned throughout Nicaragua in 1966, he mentioned women's rights in most of his speeches. In fact, he took credit, on
behalf of his family and the PLN, for "incorporating into political life [the
nation's] most beloved being . . . the Nicaraguan woman."[64] Somoza
Debayle repeatedly pointed out that "the party that gave women equality
before the law was the Nationalist Liberal Party."[65]

Others in Nicaragua agreed with Somoza's interpretation, even though
Somocista Liberals had delayed the vote for women throughout the 1940s
and early 1950s. Thus, in 1974, journalist and Ala co-founder Lucrecia
Noguera Carazo noted: "General Somoza García, in granting [the Nica-
raguan] woman her political rights, gained inspiration in the principles
of the Nationalist Liberal Party . . . [, which stated,] 'In civil and political
matters, all Nicaraguans are equal before the law. . . .' That is how the
Nicaraguan woman entered the . . . political life of the nation."[66]

Both Anastasio Somoza Debayle and Lucrecia Noguera Carazo failed to
mention the feminist contribution to the struggle for women's suffrage.
Ironically, Noguera Carazo did mention Josefa Toledo de Aguerri in her
presentation, but described her only as a "prestigious educator who had

great meaning for the cultural life of the Nicaraguan woman."[67] What Noguera Carazo and Somoza Debayle did mention was the contribution the "dynamic . . . women affiliated with the Nationalist Liberal Party"[68] had made to political life. In Somoza's words, these women, "with their tenderness and delicate [nature], serve as inspiration to us men."[69] In Noguera Carazo's words, the Ala Femenina was a "powerful Nationalist Liberal Party association."[70]

For Noguera Carazo, the Ala's organization was "perfect." To prove her point, she stressed the fact that women had come to constitute "a respectable and decisive bulwark in electoral results." In the 1974 elections, she pointed out, "60 to 67 percent of the votes for the Nationalist Liberal Party were women's votes."[71] Author Bernard Diederich supports Noguera's affirmation that women voted in large numbers for the Somozas. He notes that in the 1967 elections "Somoza declared he had received 480,162 of the reportedly 652,244 votes cast. The majority of votes were cast by women."[72]

The Ala's Electoral Work

Between 1957 and 1974, Ala members participated actively and creatively in four successful electoral campaigns. Their propaganda was specifically targeted toward Liberal women. In 1956, a song was composed by and for "señoritas liberales." These were its lyrics:

> Soon we will vote
> Soon we will vote
> and Somoza will win. . . .
>
> *compañeras,* let's go vote
> *compañeras,* let's go vote. . . .
>
> With God's blessing
> With God's blessing
> we will win the election
> with the Boogie-Woogie SO
> with the Boogie-Woogie MO
> with the Boogie-Woogie ZA.[73]

Songs were a very popular way of expressing female support for the Somozas. Presumably, it was an easy way to reach a largely illiterate population. The next two songs were also written by women for the 1957 elections:

> The elections are coming
> the entire population
> will vote
> vote for Luis Somoza
> the governor who will win
> *que viva que viva que viva ya*
> all the people are coming
> each with a ballot
> vote for Luis Somoza
> the good man of the nation
> *que viva que viva que viva ya*

> I want Luis Somoza
> to be president of the nation
> I am sure
> that Luis Somoza will govern
> *que viva que viva que viva ya*.[74]

> My land is of the lakes
> Nicaragua and Xolotlán
> where masses of Liberals
> will go vote.
> Genuine Liberals [Las Liberales Genuinas]
> and those of the "Popular Fronts,"
> the members of the "Ala Femenina"
> for Luis Somoza
> will vote.[75]

Although charged with mobilizing women to vote for the Nationalist Liberal Party, the Ala Femenina was more than a tool the Somozas used for gaining women's votes. The Ala gave middle-class Liberal women an acceptable and respectable way of participating in the traditionally male-dominated world of politics. Through their participation in the Ala, this group of women became incorporated more fully into the upper echelons of that world. Many women—among them Núñez de Saballos—were able to occupy important national and international political posts within the Somoza administration, while other women obtained posts within the party. In 1975, for example, 12 percent of the PLN's 240 convention representatives were women (compared to 5 percent of the Conservative Party's convention representatives).[76] At that time there were also thirteen women mayors, one woman senator, one woman vice minister of the National District (Managua), one woman vice minister of public education, one woman chief of commerce, one woman president of the Social Security and Welfare Department (Junta Nacional de Asistencia y Previsión Social) and eleven local female judges.[77]

The 1950s, 1960s, and early 1970s, in part because of the relative economic stability Nicaragua enjoyed during these decades, constituted the Ala's golden age, a period all Somocista women, but particularly those of the middle classes, were proud to have lived through. During those years, the Somozas stressed a new role for women, that of full citizens, and Liberal women responded enthusiastically to the new responsibilities they were being awarded. The Somozas made a special effort to showcase Ala members and their achievements, and Somocista women were pleased with the attention. When Luis Somoza fondly called Ala members his "breast" (pechuga), the most savory part of a chicken and the part closest to its heart, Somocista women flocked to hug and kiss a president they considered to be "a very cultured, very sensible man, who was open to poor people and very open to the public."[78]

Opposition to the Ala

Although most Somocistas agreed that Luis Somoza was a populist, most anti-Somocistas believed that the Ala was an exclusive housewives' club that only sought to make money. In 1956, a schoolteacher wrote a letter to La Prensa in which she complained about being lied to by the Ala leadership: "Everything is a matter of money," she claimed. "Entry into the famous Ala Femenina Liberal costs five córdobas. One must pay three for the affiliation card [carnet]. And then there is a monthly fee of two córdobas. How is it possible to ask so much from poor teachers?" This woman also complained that Ala leaders spent most of their time in social gatherings gossiping about other women.[79] Those who did not reap the benefits of Somocismo—many if not most Nicaraguan women and men—shared this view of the Ala, and it is the view that still persists in Nicaraguan society at large.

Although it is true that the leadership of the Women's Wing of the Liberal Party held many social functions, it is also true that those who participated out of their own free will in the Ala were committed to their political ideals and did a great deal of political work. Maritza Zeledón claims that she does not know of another Nicaraguan political organization that worked as hard as the Ala did. According to Zeledón, the Ala's greatest legacy was "to have awakened [in Liberal women] dormant ideals to the whisper of redemptive ideas."[80] One cannot dispute this legacy. On the other hand, we must keep in mind the price the rest of the Nicaraguan population paid for Nationalist Liberal women's twenty-five-year experimentation with politics: exclusion, co-optation, and repression.

Conclusion

It is easy to dismiss the fraudulent elections under the Somozas as unimportant, as indeed they were to those Nicaraguans who opposed the dictatorship. But they mattered a great deal to Somocistas. This is one reason why they deserve our closer attention. Another reason is that they shed light on exactly how the Somoza dictatorship functioned and on how women experienced and shaped clientelistic citizenship.

The Ala became the primary channel through which urban working-women participated in the Somozas' clientelistic system. Their participation gave these women concrete proof of their support for the dictatorship, which they then used to bargain directly with the Somozas for material goods. That bargaining was expressed as an intimate reciprocity. Ala membership gave women a collective Somocista identity that made them feel they had a right to be heard by the Somozas. The Somozas—particularly Luis Somoza—honored this "right," thus personalizing the clientelistic exchange.

From Somocista women's perspective, the PLN proved its commitment to them by enfranchising women and by encouraging them to participate fully as workers and citizens in Somocismo. In exchange for these political and economic opportunities, large numbers of middle- and working-class female Somocistas were quite eager to devote themselves entirely to their country, their party, and their president. They believed the dictatorship when it told them, time after time, that women were integral to Somocismo and the Nationalist Liberal Party. These followers of the Somozas became intoxicated with Somocismo and Somocista rhetoric.

In Antonia Rodríguez's view, women were of central importance to Liberalism. Looking back to the mid-twentieth century, she proudly notes that "we all were the Liberal Party [el Partido Liberal eramos todos]."[81] Rosa Alvarez (pseudonym), a Somocista seamstress who was involved in politics against her husband's wishes, and who was jailed for political reasons under the Sandinistas, stated in 1998: "Within Liberalism you feel like family. If I were a hundred or two hundred years old, I would still be a Liberal." Alvarez fondly remembers that her grandmother was the first woman to vote in her hometown: "My grandma was proud to have Liberal granddaughters."[82] This legacy of pride in Liberalism is the legacy embraced by working- and middle-class Somocista women alike.

FOUR

SOMOCISTA WOMEN'S LIVES

"Luis Somoza was my political mentor." Those were the first words Marta García (pseudonym) shared with me after I told her why I was interested in interviewing her. Significantly, this remark represents not only one woman's personal experience with the Somoza family but also that of an entire generation of Somocista female leaders: Liberal women born in the mid- to late 1920s who came of age politically under Luis Somoza Debayle's rule (1956–61). These urban women occupied important posts under the Luis and Anastasio Somoza Debayle administrations while providing leadership for the Women's Wing (Ala Femenina) of the Nationalist Liberal Party up until the Somozas' defeat in 1979. They constitute the first generation of women to obtain university degrees and hold political power in Nicaragua over an extended period of time. As noted in the introduction, they include Nicaragua's first women attorneys, first women mayors, and first women members of Congress. Most important perhaps, these are the women for whom Somocista Liberalism made the most sense.

To help explain the appeal the Somozas had among their women supporters, this chapter delves deeply into the lives of seven Somocista female leaders of this generation of firsts. It shows the personal reasons Nicaraguan women had for supporting the regime and how they made sense of Somocismo—a side of the Somoza regime that has been largely ignored until now; it also briefly discusses the anti-Somocista relatives and friends of Somocista women.

The chapter also addresses the lives of women who did not occupy the upper echelons of Somocismo but who nonetheless were strong supporters of the dictatorship. It examines the intersection between official (male) Somocista propaganda, Somocista women's interpretations of the official rhetoric, and their own personal experiences, focusing on the narratives they use to tell the stories of their lives. From the oral histories I gathered between 1994 and 2009, I conclude that Somocista women at once supported and subverted official accounts of Somocismo.

As I sought out potential informants in the late 1990s and the early 2000s, I encountered the Liberal women's movement that developed after the Liberals returned to power in 1996. This new movement, I quickly discovered, had little in common with the Liberal women's movement before the revolution of 1979. Whereas Somocista women of that time had advocated the expansion of state services and women's incorporation into the workforce, the "new" Liberal women supported the neoliberal privatization of state services and a "return to family values." The main commonality between "new" Liberal women and the Somocista women I was looking for was their hatred of the Sandinistas. Given the differences in the two groups, I was surprised to find that a large contingent of young women in the "new" Liberal women's movement identified as Somocistas. Although these women, whom I call "neo-Somocistas," did not live through what they perceived to be Nicaragua's golden age as adults, they were mesmerized by the Somoza years. Largely unaware of the history of Somocista women who came before them, they believed they were the first generation of Liberal women to organize on a massive scale.

The primary way in which Somocista women's lives can be documented is through oral interviews. Because personal and institutional archives were burned in 1979 by both Somocistas and anti-Somocistas, there are hardly any written sources available. Virtually all of the Ala papers were destroyed by the Ala leadership; only a few documents have survived in Managua's National Archive and the Central American University's (UCA) Institute of Nicaraguan and Central American History (Instituto de Historia de Nicaragua y Centroamérica or IHNCA). This chapter discusses the promises and problems of documenting Somocista women's lives through oral histories. It also addresses some of the concerns this study raises in contemporary Nicaragua, a topic touched on in the preface. And because women's history benefits greatly from a comparative perspective, the chapter briefly compares the lives of Somocista women with the better-known lives of right-wing women in South America and Europe.

Doing Oral History: Telling Right-Wing Women's Stories

> Suppose you want to write
> of a woman braiding
> another woman's hair—
>
> . . . .
> you had better know the thickness
> the length   the pattern
>
> . . . .
> what country it happens in
> what else happens in that country
> —*Adrienne Rich*, "North American Time"

One of oral history's original claims was to give a voice to the voiceless, to those who would not normally enter the historical record. Women's history originated with a similar goal. But what happens when a researcher attempting to document the lives of right-wing women does not support their political agenda? There are different ways of addressing this issue. For pioneering authors in the field such as Kathleen Blee, Nancy MacLean, and Glen Jeansomme, giving right-wing women a voice is simply not a consideration.[1] Nonetheless, Blee, MacLean, and Jeansomme are careful to portray rightists as active historical agents. In their accounts, Ku Klux Klan women and anti-Semitic Fascist mothers are not pawns of men or misguided tragic figures. Such women, like their male counterparts, make choices, whether based on deeply held beliefs or opportunism. Although readers of the works of these three authors are not encouraged to identify with the women being studied, they do gain a better understanding of their experiences, actions, and possible motives, albeit from the authors' antiracist perspective.

Rebecca Klatch, on the other hand, explicitly states that giving right-wing women a voice is indeed one of her objectives. She quotes from interviews at length, allowing readers to understand how Conservative women in the United States view their own lives; moreover, she claims that "the aim throughout [her] study has been to try to suspend judgment."[2]

Like Klatch, my objective is not to judge the right-wing women I study. But, like Blee, MacLean, and Jeansomme, my goal is also not to give these women a voice, although I am, of course, intent on portraying them fairly and accurately. Most important perhaps, like Blee and many Nicaraguans, I worry that, by simply documenting Somocista women's stories, I am providing a platform for right-wing views and empowering right-wing women. Blee notes: "Perhaps the nature of oral history research— . . . eliciting and conducting interviews with former . . . members [of a right-wing group]—itself empowers informants, by suggesting to them, and to their political descendants, [their] importance . . . [in] history."[3] This concern became a real one when many former Somocistas came back on the political scene as a result of the 1990, 1996, 2001, and 2006 presidential elections, although it is easy to overestimate the effect a modest study such as this one might have on contemporary politics.

What, then, might its effect be? There is no doubt in my mind that my research results have helped some Somocista women make sense of their lives in the context of Nicaraguan women's history and, indeed, have helped ensure them an important place in this history. Moreover, my results and the few remaining documents on the Ala Femenina have helped them find one another.[4] These results are of crucial importance to the dozens of anti-Somocistas I have spoken to over the years.

In contemporary Nicaragua, many anti-Somocista activists still feel that women who supported the abuses committed by the Somozas or who committed abuses themselves lost the right to have a history and that their existence needs to be erased from the nation's memory. Some women's rights activists feel that only "good" things done by women should be told and that Somocista women's stories will tarnish the reputation of all women. Still others, as noted in the preface, argue that if Somocista women's stories are to be recorded, these women should be portrayed as having been manipulated by the regime. They contend that not doing so gives the dictatorship credibility and respectability.

I strongly disagree with those who argue that explaining the appeal of Somocismo for women and addressing women's participation in Somocismo automatically legitimize the dictatorship. Nonetheless, I take this concern and others seriously. In the discussion that follows, I address three questions raised by my work that are not covered in the preface.

The first and second questions are almost inseparable: How will the Somoza period be remembered? And who will write the history of Somocismo? The third question arises in debates over history throughout the world: If we spend time and effort studying one group of people—in this case Somocistas—are we not doing it at the expense of studying another group's history? As one anguished Sandinista woman asked me, "What about *my* story? Who will record *my* experiences? Why are Somocista women more important than we are?"

These concerns have to do, in part, with individual and collective beliefs on class, agency, and victimization that are commonplace in politically polarized societies such as Nicaragua. For political purposes, anti-Somocismo, like most other political movements, propagated myths—many of which are still very much alive. Anti-Somocista myths tend to rest on the notion that someone is either with you or against you. This way of understanding politics turns average Nicaraguans into either perpetrators or victims/resisters in relation to Somocismo. Who fits into which category is decided a priori and working-class women and men, according to this interpretation, overwhelmingly fall into the second category. Anti-Somocista myths hold great power even though they do not correspond to the lived experiences of most Nicaraguans. The myths are constantly reinforced and reproduced in the media and in political propaganda.

The results of my research challenge some of the most appealing and some of the most powerful anti-Somocista myths: that Nicaraguan women first became politically active against the Somozas, that right-wing women were manipulated by the Somozas, and that no working-class people ever willingly supported the dictatorship. I propose a rethinking of the nation's twentieth-century history based on the acknowledgment that Nicaraguans were not simply victims or resisters of the dictatorship. My results and proposal make many Nicaraguans uncomfortable, however. The finding that Somocismo was forged by thousands of Nicaraguans actively engaged in upholding the dictatorship threatens the established version of Nicaraguan history taught to an entire generation. That this finding is not easily transferable into everyday political practice also makes it difficult to digest by those who are interested in concrete political solutions to concrete social problems.

Precisely because the critiques of my work came from people who were (and still are) genuinely interested in solving pressing contemporary problems, I have thought long and hard about the questions and concerns they have raised. Unfortunately, I have concluded that there are no easy answers. Nicaragua has not yet healed from decades of warfare. It was only in the late twentieth century that the field of history in Nicaragua started developing as a nonpartisan, professional endeavor. Before then, political parties and movements wrote their own histories and tried to impose them on the population whenever they were in power.

Although many books and articles were written on Nicaragua by foreign academics during the 1980s, most were not historical. Moreover, most were never translated into Spanish, making them inaccessible to the population at large. Inexplicably, the many works on Sandinista women that emerged in the 1980s and 1990s tended to tell the same story over and over again. They described the rise of AMPRONAC in the 1970s, its conversion into AMNLAE, and the eventual rise of the independent women's movement. A handful of books and articles consisted primarily of oral interviews with individual women. At its best, the *testimonio* genre, perfected by Margaret Randall, presented invaluable insights into specific moments of Nicaraguan history. At its worst, it provided a simplistic and misleading representation of Nicaraguan women's realities, an issue discussed in the preface.

Against this backdrop, it is no wonder that my findings are considered politically suspect. In response to the specific concerns discussed above, however, I acknowledge that my findings might support some of the claims made by the Right about Somocismo. Nonetheless, I also believe that most Nicaraguans, regardless of their political persuasion, are tired of one-dimensional portrayals of their collective past. Most people who lived through the dictatorship and the revolution know that these were complex periods full of contradictory and counterintuitive policies and outcomes. Thus Nicaraguan history should reflect these realities.

With regard to the question of who will write the history of Somocismo, only time will tell. So far, that history has been written largely by men and about men. U.S. historians Jeffrey L. Gould, Knut Walter, and Richard Millet have written excellent book-length studies. Nicaraguan historians, among them Miguel Ayerdis and Ricardo Baltodano Marcenaro, are also writing about the Somoza period. And accounts written by former members of the Somozas' National Guard have become popular in the last few years.[5] Whatever the author's point of view, however, we should remember that nobody has the exclusive "right" to tell the stories behind Somocismo.

In sum, the history of Nicaraguan women has yet to be written and, for better or worse, will have to depend largely on oral histories. This raises additional concerns about informants' privacy and safety and the accuracy of oral accounts. It is my hope that the need to rely on oral sources will provoke a national debate on memory and the promises and pitfalls of oral history, an endeavor that has already started taking place among historians in Nicaragua.

Interviews with Somocista Female Leaders

Between 1994 and 1999, I interviewed seven high-level Somocista female leaders who gained prominence in national politics before 1979. Three were co-founders of the Ala and formed part of the Ala's inner circle throughout the dictatorship. Moreover, they held important posts within the Somoza administrations. These three women were the only surviving Ala co-founders available for interviews. The other four women I interviewed also held significant positions within the Ala, but not at the highest levels; of these, two were deeply involved in departmental politics and one worked for the Ministry of Health. At least two of the seven Ala leaders I interviewed have already died.

At the time of the interviews, six of these seven women were in their seventies, one was in her late sixties, and all but one were retired from official posts in national politics. Eugenia Robleto (pseudonym) held a highly controversial government position in Arnoldo Alemán's administration (1997–2002) when I interviewed her in the late 1990s. I asked Robleto why she took the job Alemán offered her, implicitly acknowledging her age and ailing health. Her brother, who was present during the interview and had already expressed concern for her safety, responded first: "Because she's crazy." She smiled at this and, with a twinkle in her eye, replied, "Yes, I'm crazy about politics." Azucena Campo (pseudonym) was also offered a position but declined it, in her words, because she "didn't want Alemán to appear to have had close ties with the Somozas."

Of the seven leaders I interviewed, only one had married a high-ranking military man. Four others married men who held neither military nor political posts. The two unmarried women had the highest degrees: one was in the legal profession; the other was a health care professional. Of the five married women, four had children. The unmarried women had none.

All of these women were used to speaking in public, giving orders, and facing difficult political situations. After 1979, their fate was uncertain, and one of them landed in jail. Of the seven, only one remained in Nicaragua throughout the entire Sandinista period. Two fled to other Central American countries. Four went to live in the United States; of these, one ended up living in Miami; the other three spent time in other cities, where they had family ties. Those who went into exile returned to Nicaragua during the 1990s, some permanently, others temporarily, in part to try to recover properties that had been confiscated by the Sandinistas in 1979. At the time of the interviews, two informants were still living in the United States; I traveled to their respective states for the interviews. The other five interviews were conducted in Nicaragua.

Of the seven women, at least two were actively trying to recover properties. In talking about her confiscated properties, Maritza Zeledón (pseudonym) mentioned several times that she came from a working-class family and that she had worked hard for the two homes the Sandinistas had taken away. Marta García noted that she came from a middle-class background and that she, too, had had two homes, one in Managua and one in the beach resort of San Juan del Sur, both of which were confiscated. Azucena Campo also had her house taken away. She was particularly upset because its current occupant was an upper-class Sandinista who came from a wealthy family with long-standing ties to the Somozas.

I interviewed four of these women in their current homes, one at her workplace, one at a shopping mall, and one at a relative's house. In all cases except one, I met with at least one relative (a husband, sibling, child, grandchild, etc). The husbands of two of these women were eager to showcase their wives' achievements. In general, the women's families seemed to take great pride in them.

All the women took great care of their physical appearance and were keenly aware of their differences. They made many references to details about each other that were still vivid in their minds, even though most had not kept in touch for twenty years. "Oh yes," remembered one, "[so and so], even though she was fat, was a great dancer." These women were also eager to know more about the current lives of the other leaders I had interviewed.

The shortest interview lasted approximately two hours; the longest, with two of the women, lasted more than a dozen hours. I videotaped parts of the longest interviews but simply took notes or used a tape recorder in the other five.

Six of the seven women maintained ties to the Liberal Party in the late 1990s and did not seem to regret their participation in Somocista politics. Only one woman was active in a different party, the non-Somocista Independent Liberal Party (Partido Liberal Independiente). Alejandra Flores (pseudonym) was, in fact, the only one who was highly critical of the Somozas—Anastasio Somoza Debayle in particular—and the Ala.

Even though four of the women I interviewed were trained as teachers under the tutelage of Josefa Toledo de Aguerri (1866–1962), Nicaragua's foremost women's rights activist, Flores was the only one who remembered Toledo de Aguerri as a feminist. Moreover, Flores claimed that she herself was a feminist and that the feminist movement should be renewed in Nicaragua (she was unaware that a feminist movement existed in Nicaragua during the 1990s). But she clearly differentiated her feminism from the type of feminism that pitted men and women against each other.

As a group, Ala leaders disapproved of feminism because they disapproved of anger toward men. Eugenia Robleto stated in her interview: "We fought for women's rights, but we were not confrontational." Moreover, most Ala leaders did not see a need for feminism because they did not perceive Nicaraguan middle-class society to be particularly sexist. Maritza Zeledón told me that "in Central America there was never a declared patriarchy, although machismo did exist."

Ala leaders truly believed they had reached a high degree of equality with men and that they had earned that equality. They did not see themselves as victims of a male-dominated society and felt they could deal with individual instances of sexism. Nonetheless, in response to a question about institutionalized sexism, several did admit that they earned less than men in similar positions of power and that discrimination against women did exist. Marta García, in particular, believed it had existed under President René Schick (1963–66).[6] And when I asked her why the vote took so long to achieve, she responded: "Because of societal prejudices." Other women stated that they had to struggle as women to obtain the professional degrees they wanted. Maritza Zeledón, for instance, went against her mother's wishes in choosing her career. Zeledón came from a family of female teachers: both her mother and grandmother had been teachers, and she herself taught for twenty-five years. Zeledón also obtained a professional degree and, as the first woman in her family to become involved in politics, went on to hold several high-level posts under the Somozas. Zeledón's mother had wanted her to become a pharmacist instead; that way, Zeledón could have opened a pharmacy and worked from home.

In terms of gender relations, Ala leaders envisioned a world where a woman and a man would complement each other as sexual partners and as companions. Heterosexuality was fundamental to their worldview, but marriage was not. "The Liberal Party always thought about the family, the home," Marta García told me, "but not all women have to get married." Women could choose to remain single, as long as they remained, or appeared to remain, virgins. One Ala leader told me: "I always had to be careful so that I wouldn't be slandered." Women could also choose to obtain a divorce without stigma if the man was considered to be at fault (i.e., if he was an alcoholic, a wife beater, had public extramarital affairs, or had abandoned his wife).

Although Ala leaders' view of proper gender roles did not differ significantly from that of society at large, their actions sometimes did. One woman, for instance, while on a business trip to Europe and the United States did not call her husband for three weeks. Her husband was the one who told me this story; she only laughed about it, a quarter of a century after it happened.

Ala leaders who never married had a complex view of their status as single women. Maritza Zeledón, for instance, believed that, ideally, women should get married and have children. But she had a hard time meeting a man who supported her political and professional aspirations: "My boyfriends wanted me to stop studying." Zeledón was also unable to find a man "who knew more" than she did. In the end, she never married and never had children. Although she stressed that these choices were ones she made based on the options available to her, Zeledón also stressed her lack of agency in the face of divine intervention: "Marriage and death are heaven sent [*Casamiento y mortaja del cielo bajan*]."

When it came to other women, some Ala leaders were sympathetic to widows and abandoned women, especially if they had children. They believed that mothers carried greater burdens than nonmothers: "Motherhood slows you down because of the responsibilities."[7] To ease the burden of these responsibilities and allow women greater participation in Liberal politics, Ala members provided babysitting services for working-class Liberal mothers on voting days.[8]

The Ala leadership believed poor women were to be pitied and not blamed for their fate. They claimed they felt a bond of "sisterhood" with poor Liberal women, with whom they came in frequent contact. Those who were teachers knew the realities of the poor quite well, as did those who worked in the health and legal fields.

As a group, Ala leaders felt they were part of a larger Somocista project to bring progress to Nicaragua. But progress was not meant to happen overnight, nor was it meant to come about by violent means. Moreover, in exchange for their leadership roles and their hard work, they expected substantial material rewards. Even though some Ala leaders claimed to have "humble" origins, they saw themselves as different from the poor. They had risen above the majority, and they deserved to be rewarded for their work. They saw this as a fair and just situation, for they were educated, and that, in and of itself, merited recognition. Ala leaders felt their status was based on their hard work, although they also acknowledged that good luck or family connections may have helped them to advance in Somocista ranks.

My wanting to document their stories took them by surprise. Most of them noted my age and were curious to know why someone who had not experienced Somocismo as an adult was interested in their lives. But they were not shy about sharing their life stories with me. Indeed, I sometimes felt they had been waiting for someone to come along so that their stories could be told to the world.

In general, the women I interviewed did not go out of their way to defend themselves or attempt to justify their support for a dictatorship. They did not make excuses. Instead, they reminisced. Several showed me photo albums and scrapbooks. One even gave me her scrapbook as a gift. Another showed me over a dozen photos of herself with a headless man. In 1979, she cut Anastasio Somoza Debayle's head off in all the photographs she had of him, so as to protect herself in case she was arrested by the Sandinistas. Having photos of oneself embracing Somoza would have been sure proof of one's involvement in the dictatorship. Hugging a headless man was less dangerous.

Although they offered no meaningful reflections on their support for the Somozas, the women I interviewed did appear to have thought about the subject. I soon found out that the primary way Somocista female leaders came to terms with the terror and violence brought about by the Somozas (terror and violence they themselves sometimes participated in or oversaw) was by differentiating among the three dictators. As a group, they identified quite strongly with the second dictator, Luis Somoza Debayle, and this made it easier to claim that Luis was "el bueno" and that "el malo" had been Anastasio Somoza Debayle, the third dictator. Another way they dealt with the abuses committed by the Somozas was to focus on the positive and minimize the negative by arguing that anti-Somocistas had brought on the violence themselves, that the Somozas were simply acting in self-defense. A third way was to actually help out those who were victimized by the Somozas. Several Somocista female leaders mentioned that they helped out friends and relatives who were not Somocistas escape from persecution. At the time, these actions probably eased their conscience and made them feel better. Some Somocista women might have also been genuinely horrified by the terror their non-Somocista relatives were experiencing. Alejandra Flores, for instance, helped the surviving members of a cousin's family escape further persecution by the National Guard. In an infamous massacre, Guard members killed four members of that family in the 1970s. Not surprisingly, perhaps, given such a blatant disregard for human life, Flores was extremely critical of the last Somoza.

Yet another way female leaders came to terms with Somocismo was to claim that they did not support everything the Somozas did, even though they supported the regime as a whole. One informant, for example, claims that she did not support the jailing of the Sandinista revolutionary Doris Tijerino. She knew Tijerino's family personally and seemed to regret her capture and subsequent torture and rape. My informant also noted that, at times, Somocista women's names were attached without their knowledge to public petitions or statements for causes they did not support. Protesting against this common practice would have put Somocista women's standing within the party at risk.

Antonia Rodríguez's Story

Although Antonia Rodríguez's house was not confiscated, and even though she never left Nicaragua, remained at her job after the revolution, and worked for the new administration until her retirement, her story is important not because it departs from other leaders' stories but because it is so similar. All these women's stories overlap with the official story of the rise of Liberalism in twentieth-century Nicaragua.

In all of them, hard work is a constant, as is women's work and the intersection between larger political events and family life. All the leaders I interviewed did well financially under the Somozas, and their families appreciated the relative peace brought about by the defeat of Augusto C. Sandino in 1934.

In an extensive interview, Antonia Rodríguez (pseudonym) shared her family history with me. Rodríguez was a first-generation university graduate who came from a rather poor family. Her maternal grandfather had been a bricklayer and her maternal grandmother sold homemade soap for a living. Her grandmother's family also sold tripe soup (*mondongo*) in the market. "I don't remember much about my grandma, but I know that she was thin, tall, very active, very friendly. I've been told she knew all sorts of things, how to make things. She was always trying to improve her [economic] situation."

Politics, economics, and family are intertwined in Rodríguez's life story: "My grandfather went off to fight in [Conservative rebel Luis] Mena's war, on the Atlantic Coast [in the early twentieth century] and got lost over there. . . . My grandmother's oldest brother went to look for him . . . until he found him . . . ! He had stayed on the Atlantic Coast. When he came back, [his daughter] had already been born. . . . He hadn't met her yet. . . . [Then] came [General Emiliano] Chamorro's war. . . . My grandmother died during those years. . . . She died in the war. . . . She was in the [1927] Chinandega fire."[9]

On Rodríguez's paternal side, her grandfather had been "a very distinguished gentleman . . . and the entire town respected him a lot. He was very fond of . . . the Church and all that." He died when Rodríguez's father was about fourteen years old: "Then my grandmother, widowed, with two sons, and poor . . . took her two sons to León. . . . [There] . . . she put them in school to learn a trade. My grandmother [meanwhile] sold . . . clay pots . . . in the market."

Rodríguez's father became a musician at an early age, and her mother earned a living as a seamstress: "My dad earned . . . 60 centavos playing at the Church. And a dozen bananas cost 5 centavos. . . . So my mom said to him, 'The day I have some money, I will open up a store.'" A priest then helped her get a loan: "That is how my mom's store started, buying vegetables, bananas, pieces of cheese, and things like that. . . . My father says that he was embarrassed when my mom opened the store [because it was so small]. That's how they started. . . . My mom was the one in charge of the store. She loved business."

> Politically speaking, all [my family members] were Liberal. I've been told that during the war [in the late 1920s] aunt Heriberta would carry pistols in her basket under the soap she took to market to sell. . . . They were obsessed Liberals. All of them. All of them. All of them. On the other hand, since they lived in León, there were also no Conservatives around.
>
> My mother was very Liberal and so was my dad. So, when they came [to the Central Highlands], during the war [in 1926], my poor father had to hide because the Conservatives forced people to display green flags. . . . My father [also] hid because the Conservatives would stop by my mother's store, which was very small, and asked for rations of everything: 'give us vegetables for the troops' soup, give us such and such a thing.' And since the Conservatives were backed by the Yanquis. . . .
>
> Yes, young lady, that is the way it happened. That is the way history is written. . . .
>
> My mother's sister did become a Conservative [when she married a Conservative]. Of course! She voted as her husband did. She adored him. She became a Conservative, just like [her] old man. When she got married he dominated her in that respect.

Eventually, Rodríguez became the first person in her family to obtain a university degree. She then left her hometown and moved to the capital in search of employment. She was successful in her field and eventually obtained a high-level post in the ministry where she worked.

Rodríguez's story sounds similar to the one Anastasio Somoza Debayle himself told in his campaign speeches during the 1960s. Certain themes are stressed: women's work, women's suffering, childbearing in difficult circumstances, and husbands being persecuted by the Conservatives. "My grandfather, Luis H. Debayle, told me how, a few days before my mother was about to give birth to me, the Conservatives broke into my family's home at night and took my father away to kill him. If it had not been for his [schoolmates, they would have done so]. . . . My mother gave birth to me without the assistance . . . of a midwife, which almost caused her death and mine."[10]

Two other important themes in both Rodríguez's and Somoza Debayle's stories are those of generational and regional commonalities. Born a year apart, both believed they were part of the generation that was reaping the benefits of Liberalism. Moreover, even though they lived in Managua, they also identified as natives of León, a characteristic that made them true Liberals. Somoza noted in the speech quoted above: "I, along with all other men of my age in Nicaragua, and especially those of León, owe a debt to all Liberal heroes. . . . We owe those men the peace, the tranquility, and the high level of socioeconomic development that our nation has achieved and will achieve with the revolutionary ideals of the Nationalist Liberal Party."[11]

Antonia Rodríguez's life story just happened to coincide with the established story of Liberalism in many respects. On the other hand, she was quite familiar with that story. She was, in fact, the person who gave me the book in which Somoza's speech appears. There can be no doubt that many Nicaraguans of Anastasio Somoza Debayle's generation could relate to the Somocista discourse and that the Somozas knew this. This helps explains why Somocismo made sense to those who supported the dictatorship. But it is also possible that Antonia Rodríguez and other Somocistas organized their memories through the framework provided by Somocismo (fig. 14).

Other Stories: Somocistas' Relatives and Friends

What surprised me the most about the relationships between Somocistas and anti-Somocistas who managed to remain close—an unavoidable subject during my fieldwork—was not that they refused to talk about politics with each other. That would appear to be only common sense. It was that many anti-Somocistas honestly wanted to know why their female relatives and friends supported the Somozas. In one case, a Sandinista woman I interviewed agreed to help me arrange an interview with her elderly Somocista mother on one condition: that I ask her whether she would have been a Somocista if her husband had not been a Somoza supporter. In another case, an anti-Somocista woman recommended I interview a good Somocista friend of hers, but asked me to tell her why her friend had chosen to back the dictatorship. Clearly, these examples demonstrate the difficulty some anti-Somocistas have in understanding why women supported the Somozas.

Some Sandinistas knew exactly why their relatives and friends participated in pro-Somoza rallies and events: they had to. Thus Sergio Gutiérrez (pseudonym), a Sandinista man I interviewed, explained to me that his working-class mother had been a public employee and that, to keep her job, she had to vote for the Somozas and participate in pro-Somoza activities. She eventually quit her job after being subjected to sexual harassment by the head of the National Guard in her hometown.[12]

Many Sandinista sons and daughters of Somocistas assume that their mothers' participation in the Ala Femenina was involuntary and unimportant. Obviously, many working-class women, like Sergio Gutiérrez's mother, did indeed vote and work for the Somozas because of their dire economic circumstances. But what about the women who were "true" Somocistas? How is it that their Sandinista children, relatives, and friends did not understand what led them to support and contribute to Somocismo? This subject deserves to be explored in greater detail elsewhere. But I want to point out here that at least some of the Sandinistas I spoke with did in fact understand what Somocismo meant to Nationalist Liberal women. "The Somocista women you write about," one Sandinista woman told me, "are exactly like my mother-in-law."

Neo-Somocista Women at a Liberal Women's Assembly

Over a thousand women gathered at the Liberal Women's Assembly that took place in Managua's Olof Palme Convention Center in May 1998. Having decided to interview the oldest-looking women in the group, I first approached a petite and fragile-looking woman who appeared to be in her eighties. Her hair was entirely white, and she could barely walk on her own. It turned out she was only sixty-eight and not even a Liberal. Her life story, however, like that of so many Nicaraguans, was intertwined with the history of Somocismo and Nicaraguan politics in general. Margarita Chávez (pseudonym) had been a teacher in southern Nicaragua during the Somoza years. She was a Conservative and was eventually fired for her political beliefs, never to be employed again, because she refused to vote for the Somozas.

At the insistence of her daughter, Maribel López (pseudonym), I visited Chávez in her home in a poor Managua neighborhood several days later to continue my interview and to speak with both women. López, a vocal woman in her early forties who identified as a Somocista, had invited her mother to the Liberal Assembly. What these two women had in common was their anti-Sandinismo, fueled in part by their opposition to the draft.

So great was the family's opposition to the FSLN that one of Chávez's sons had joined the Contras in the 1980s.

Maribel López went out of her way to introduce me to Liberal women in her working-class neighborhood; we spent almost an entire day visiting their homes and talking to them. They all told the same story: the Somozas had been good for the people; under the Sandinistas, Somocistas had suffered a great deal; but now they were happy to have the Liberals back in power. Given that López was the Liberal Party representative in her neighborhood, it is hard to know how truthful these women were, but they certainly appeared to be sharing their true opinions. A few even brought out Somocista magazines from the 1970s to prove to me that they were long-standing Liberals.

Although I do not doubt the sincerity of Maribel López and the women she introduced me to, it turned out that hardly any of them had been politically active during the Somoza dictatorship. In 1998, most were in their early forties, which means they were teenagers in the 1970s. These working-class urban women belong to a new generation of Liberal women I call "neo-Somocistas." They claim the Somocista legacy as their own, but their knowledge of Somocismo is based on the experiences of others. These women are literally reactionaries in the sense that they are reacting against the Sandinistas and want to go back in time to Nicaragua's supposed golden age.

Neo-Somocista Market Women

Many contemporary Liberal market women are also part of the neo-Somocista contingent that arose after the Liberals' return to power in 1996, under the leadership of Arnoldo Alemán. These women were highly vocal at the 1998 Liberal Women's Assembly. Wearing their trademark aprons with the frilly pockets, they were also easy to spot. I spoke to a few market leaders briefly at the 1998 assembly. Then, in June 2000, I spoke at length to several market women at Managua's Mercado Oriental, Nicaragua's largest open-air market. What I learned was that most Liberal market women at the time were in their forties and were becoming politically involved in Liberalism for the first time under the Alemán administration. Like Maribel López's neighbors, what motivated them was their anti-Sandinismo and the belief that they could turn back the clock to the 1950s and 1960s, the Somocista golden age.

At the beginning of the twenty-first century, there were approximately 20,000 women working in Managua's Mercado Oriental and thousands more working in open-air markets throughout the nation. Market women were among the staunchest supporters of the Somozas. They were also some of the Sandinistas' harshest critics. Karen Kampwirth, in her study on Contra women, writes about the small merchants who became counterrevolutionaries during the 1980s:

> Rationing was one of the Sandinista actions that particularly angered the women who became Contras. . . . Several mentioned resentment at the periodic shortages of white sugar that forced them to buy "black sugar," something that never happened before: "General Somoza gave that sugar to animals."
>
> Sandinista rationing and rules against hoarding created particular hardships for small merchants. Andrea, who was born in 1945 in the provincial city of Chinandega, was a merchant who supported the Sandinista struggle against Somoza. "I was part of the insurrection, I carried arms, I even made Molotov cocktails." But after the Sandinistas took power, she was unhappy with some of their policies. "I didn't like the way Sandinismo worked . . . the rationing of food, the abuse against teenagers [who] had to carry out military service. MICOIN [the Ministry of Interior Commerce] did not allow one to work, it took everything away and my poverty was what made me join. . . . Because of that I decided to go with the Resistance [the Contras]. When I looked at the rationing of food, no, that was not for me." To continue working as a merchant, she had to violate the rule that "nobody could buy more than 3 pounds [of meat] at a time, that nobody could buy things wholesale."
>
> The purpose of the Sandinistas' rule was to ensure that meat was available at affordable prices for all. But the same rule that made life easier for some who had not been able to afford meat under Somoza, made life harder for women like Andrea. Moreover, by forcing them to make illegal purchases, it turned them into enemies of the state. Once she had become a Sandinista enemy through an action that she felt she had to take to preserve her livelihood, it was not such a great leap to join the Contras.[13]

As Kampwirth notes, small merchants tend to value a free-market economy. The Nicaraguan market women were no exception. For them, the freedom to purchase and sell the products they wished in the quantities they wished was an essential component of their political "freedom," which they associated with the Somoza period. Given their political and economic priorities, it is understandable that many market women in the late 1990s supported the Alemán administration and its neoliberal economic policies.

Neoliberal Women and the New Liberal Women's Movement

Although they did not focus primarily on motherhood or on women's retreat into the home, neo-Somocista Liberal women were much more in line with traditional right-wing women's movements in other parts of the world than Somocista women ever were. Contemporary Liberal women constantly looked backward to better times, as did Fascist women in Italy under Mussolini and right-wing women in Chile under Pinochet. Moreover, unlike the discourse of Somocista women, theirs did stress "a return to family values," an important characteristic of Nicaragua's "new Right" discussed in greater detail in chapter 6.

Surprisingly perhaps, given their constant references to the golden age of Somocismo, the younger women of the "new" Liberal women's movement did not appear to establish links with the aging women of the "old" Liberal women's movement during the late 1990s or the early 2000s. This is understandable, however, once we remember that these contemporary Liberal women had different priorities from their foremothers.

Unlike the Somocista women's movement, the new Liberal women's movement, which included non-Somocistas as well as neo-Somocistas and which developed in reaction to the Sandinista revolution and its socialist economic policies, did not emphasize citizenship or employment as the primary attraction of Liberalism for women. The movement had two goals in mind: to establish neoliberal economic policies (privatization of state services, end of state subsidies, etc.); and to prevent the Sandinistas from achieving power again. Ironically, Daniel Ortega's reelection in 2006 was a result of the power-sharing deal, "the pact," reached between the FSLN and Arnoldo Alemán's Constitutional Liberal Party (PLC) earlier that year. The pact placed Liberal women, particularly neo-Somocista women, in a difficult position. The fate of Liberal women (non-Somocista and neo-Somocistas alike) after the pact is a fascinating subject beyond the scope of this book and one that merits greater attention elsewhere.

The Constitutional Liberal Party Convention: Rosa Alvarez's Story

Seeking to enlarge my pool of Somocista informants, I approached as many women over forty as I could at the July 1998 PLC Convention, which took place in Managua. Because important political deals were being forged at this convention, many attendees were too busy to grant me extended interviews, even though they proudly admitted they had been supporters of "the General." Some women, however, were more than willing to talk, and Rosa Alvarez (pseudonym) was one of them.

When I approached potential informants, I normally began by stating that I was interested in interviewing women with long trajectories in the Liberal Party, attempting in this way to weed out recent converts to Liberalism. Alvarez's response surprised me, for she clearly interpreted my inquiry as a compliment: "How did you know I have dedicated my life to Liberalism?" I had to admit to her that I had not known and that I had actually approached her quite randomly. Although she seemed disappointed by my reply, she invited me to sit down with her and began a conversation that would lead her to tears.

Alvarez told me that she came from a poor family, that she had always been poor, and that she had physical ailments she had been unable to treat because of her financial situation. She was proud that she had never benefited financially from her political activism, that she was a "heart Liberal" (*liberal de corazón*), unlike others who were in it for the money. And yet she expected some recognition at least of her commitment to the party, something she felt she had not received. But that was just the beginning of her story.

Alvarez told me that her husband and children disapproved of her political activism. Since she felt so strongly about being a Liberal, however, defying them had never been a problem, at least not until 1998. "How can I support a man who is starving his country?" she sobbed. She repeated the question several times and wondered out loud how she could reconcile her Liberalism with support for the Alemán administration, the heir of Somocista Liberalism. In her view, Alemán was not a liberal de corazón. He was in politics for the money, using the Liberal Party to profit from the people. Equally upsetting in her view was Alemán's disregard for local political players. He did not respect or acknowledge grassroots Liberals like her who had given their lives to their local communities. Instead, he imposed outside leaders on communities, with disastrous political results for grassroots Liberalism. The damage she felt Alemán was doing to the Liberal Party pained Alvarez deeply.

Since the original intent of this book was not to cover the current period of Nicaraguan politics, I did not deliberately set out to gather Somocista women's opinions about the Sandinista revolution, the Liberal administration of Arnoldo Alemán, or the return to power of Daniel Ortega. But I found that Somocista women's view of the Somoza years was inevitably mediated by their experiences since then. For Alvarez, the Somoza regime was everything the Alemán government was not. She could not help but contrast the two. In her view, the Somozas took care of their people, whereas Alemán was letting them starve. Under the Somozas, she had held political power and had been recognized as a local leader; under Alemán, she felt she had neither power nor recognition.

Several aspects of Alvarez's story need to be stressed. Her complaint about not being recognized by Alemán was a very common one among the Somocista women I interviewed. It does appear that Alemán did not take women into account to the extent that Luis Somoza Debayle, or even Anastasio Somoza Debayle, did. On the other hand, however, Alvarez's complaint about Alemán's imposition of outside leaders on local communities was one that was made often during the Somoza dictatorship, as were complaints about corruption.

Since Alvarez's recollections of the Somoza period do not correspond with established historical fact, what are we to think of her opinions of Alemán? Among my informants, Alvarez was not alone in her positive assessment of the Somozas and her negative assessment of Alemán. Like her, many other working-class Somocistas had voted for Alemán because they wanted a return to the Liberal clientelistic populism of the 1950s and 1960s, a return that never took place. That yearning for the past, the one captured in the Granada study mentioned in the introduction, was felt not only by established Somocistas like Alvarez but also by neo-Somocistas like Maribel López. Some Somocista women became disillusioned with Alemán early on in his administration, before he was convicted of stealing millions of U.S. dollars from Nicaragua's coffers, when neo-Somocista women's support for his administration was at its highest levels. The impact of Alemán's conviction and the effects of the FSLN–PLC pact on Somocista and neo-Somocista women has not been studied. Thus, we do not know how Somocista and neo-Somocista women's political identities have been transformed under Daniel Ortegas rule (2007–11).

Remembering Somocismo

In his study of contemporary Peronism in Argentina, Javier Auyero notes that "to be a Peronist means, and has always meant, many different and competing things. . . . These different meanings are anchored in different relational settings, entailing diverse narratives and memories." Auyero goes on to argue that "in ideal-typical terms, there are not one but two memories of Peronism. On the one hand, the *heretical memory* narrates the history of Peronism in terms of social justice. The *distributional memory*, on the other hand, narrates the history of Peronism in terms of 'what we got from the government.' . . . [T]hese different memories and narratives are neither clear-cut nor mutually exclusive: the difference is mainly a matter of emphasis within a master narrative of Peronism as a 'wonderful time.'"[14]

I found Auyero's analysis quite useful in my study of Somoza supporters, for Somocismo, like Peronism, is remembered both in "heretical" and in "distributional" terms. The emphasis on social justice and the rise of the middle class constitutes the basis for the heretical memories of my informants; the emphasis on the distribution of goods, services, and jobs, the basis for their distributional memories.

Depending on their personal circumstances and experiences, different informants emphasized different aspects of Somocismo in their interviews. Rosa Alvarez, like Maribel López, stressed certain parts of the official story of Somocismo. Perhaps due to their working-class background and to their concern over basic needs like food, they focused on the part that contends the Somozas provided for the people in the 1950s and the 1960s. That is the mythical Nicaragua they wish to return to; they are willing to work hard in order to re-create a clientelistic system that, in their view, functioned fairly. Alvarez's and López's accounts can thus be considered distributional memories of Somocismo.

Marta García, a middle-class Ala co-founder, identified with a different aspect of Somocismo: the rise of the middle class. "Before Liberalism, only the upper and lower classes existed. Liberalism founded [high schools] and the middle class was created through them. . . . Somocismo can be defined as the era in which the middle classes developed in Nicaragua."

Eugenia Robleto, another Ala leader, emphasized the importance of progress and social justice in Somocista politics. She noted that she became involved in mayoral electoral politics under the Somozas because of the poverty she saw in her hometown. In an effort to relieve that poverty, she oversaw the installation of potable water facilities in her region.

Somocista women who stressed the "heretical" aspects of Somocismo were highlighting aspects of Somocismo that the Somozas themselves emphasized, as reflected in a 1967 speech by Anastasio Somoza Debayle:

> In 1946, when I arrived at a hacienda in Chontales to buy cattle, the peons greeted me with their hands joined together [in sign of reverence]. . . . I felt profoundly depressed to see human dignity so trampled by customs imposed by Conservative families, the owners of that hacienda.

I protested to the men, asking that they not disrespect their God, because I was equal to them and such reverence is reserved for God, not for men.

Let not Nicaraguans be surprised by my Nationalist Liberal fervor! For it is our Party which holds the principle that "all Nicaraguans, in civil and political matters are equal before the law. . . ."

That is why I am not impressed by family lineages, or transitory titles or posts like those used by the speaker of the Conservative Party. It is time we, the Nationalist Liberals, and all the workers who are treated feudally by Conservative capital, that we make Conservatives comply with these principles of National Liberalism, for their own happiness and for the happiness of the people of Nicaragua. Here I repeat what I said before the Great Convention: "In my eyes, there are no social classes!"[15]

Although Somocismo meant different things to different people and its meaning changed over time, most Somocistas would agree that it was about "helping people" by bringing peace, progress, and social justice to Nicaragua; about the rise of Nicaragua's middle class, the formation of a modern state, and the creation of jobs; and about anti-Communism.[16] Lucrecia Noguera Carazo, an Ala co-founder, brought up most of these points in an article she wrote for *Novedades*, the Somocista newspaper, in 1969:

The Liberal Party in all periods has been the one that has given the Nicaraguan people their most precious achievements: the Labor Code [Codigo del Trabajo], Social Security, Labor Reforms, Constitutional Rights, the freedom to work, university autonomy, the Agrarian Reform, under the wing of peace. That is why the Nicaraguan people do not need the lure [*canto de sirena*] of the Communists, because the PLN has given, and continues to give, all that is necessary to the people so as to live democratically. And that is why . . . the people will not be able to welcome the Communists, who are a symbol of terror and anarchy, of plunder, hate, crime, and death.[17]

Because female Somocista leaders were policy makers, they had to think in broader political terms than grassroots Somocista women. We can see, however, that there were many intersections between these two groups in their understanding and experience of Somocismo, especially at the personal level. All the women had to find a balance between politics and family matters, often confronting unsupportive husbands (Marta

García, Rosa Alvarez) and parents. Unlike Alvarez, García came from a middle-class Liberal family, although she was "not rich." She married in 1960 and had a child soon after. Even though García's husband was in the Somozas' army, he did not want her to participate in politics. This did not keep her from participating, however, and after her husband left her for another woman, she devoted herself completely to Somocismo and to her child. "I had two children," she explained. "The other one was the Ala." Even while she was married, she noted, "my husband was not able to dominate me completely." For example, against his wishes, she refused to use her husband's last name.

Another commonality between working- and middle-class Somocista women is that, in their versions of their lives, they are the heroines and the true Somocistas. On the one hand, they are the "liberales de corazón," the ones who followed all the rules. On the other hand, they are the ones who went against established societal rules by struggling against un-supportive husbands and parents in order to forge a new nation. They are also the ones whose political careers were slowed down by mother-hood, who had to watch what they did so as not to damage their sexual reputations, and who, implicitly, had to work harder than Somocista men to advance within Somocismo, and harder than subsequent genera-tions of women to advance in politics. "My daughter says, 'I'd like to be just like my mom,'" Eugenia Robleto told me. "But she doesn't like to struggle."

As other scholars have noted about oral histories with women else-where in Latin America, "'tales of resistance against ingrained male stereotypes of femininity' may be placed alongside 'narratives of obedi-ence and conformity'" to party lines.[18] It is in this apparent contradiction in the discourse of Somocista women of different classes that we find that they both supported and subverted the official story of Somocismo. But is there an official Somocista story of Somocismo? If, by "official," we mean dominant versions created and promoted by those who label them-selves "Somocistas," I argue that there are actually two official stories: the pre-1979 story Somocistas told about Somocismo, in which women played a central role; and the post-1996 story contemporary Liberals tell of Somocismo, which ignores Somocista women's participation and por-trays Somocismo as a masculine endeavor. It is important to reiterate that Somocista women (those active in Somocista politics before the revolu-tion of 1979) are largely absent from the story contemporary Liberals tell of Somocismo, the second official story of Somocismo.

Regarding the creation of a dominant popular memory, England's Pop-ular Memory Group wrote in the early 1980s,

It is useful to distinguish the main ways in which a sense of the past is produced: through public representations and through private memory (which, however, may also be collective and shared). . . . In thinking about the ways in which these representations affect individual or group conceptions of the past, we might speak of "dominant memory." This term points to the power and pervasiveness of historical representations, their connections with dominant institutions and the part they play in winning consent and building alliances in the processes of formal politics. But we do not mean to imply that conceptions of the past that acquire a dominance in the field of public representations are either monolithically installed or everywhere believed in. Not all the historical representations which win access to the public field are "dominant." The field is crossed by competing constructions of the past, often at war with each other. Dominant memory is produced in the course of these struggles and is always open to contestation. We do want to insist, however, that there are real processes of domination in the historical field. Certain representations achieve centrality and luxuriate grandly; others are marginalized or excluded or reworked. Nor are the criteria of success here those of truth: dominant representations may be those that are most . . . obviously conforming to the flattened stereotypes of myth.

The authors go on to state: "There is a second way of looking at the social production of memory which draws attention to quite other processes. A knowledge of past and present is also produced in the course of everyday life. There is a common sense of the past. . . . Usually this history is held to the level of private remembrance."[19]

After 1979, Somocista women's memories of Somocismo exist only at the level of private remembrance. They do not form part of the contemporary Liberal version of Somocismo, for that story holds that Somocismo was about "the people," rather than about women as a group. Ironically, it was the contemporary version of Somocismo that drew neo-Somocista women to Liberalism, leading many of them to think that they were the first Liberal women to organize politically in Nicaragua.

In short, Somocista women's memories greatly coincide with the official Somocista discourse of thirty years ago, but not with the contemporary Liberal version of what Somocismo was. According to my informants, women's past contributions to Liberalism were not acknowledged by Arnoldo Alemán in the Liberal resurgence that took place after 1996, and, with a few exceptions, older Somocista women at that time were not invited to participate in the rebuilding of Liberalism. Marta García, for instance, felt that the Alemán administration did not take women into account, even though she, like many other Somocista women living outside Nicaragua, raised funds for Alemán's campaign in 1996 and even though she knew Alemán personally. Indeed, the Liberal propaganda of the late 1990s made hardly any mention of women's long-standing participation within Somocismo. The Liberal officials I spoke to knew nothing about the history of Liberal women. In the late 1990s and the early 2000s, they told me only that "Liberal women are in the process of being organized." Given this situation, it is no wonder that Marta García said to me: "History might have been erased, but we are [still] here."

Somocista Women in a Comparative Perspective

Comparative analyses of women in right-wing politics were rare before 2000. In fact, the study of right-wing women itself is relatively recent, particularly in Latin America. However, two studies in particular stand out, those of Sandra McGee Deutsch and Margaret Power.

The case of Somocista women is in many ways different from that of the right-wing women in Argentina, Brazil, and Chile studied by McGee Deutsch and Power. McGee Deutsch's research is on women in these three countries between 1900 and 1940. She concludes that these decades "gave rise to three distinct periods of rightist activity. . . . In the years before World War I, the extreme right originated in a Catholic-influenced cultural context; during the war (and in the early postwar years), the bourgeois Leagues—with state assistance—battled militant workers; finally the late 1920s inaugurated an age of fascism. Each period had its own characteristic forms of female involvement. Despite some differences among the women and countries under study, the similarities were paramount. The women's main goal was to safeguard rightist notions of family, country, and religion."[20]

Nicaragua was not industrialized in the early twentieth century and did not share with Argentina, Brazil, and Chile (the ABC countries) massive European immigration in the late nineteenth and early twentieth century. These two factors, among others, prevented the development of a strong traditional left and right before the mid-twentieth century. And Fascism, not surprisingly, never developed many adherents in Nicaragua. Moreover, because of the Somozas' Liberal roots, Catholicism was not as important in the development of Somocismo as it was in the formation of other right-wing movements elsewhere. These differences make for a somewhat unusual situation. Nonetheless, there are also important similarities between right-wing women in the ABC region and those in Nicaragua: as it had been in Argentina, Brazil, and Chile between 1920 and 1940, defending family and country against Communism was at the center of Somocista women's mobilization, albeit much later, in the late 1960s and the 1970s.

How do pro-Pinochet and pro-Somoza women compare? Margaret Power has conducted one of the most extensive studies of pro-Pinochet women. She argues that "many of Pinochet's female supporters agreed with him that motherhood is the fundamental expression of womanhood. Disturbed by what they perceived to be the chaos and uncertainty of the Allende years, they looked to the military to restore patriarchal order in society and their families and welcomed the assertion of traditional gender roles." Power goes on to note that "one of the most remarkable qualities of right-wing women during this time is the rapidity with which they transformed their public identity. Since 1973, the military and conservative women had defined women as mothers outside the political sphere whose function was to serve their families and the nation. . . . The overtly political nature of the [1988] plebiscite . . . forced a change in the definition of conservative Chilean womanhood: instead of being apolitical mothers women had to become citizens who actively defended the military regime."[21]

Unlike Pinochet, the Somozas did not mobilize women primarily as mothers, nor did they attempt to turn back the clock to a golden age in Nicaragua's past. To the contrary, Somocistas believed they were forging a radically new and modern Nicaragua, one in which women were new and public participants. Most important perhaps, Somocista women played a crucial role as citizens in presidential elections (albeit fraudulent elections) for almost twenty years (1957–74). Under the dictatorship in Chile, right-wing women had this experience only in 1988.

If the situation of Somocista women differs greatly from that of right-wing women in South America, it differs even more from the experiences of Nazi women in Germany under Hitler and Fascist women in Italy under Mussolini, the two most studied cases of right-wing women in Europe. As in post-Allende Chile, right-wing forces in Germany and Italy were attempting to restore a "gender order turned topsy-turvy"[22] in the years before they came to power. Thus Hitler and Mussolini attempted to push women back into the home so that they could dedicate themselves to motherhood.

According to Victoria de Grazia, women's duty under Fascism was "to bear the nation's children."[23] This emphasis on motherhood was not arbitrary; it reflected a well-developed ideology. Claudia Koonz notes that "to a degree unique in Western history, Nazi doctrine created a society structured around 'natural' biological poles . . . based on race and sex as the immutable categories of human nature."[24] Because of this ideology, Koonz finds that there was a sharp distinction between Nazi men and Nazi women but not between Nazis and non-Nazis. In the Nicaraguan case, I found the opposite to be true: there was a sharp distinction between Somocistas and non-Somocistas but not between Somocista men and Somocista women. Thus an interview with Gilberto Cuadra (b. 1934), an engineer who worked for the Somozas, sounds quite similar to the interviews I conducted with Somocista female professionals:

> I had my first job with the government in 1954; it was a small assignment, with no connections to politics. I continued doing work for the government until 1967. . . . I knew Somoza slightly, just a little. To be frank, working for the government had its advantages. That was the time that Nicaragua really began to develop. Almost everything that we have that is new or modern is a product of that epoch. We progressed because of the labor of many people, but especially through the mechanization of agriculture, which allowed cotton production to increase; the technical improvements in coffee-growing; and a more scientific approach to cattle-raising. Production in these areas meant that the country needed to provide more electricity and better means of communication and transportation. All this was a sudden, swift development for an extremely underdeveloped country.
>
> For me and for many others, those sweeping changes permitted us to develop ourselves much more than we would have been able to do in other countries. For an engineer, modernization on that scale was an exciting adventure. The good and the bad of it is that I still feel that way about myself and about that epoch. It was a privilege to live at a time when I felt like I could be a pathfinder.[25]

Since the Somozas did not set out to create a separate female sphere, as the Nazis did, it seems reasonable that Cuadra's comments would sound similar to those made by Marta García or Antonia Rodríguez.

Comparing and contrasting right-wing women in different regions of the globe can help us understand the reasons behind their differences and similarities. A comparative approach can also help us think differently about the individual countries we study, suggesting new approaches and new questions to be asked.

Conclusion

Kathleen Blee, in her study on women and radical protest, suggests that women in extremist or right-wing groups do not always agree wholeheartedly with their organizations' ideologies. Blee argues that "the ideological engagement of members with [these] groups may be far less comprehensive—and reflect far lower levels of personal commitment—than is commonly understood. Differences between organizational propaganda and personal belief therefore provide a possible avenue for the recruitment of members out of the movement."[26] In the case of Nicaragua, there was no clearly formulated Somocista ideology. This left women free to identify with those aspects of Somocista discourse which made most sense to them. It also made it easier for women to stop supporting the dictatorship when they no longer felt they could identify with Anastasio Somoza Debayle's rhetoric.

This reasoning can help us understand why so many women supported the Sandinista revolution of 1979, for I cannot help but assume that women's widespread support for the FSLN meant that many women left Somocismo in the late 1970s. Unfortunately, my research does not address this important question. I did not interview Sandinista women who were once Somocistas. In any case, it makes sense that both men and women make political choices based on their current situations and the political options available to them at the time. Somocista women believed Liberalism best met their needs under the dictatorship. The women of the post-1996 new Liberal women's movement (including neo-Somocistas) also believe in Liberalism, for economic and political reasons. How Liberal women have fared under the Ortega-Alemán pact and how they have shaped and transformed Liberalism under the new rules remains to be studied.

FIVE

THE ACTIVISM AND LEGACY OF NICOLASA SEVILLA

We cannot properly understand the Somocista women's movement unless we take into account Nicolasa Sevilla's support for the Somoza regime. This chapter documents the role Sevilla played in the dictatorship. Unlike the Ala, which originated as a means to channel middle-class women's political participation into "proper" and acceptable expressions, "la Nicolasa" symbolized the unrestrained manifestation of working-class women's political passion.

The middle-class respectability of the Ala depended on the continuous stereotyping of the Ala's counterpart: working-class Somocista women activists like Nicolasa Sevilla who were accused, justly or unjustly, of being prostitutes, madams, or both. Given their reputation, women like Nicolasa Sevilla were able to engage in political activities middle-class Somocistas sought to avoid. Whereas the Ala was charged with tactfully gaining women's support for the Somozas, Sevilla and her followers, both men and women, were given free rein to heckle, torment, humiliate, and attack those who refused to be swayed by "polite" tactics. The distinction between Ala members and Sevilla's followers, however, was not always clear-cut. Sevilla was sometimes invited to attend Ala functions, as were market women, who made up Sevilla's female constituency.[1] Although there was some overlap between the two groups, the state-sponsored violent gang politics of Sevilla's working-class followers served to high-light the pacific nature of the Ala's activism.

Nicolasa Sevilla's Activism

Because she was a woman, one willing to engage personally in violent acts during her early years of political activism, Sevilla was most effective at intimidating other women, particularly those who belonged to the mid-dle and upper classes. The primary targets of Sevilla's "turbas" (gangs), as they were called by their detractors, were the wives, sisters, and daugh-ters of politicians who opposed Somoza. From the mid-1940s onward, whenever "the wives of [anti-Somocista] ministers protested in public, Nicolasa would make them run."[2] Although there are no claims that she ever killed anyone personally, with her bare hands, rumor has it that Sevilla always carried a gun in her purse and that she was always accom-panied by several armed male bodyguards.[3]

Nicolasa Sevilla's political life, most of which was centered in the cap-ital, spanned almost the entire Somoza dictatorship. She supported all three Somozas. Imprisoned by the Sandinistas in July 1979, she was held at the Modelo Prison in Tipitapa, just outside Managua. She was released by FSLN Comandante Tomás Borge on October 13, 1980, because of her advanced age (seventy-seven), without having to go before the popular tri-bunals that other political prisoners faced.[4] According to journalist Luis E. Duarte, "Tomás Borge in consultation with the [FSLN's] National Direc-torate wanted to demonstrate with the pardon a magnanimous gesture."[5] She left Nicaragua immediately after gaining her freedom and lived with family in the United States until her death more than a decade later. Her daughter Ivonne Solorzano came to Nicaragua to pick her up from jail so that she could be reunited with her children and her many grandchildren.[6]

Sevilla's personal life is the subject of great debate. Among Sandin-istas, she is remembered as a "former prostitute and intimate friend of Somoza García," one who caused the jailing and death of many anti-Somoza activists.[7] Josefa Ortega (pseudonym), a Sandinista woman who knew Sevilla's son, best summarizes the Sandinista perspective on Sevilla: "Nicolasa was a bad woman."[8] The recollections of Somocistas are more nuanced. Antonia Rodríguez (pseudonym) remembers Sevilla had a child with Liberal attorney and former vice president Enoc Aguado in the 1930s or 1940s.[9] After her relationship with Aguado ended, Sevilla "lived with other men," eventually settling down with Eugenio Solorzano, a retired National Guard captain.[10] Solorzano was a founder of the Association of

Retired Military Officers, Workers, and Peasants of Nicaragua (Asociación de Militares Retirados, Obreros, y Campesinos or AMROC) and a high-level administrator of the National District (the city of Managua). His position as director of the National Slaughterhouse, the only slaughterhouse in the country, helped Sevilla come in contact with the people her enemies would later call "thugs": garbage collectors, street sweepers, slaughterhouse employees, and other city workers whom she recruited to vote for the Somozas.[11]

Luis Duarte notes that some Nicaraguans refuse to believe that Nicolasa Sevilla had a sexual relationship with Enoc Aguado, much less that Aguado fathered her son, a persistent rumor that Sevilla herself, according to Duarte, confirmed in 1980, giving the name of her son as Denis Aguado Sevilla. Duarte quotes anti-Somocista Joaquín Absalom Pastora as saying that Aguado, a married man, was too much of a "puritan Conservative" to be involved with someone like Sevilla. They also refuse to believe rumors that Sevilla had sexual liaisons with Anastasio Somoza García and Guillermo Sevilla Sacasa, Somoza's son-in-law, or that she was a prostitute. Bayardo Cuadra, a historian interviewed by Duarte, does not think these rumors are based in reality. Nicolasa Sevilla's relatives also dismiss the rumors about Sevilla being a prostitute and madam. One relative I spoke to explained to me that Sevilla had simply engaged in serial monogamy, which was then labeled "prostitution" for political purposes. Whether or not she ever exchanged sex for money or for favors is almost irrelevant. The fact that most people believe she did, however, matters a great deal since this has had long-standing negative consequences for her family, for working-class political activists, and for all Nicaraguan women involved in politics.

It is difficult to know what sort of an impact Sevilla's physical appearance had on her political career. Since many people mention her looks, this probably means that they mattered. Most interesting is the fact that Sevilla was light skinned and "did not have indigenous features."[12] Her light skin and her "presentable" clothes meant that she would not have immediately been identified as a working-class woman, much less a prostitute (fig. 15). On the other hand, in Luis Duarte's view, "Sevilla was not a pretty woman."[13] And Joaquín Absalom Pastora, one of Sevilla's victims from the 1958 attack on the Radio Mundial, agrees: "To me, she was not attractive, but those are personal tastes." Duarte goes on to write that Sevilla "had a hard face, while her husband or life partner [Solorzano] was the typical hard-rock-faced assassin type."[14]

Although some Nicaraguans today remember Sevilla as the president of AMROC,[15] this was not the case. She was, however, the founder and leader of the Somocista Popular Fronts.[16] In the late 1950s, these fronts had exclusively female committees throughout the nation.[17] Later on, they consisted of anti-Communist gangs made up of urban working-class men in their twenties and thirties, some of them members of the Somocista youth organization, the Juventud Somocista. In the eyes of their opponents, the later Somocista Popular Fronts functioned as a paramilitary terrorist organization[18] and might indeed have been related to the "Mano Blanca" (White Hand), a government-supported anti-Sandinista clandestine terrorist group that emerged in the late 1970s.[19] Regardless of whether this allegation is true, there is no doubt that Sevilla wielded great power among her followers at the grass roots and instilled fear among the population at large.

In addition to her privileged position within working-class Somocismo, Sevilla held a special place within the middle and upper echelons of the dictatorship. She participated in electoral campaigns, published articles in Somocista newspapers, and had a say in the government's upper circles. According to Antonia Rodríguez, "there was a Sevilla representative in every electoral district."[20] She was also "given the run of two pro-government newspapers," in which she "vilified Managua society."[21] Moreover, Sevilla "could go to any Ministry and the secretary there could not tell her to wait. Her power was extraordinary."[22] Most important perhaps, Sevilla was perceived as being always at the president's side: "Wherever Somoza [García] went, there she went."[23] William Krehm, a *Time* reporter who witnessed Sevilla's activism firsthand in the 1940s, notes that Sevilla, the "skinny, blue-eyed . . . owner of a cut-rate brothel,"[24] had indeed become "a pillar of the regime."[25]

How exactly Sevilla came to wield so much power remains unclear. "Leaders are not born, they are made," Antonia Rodríguez told me. "Somoza [García] saw something in [Sevilla] and knew it would benefit him to have her on his side. . . . She was like attorney Olga Núñez de Saballos, but in a different realm. She made her own organization. But as I said, she was not upper-class, she was of the people."[26]

According to Reina Zambrano (pseudonym), a well-known anti-Somocista activist who had many confrontations with Sevilla, la Nicolasa became a Somoza supporter because Enoc Aguado, a high-level Liberal politician who turned against Somoza, had refused to marry her. Aguado, the founder of the Independent Liberal Party (PLI), turned against Somoza in the 1940s. It is rumored that Somoza later poisoned him on Sevilla's request.[27] Although Sevilla's relatives emphatically reject this rumor as false, they are unable to explain why exactly Sevilla devoted so much time and energy to the Somocista cause over so many years, at great personal expense.[28]

Nicolasa Sevilla's activism took a toll on her family. The social discrimination against her children may well have influenced her son's decision to take his life. Douglas García Sevilla, a Somocista activist like his mother, committed suicide in 1955, months shy of finishing work on a degree in arts and letters.[29]

Personal encounters like those Reina Zambrano, Antonia Rodríguez, and William Krehm had with Sevilla and her followers helped turn la Nicolasa into a legendary figure of national and international proportions. Because she became such a controversial figure, it is often hard to separate fact from fiction in the stories told about her. Nonetheless, certain events did in fact take place and deserve special notice. Actions Sevilla took in 1944, 1958, 1962, and 1969 are especially important to address in detail.

By most accounts, Sevilla first gained national and international attention in 1944, when she was forty-two years old. Sources agree that, on June 29 of that year, Sevilla led a counterprotest to an anti-Somoza protest taking place in Managua. Both groups were made up of women. However, the anti-Somocista forces were made up of middle-class women and the pro-Somoza faction was working-class.[30]

According to the Conservative newspaper *La Prensa*, Sevilla's followers were "a rabble of market vendors and women of ill repute."[31] William Krehm's article "Call All Trulls" in the August 7, 1944, issue of *Time* presents a detailed description of events:

> A procession of dignified, black-clad . . . elderly mothers, respectable wives and daughters . . . [were] protest[ing] the mass arrest of more than 600 opponents of Dictator Anastasio Somoza [García] . . . [when o]ut of the Managua slums rushed mobs of prostitutes. They pressed around the horrified women and girls, slapped them, spat at them. Male relatives came to the rescue [and] dispersed the screaming trulls. Then, from an official Government auto jumped . . . Nicolasa Sevilla. . . . Threatening the older women with a knife, she spluttered filth at the prettier girls. . . . [T]he harlotry then receded into the slums. But the President invited Nicolasa to the Palace, called her his "very good friend," and introduced her to outraged callers.

Later that year, Krehm's article goes on to say, Sevilla "invaded the Chamber of Deputies and slapped a speaker."[32] Confronting anti-Somocistas inside governmental buildings would become one of Sevilla's trademarks. The tactic was seemingly supported by the Somozas themselves, for similar events took place years later. Author Bernard Diederich tells how, in 1962, an anti-Somoza crowd entered the Congress Building to protest [a law under consideration]. They were expected. Waiting for them was a gang of eighty government thugs headed by Nicolasa Sevilla, a tough-looking woman who commanded the Somoza male street gangs in Managua. When the demonstrators cried "Liberty" and "The Somozas must go" they were met with knives and sticks. Some of Nicolasa's boys even drew pistols and fired into the crowd. When the half-hour melee ended and the demonstrators had retreated, there were no dead, but there were thirty-five wounded, including "la Nicolasa," who had been hit on the head by a chair. The congressmen continued their session and passed the new broadcast law in the presence of the National Guard, guns drawn.[33]

Attorney Miriam Argüello, the most prominent female activist in the Conservative Party, recalls "having been there that day, when the Congress was going to discuss what came to be called the 'Black Code,' a law against freedom of the press. We decided, those of us in the opposition, in the Conservative Party, to go to Congress on the day of the debate, to protest that law. So we went. When we got there, Nicolasa came in with her gangs, armed with sticks. Guns went off, people were injured."[34] Luciano Cuadra Vega was also present: "The Somocista gangs injured me . . . when we went to protest against the 'Muzzle Law [Ley del Bozal].' One of Nicolasa Sevilla's bodyguards hit me with a metal-encrusted stick."[35]

On August 20, 1969, Nicolasa's gangs were involved in harassing and beating anti-Somocista teachers who had gathered at the House of the Teacher (Casa del Maestro) in Managua. According to the anti-Somocista newspaper *La Prensa,*

> approximately 100 workers from the National District [city employees] . . . attacked the House of the Teacher [a place where teachers came together to organize] armed with sticks, machetes, and other weapons . . . about fifty street sweepers tried to enter into the House, but they were unsuccessful, since the teachers had closed the door.
>
> Nonetheless, the city employees were eventually able to make a big hole in the front door. . . .
>
> Outside, on a street corner, were Nicolasa and Leonel Betanco, from the National District, leading 100 individuals armed with sticks. . . . One of the leaders of Nicolasa's gangs opened fire into a group of students who were supporting the teachers.[36]

Thirty-one years after this event, Dionisio Herrera y Canales recalled in detail what transpired. He contends that the attack perpetrated by the "Nicolasian hordes" was planned and financed by Ala leaders Mary Coco Maltez de Callejas, the vice minister of education at the time, and Zaida Fernandez de Ruiz, vice minister of Managua, who were present at the confrontation. The attack was an attempt to disrupt political activity on the part of teachers organized in the left-leaning Federation of Nicaraguan Teachers (Federación Sindical de Maestros de Nicaragua or FSMN), a group the Somozas accused of being "Sandino-Communists."[37] Not surprisingly, the assault had the opposite effect on the teachers, inciting even more opposition against the regime.

Hundreds of teachers affiliated with the FSMN had peacefully gathered the morning of August 20 to discuss demands for better wages and better retirement packages when Nicolasa Sevilla and her gangs attacked them. Students in the Ramírez Goyena and Maestro Gabriel Public Schools nearby, upon hearing of the events, left their classrooms and joined the melee in support of the FSMN teachers, battling Sevilla's forces with rocks. The confrontation ended with many injured, including Monsignor Julian Barni, who had been called in to negotiate between the two groups.

In response to the attack, 95 percent of all public school teachers quickly went on strike, forcing the Somozas to negotiate with the union.[38] Less than a decade later, in 1977, the FSMN would become part of the National Association of Nicaraguan Educators (Asociación Nacional de Educadores de Nicaragua or ANDEN), which would support the Sandinista revolution of 1979.[39]

On August 5, 1958, Sevilla and her followers had attacked Radio Mundial, a popular radio station, and savagely beaten its owner, Manuel Arana, and the journalist Joaquín Absalom Pastora, among others.[40] This event is perhaps the most well-documented event in which Nicolasa Sevilla participated. Women had gathered at the station to protest the detention of their husbands by the Somoza administration. Nicolasa Sevilla was there to stop the women and to intimidate the Radio Mundial staff, longtime advocates of freedom of the press. According to Guillermo Rothschuh, the Somozas, "having been unable to co-opt the station . . . attempted to destroy it. Somocismo showed itself to be faithful to its motto: Silver for friends, sticks for those indifferent, and lead for its adversaries. With Radio Mundial they failed, [for it] came back more vigorous and vibrant than ever." Founded in 1948, it is Nicaragua's oldest radio station.[41]

As these brief yet detailed accounts suggest, Sevilla's followers changed over the course of twenty years. In the 1940s, she led mostly working-class women; by the 1960s, her constituency comprised mostly working-class men. Two related factors might have led to this change. First, Sevilla became part of the Somoza establishment. Her new position must have required a new image, one not tarnished by the presence of working-class women of "ill repute." And, second, Sevilla's association with the National District and AMROC gave her access to a different sector of the population and to a certain amount of wealth. Sevilla obviously took advantage of her position to mobilize men of the popular classes. In fact, she sometimes even bought their support.[42] By mobilizing women and men for more than three decades, Sevilla became the most powerful and successful, and the best-known, female working-class broker within Somocista clientelism. She continues to be the best-known Somocista woman in contemporary Nicaragua.

Although Sevilla's followers might have changed throughout the decades, her endorsement of the Somoza family never seemed to waver. For more than thirty years, she dressed in red, the color of Liberalism in Nicaragua. In the early 1980s, the ever-feisty Sevilla was still considered someone to be reckoned with. According to Antonia Rodríguez, Sevilla constantly harassed her Sandinista jailers. Gray-haired and aged, la Nicolasa taunted them, pledging her unending support for the Nationalist Liberal Party, until they eventually freed her from jail.[43]

Once freed, however, Sevilla appears to have become more politically subdued, at least temporarily. As reported by journalist Luis Duarte, in the speech she gave outside the jail on the day of her release, she quietly stated, "May God bless you, may he help you make this land, my homeland, progress. May God bless the true revolutionaries who encountered face to face . . ." According to Duarte, Sevilla never finished her sentence, but did comment that she had been deceived by the "Liberal opium."[44] After she left Nicaragua, family members urged her to forget her mother country and begin anew.[45]

Nicolasa Sevilla and the "Patriotic Prostitutes"

As reported in the anti-Somocista newspaper *La Prensa*, Sevilla explained her support for the dictatorship by saying she did not "eat at the Somozas' table." She helped them simply because she "cared for" them and because "they did good for the people."[46] This article obviously made fun of Sevilla, for it was publicly known that la Nicolasa or "la Colacha," as she was called (a common nickname for "Nicolasa"), received money from the Somozas in exchange for her political work.[47] Moreover, since it was rumored that Sevilla had been Anastasio Somoza García's mistress,[48] the phrase she simply "cared for" the Somozas acquired a double meaning, underlining her supposed past as a mistress and a prostitute. The second so-called reason why la Nicolasa supported the regime was, from an anti-Somocista perspective, the most absurd. In the context of censure and severe restrictions on freedom of the press, to quote Sevilla as saying, in an opposition newspaper, that the Somozas "did good for the people" was a subtle critique of the government and the only kind allowed.

According to Marta García (pseudonym), one of the founders of the Ala Femenina, "Nicolasa was sincere about her work. She did it thinking she was doing a great job." Her legacy was "to have made people enthusiastic, but she caused the government [and middle-class Liberal women] conflicts. Nicolasa would call [Ala members] 'the intellectuals.' She gave us a hard time at first because she was jealous. She didn't like us, she attacked us a lot. We were a little scared of her."[49]

Despite class conflicts such as this one within the Somocista women's movement, women of different social classes worked together on behalf of the regime. And despite the fear that la Nicolasa instilled in middle-class Somocista women, Ala members benefited from Sevilla's bad reputation. The inevitable comparison with la Nicolasa helped women like Marta García appear to be more respectable and less "public" than the Somocista women of the popular forces.

But how did a supposed prostitute gain so much political visibility within a right-wing dictatorship? The "patriotic prostitute" who sacrifices herself for the nation has played an important role in Nicaraguan politics, not only within Somocismo.[50] During the 1920s, a group of prostitutes supported Augusto C. Sandino's struggle against U.S. intervention:

> What [Juan Bautista] Sacasa and his generals could not or did not do, was done by a group of prostitutes [mujeres públicas] in [Puerto Cabezas].
>
> The patriotism of these women could be felt in the strength of their feelings and they considered it their duty to assist Sandino and his men in the task of saving Nicaraguan arms from the actions of the invaders [The Marines had ordered the destruction of Sacasa's and Sandino's arms]. Led by Sandino, each one of them brought out from under her clothes a double-barrel rifle and as much ammunition as she was able to carry. This is how Sandino found himself in the early hours of the next morning with a good number of rifles and more than seven thousand cartridges.[51]

Although socially marginalized, prostitutes have played a central role in both the political discourse and politics of Nicaragua, becoming an integral part of the nation's imaginary and body politic. The figure of the prostitute is particularly useful in politics because of its malleability. In this context, the actions of "good" anti-imperialist prostitutes become no more than a tool used to question the manhood of "sellouts" like Sacasa, while the actions of "bad" Somocista prostitutes reinforce the Nicaraguan version of the Malinche story, in which women are blamed for their victimization and for the downfall of the nation.

Nicolasa Sevilla terrified Somocistas and anti-Somocistas alike. The emotional words Nicaraguans use to describe their strong feelings about her shed light on how the figure of the prostitute came to symbolize, for the regime's opponents, the evils of the dictatorship. One anti-Somocista leader remembers,

> The figure of repression for us women was another woman, a woman who undressed us in the street. Once, I went to the National Palace because a first cousin of mine who was Somocista was the personal secretary to [a high-ranking Somocista administrator]. I arrived and saw some people there, and when I was on my way out Nicolasa said she was going to beat me up and undress me in the street. But my cousin told her who I was [related to] and she didn't undress me in front of the Palace. But in Granada, in the Central Park, Nicolasa undressed the Marenco sisters, and it was in a public, virulent attack. All of us women were stripped of our dignity in the street by another woman.[52]

Sevilla's tactics were so outrageous, cruel, and public that she constantly drew attention to herself in the media. As early as 1944, La Prensa proclaimed,

> Nicolasa Sevilla is the best propaganda for the opposition. She has become a kind of "Cegua" or "Carreta Nagua," which causes horror among women and children. For the opposition, the best propaganda . . . are Nicolasa Sevilla's misdeeds and exploits, for she makes the government appear to be supported by women of her class. On Saturday, she threw some sand . . . into the eyes of Sra. Cristiana de Pasos, and she created an enormous commotion in the street when she hurled insults at Srta. Rosales, when she insulted the Barreto spinsters [niñas] and pulled out a dagger in Darío Park, when she insulted the Lacayo niñas with vile comments, threatened and insulted Sra. Nora de Aguilar, and did countless similar things. . . . She has no respect for age or political affiliation,

for she has even insulted the daughters of Liberals who collaborate with the Somozas. . . . We insist that we are judging this case as a social problem that needs to be resolved for, if we judged it as a political issue, we would wish that Nicolasa Sevilla continue dishonoring and covering in shame those who . . . counsel and . . . defend her.[53]

It is not surprising that la Nicolasa was compared to "la Cegua" and "la Carreta Nagua," two figures that have aroused great fear among the population, dating back to colonial times. La Cegua is a woman who turns into a witch by shedding her skin. According to anthropologist Milagros Palma, "in small towns there is always someone who can tell a story of the apparition of one of these women who go out at night especially to frighten men who are drinking or visiting a favorite lover. Men do not even trust their own wives; they wonder about their powers and think that they can turn into *ceguas* and that in that state they might appear to them and chase them, harm them and make them impotent from fright." The Carreta Nagua—literally the "Nagua Wagon"—frightened people for different reasons. According to Palma, "the oxen-pulled wagon was introduced to the New World by the Spanish." The wagon's "infernal sound . . . was interpreted as a new manifestation of the spirits of the night, which constantly besieged the tranquility of the [Indian] pueblos."[54]

The Carreta Nagua and the Cegua play a "moralizing role" in society, reminding the population of two contradictory points: that those who stray from appropriate behavior will be punished and that punishment can be unjust and arbitrary.[55] Comparing la Nicolasa to both the Cegua and the Carreta Nagua, anti-Somocistas suggested two possibilities: either Nicaraguans deserved la Nicolasa (especially Sevilla's female Somocista targets) or perhaps they needed to do something about this unjust situation.

Another possibility is raised in a poem about the Cegua written by Rubén Darío in the late nineteenth century. According to Darío, the Cegua lives in all of us:

En fin: en todo mortal,
algo de cegua se encuentra;
en el que se va, y el que entra
en este mundo ideal.
De todo ser terrenal,
aun del que os sea mas grato,
esperad siempre un mal rato:

que hallaréis fotografiado
en uno o en otro lado
de la cegua el fiel retrato.

In sum, in every mortal,
there is a bit of *la cegua*;
in him who leaves and him who enters
into this ideal world.
From all terrestrial beings,
even from those who are agreeable to you,
await always some bad moments:
for you will find photographed
in one place or another
the exact picture of *la cegua*.[56]

Nicolasa Sevilla's Legacy

The use of violence by Somocista working-class gangs was a phenomenon that predated Nicolasa Sevilla's entry into politics in 1944, although, before Nicolasa, the gangs had been exclusively male. Rolando Hernández Aburto, an engineer who lived in Managua's San Antonio neighborhood, recalls his experience with one such gang in 1942:

> On a sunny and tranquil afternoon . . . I was . . . sitting . . . [in a park located across from the San Antonio Church] when all of a sudden I saw a line of men appear. They were walking quickly, two at a time. . . . Some carried . . . heavy bars of iron; others were armed with pickaxes.
> "Where are they headed?" I wondered. . . . I saw them enter . . . [a] yellow building. . . . I ran . . . toward the building . . . to see what they were going to do, and this is what I saw: they started to . . . break the machines that printed the newspaper *La Nueva Prensa*, property of Sr. Gabry Rivas, who lived a few blocks away. . . .
> Sr. Gabry Rivas was a Somocista, but he had written some editorials that did not please President Somoza [García] and for that reason [Somoza] ordered the destruction of the machines.[57]

Nicolasa Sevilla would eventually become the only female leader of these Somocista "arm[ies] of street sweepers and garbage collectors."[58] Although her position points to the new leadership opportunities women had under the Somoza regime, it also demonstrates the constraints working-class women (particularly those with a tarnished sexual reputation) faced in politics. Nicolasa Sevilla was never named to an official governmental post and was never voted into office. In short, Sevilla had power but was denied dignity and acceptance.

Nicolasa Sevilla's long-term legacy is complex. On the one hand, she helped dispel the myth that women are inherently peaceful. On the other hand, she reinforced stereotypes about working-class women's "suspect" sexuality. Ironically, today she is the only woman men are ever compared to in Nicaraguan politics.

Political scientist Consuelo Cruz Sequeira notes that Nicolasa Sevilla "has become a prominent character in Nicaraguan folklore. If a woman is called 'a Nicolasa' she stands accused by that single name of being mercenary, loud, vulgar, and rough."[59] A politician who engages in public "scandalous" or violent behavior is often labeled "a Nicolasa Sevilla." Thus, speaking of Alejandro Fiallos, a Liberal municipal representative, Managua's Sandinista mayor Herty Lewites noted in March 2001: "Everyone sees Fiallos as a Nicolasa Sevilla. Can you believe the vulgarities he shouted in a place where composure and respect must reign?"[60]

Indeed, Nicolasa Sevilla has been mentioned more frequently in recent years than ever before. During the 1980s, FSLN founder Tomás Borge had called violent Sandinista working-class groups demonstrating against upper- and middle-class counterrevolutionaries "divine mobs." Critics argued these mobs were modeled after Nicolasa Sevilla's gangs and warned that they would be resurrected when Daniel Ortega returned to power, as he did in 2007.

Newspaper articles in the late 2000s were replete with references to "Nicolasas" and "Nicolasos," usually referring to Sandinista leaders of working-class groups who threatened to commit, or did commit, violent acts against their political enemies.[61] Nicolasa Sevilla's "goon squads,"[62] those "repressive mercenary mobs . . . presented as spontaneous explosions of popular fury"[63] thus continued to be a model for political action, at least in the collective imaginary. In a surprising and unexpected turn of events, however, it was Daniel Ortega and his followers who were now being labeled Nicolasa's "nefarious heirs."[64]

Conclusion

Some women of the popular classes, including those who were socially shunned as supposed prostitutes, madams, or mistresses of powerful men, were drawn to Somocismo. Nicolasa Sevilla was one of them. Although hers was a unique situation, Sevilla came to hold a great degree of power within the dictatorship. Like middle-class women of the Ala, Sevilla was able to benefit economically under the Somozas. Moreover, she was able to define Somocismo on her own terms, albeit within the constraints society imposed on those of her class background.

Most important, Sevilla's working-class heritage did not prevent her from participating fully as a broker in Somocista clientelism. She presided over what was perhaps the largest—or at least the most infamous—working-class urban client network in Managua's entire history. Although some poor people benefited economically and politically from these networks in the short term, the long-term results were not positive. Because of the existence of the Somocista Popular Fronts, many in Nicaragua today associate the political mobilization of the urban poor with violence and the crudest sort of clientelism. In the end, the participation of Managua's poor in Somocista clientelism robbed them of their agency in the eyes of their fellow Nicaraguans.

Fig. 1 Juanita Molina de Fromen. The Schlesinger Library, Radcliffe Institute, Harvard University.

Fig. 2 Salvadora Debayle de Somoza (third from left) with María Elena de Porras (center) and other Ala leaders. Courtesy Instituto de Historia de Nicaragua y Centroamérica.

Fig. 3 Luis H. Debayle (1865–1938). Courtesy Instituto de Historia de Nicaragua y Centroamérica.

Fig. 4 Guillermo Sevilla Sacasa. Courtesy Instituto de Historia de Nicaragua y Centroamérica.

Fig. 5 Anastasio Somoza García poses for a photograph, surrounded by women. Courtesy Instituto de Historia de Nicaragua y Centroamérica.

Fig. 6 Luis Somoza Debayle talking with women. Courtesy Instituto de Historia de Nicaragua y Centroamérica.

Fig. 7 Luis Somoza Debayle seated, surrounded by women. Standing behind him is his younger brother, Anastasio Somoza Debayle. Courtesy Instituto de Historia de Nicaragua y Centroamérica.

Fig. 8 Liberal Party Propaganda House for Luis Somoza Debayle in preparation for the 1957 election. Courtesy Archivo General de la Nación–Nicaragua.

Fig. 9 Ala Femenina from La Concepción. Courtesy Archivo General de la Nación–Nicaragua.

Fig. 10 Liberal Women from Muy Muy, Matagalpa. Courtesy Archivo General de la Nación–Nicaragua.

Fig. 11 Irma Guerrero Chavarría, an Ala leader from Chinandega, and Guillermo Sevilla Sacasa, September 17, 1968. Courtesy Instituto de Historia de Nicaragua y Centroamérica.

Fig. 12 Event honoring Somocista leader Carmen Lara de Borgen. Courtesy Instituto de Historia de Nicaragua y Centroamérica.

Fig. 13 Member of Congress and Ala leader Mary Coco Maltez de Callejas delivering a speech, July 13, 1978. Courtesy Instituto de Historia de Nicaragua y Centroamérica.

Fig. 14 "Batahola Loves Somoza," June 29, 1978. Courtesy Instituto de Historia de Nicaragua y Centroamérica.

Fig. 15 Nicolasa Sevilla.
Courtesy Instituto de Historia
de Nicaragua y Centroamérica.

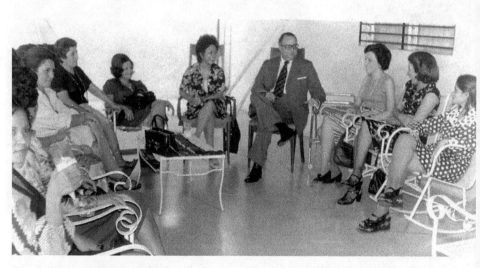

Fig. 16 Anastasio Somoza Debayle with the wives of army officers. Courtesy Instituto de Historia
de Nicaragua y Centroamérica.

S I X

SEX AND SOMOCISMO

Before the advent of the Sandinista National Liberation Front in the 1960s, the nation-building project of the Somozas' Nationalist Liberal Party was the most inclusive ever to be promoted in Nicaragua. But it was full of contradictions for women. It incorporated women into the nation's economic system, but as low-paid workers, and into the nation's political system, but as loyal voters organized in pro-government partisan groups. This Liberal legacy—radical in comparison to the Conservative one—resulted in the formation of a populist Somocista Liberalism that rested not on moralistic or maternalist ground but on the public display of exaggerated sexuality. During the Somozas' years in power, certain misogynistic sexual practices common to all social classes of Nicaraguan society—husbands' public extramarital affairs, male promiscuity, and the prostitution and rape of women—would be writ large on the national canvas. The Somozas personally exemplified promiscuity by openly engaging in countless extramarital affairs. Prostitution was institutionalized under their rule, as was state-sponsored sexual violence against female anti-Somocista prisoners.

Even as the Somozas fostered women's leadership and solidarity among Somocista women through the Ala Femenina, they worked to reinforce the sexism already present in Nicaraguan culture, with negative results for women. In this regard, Roger Lancaster's findings during the 1980s can also be applied to the Somoza period:

> Women often find their intimate emotional (and sometimes even much of their *material*) support and mutual aid in the company of other women more than in the company of men. . . .
> This female world is . . . a necessary prerequisite for the ongoing reproduction of the male world of machismo—for the package of assumptions it carries, the efforts and resources it allots, even the spheres of relative autonomy it grants for women, are part and parcel of a deeply gendered division of the world, where gender remains defined in terms of male dominion over women and children.[1]

Under the Somozas, women's work and political participation outside the home was not meant to disturb traditional family arrangements or women's relationship to their husbands or children; it was simply an added responsibility, recognized by the state. This way of thinking can be found in a Somocista grade school textbook, which stated: "Now the mother cannot stay in the house, in her home, only tending to her children, her husband, the domestic chores, etc.; now in addition to attending to her family, she has to go out to work in diverse occupations, to help in the economy of the home."[2]

Women's entry into politics through a female partisan organization and into the workforce in traditionally female fields did not radically alter gender relations in Nicaragua either for the better or for the worse. Yet, in the aftermath of the Somozas' reign, Nicaraguan and foreign anti-Somocistas remember the dictatorship as a period of extreme sexism and profound sexual exploitation of women. This understanding of the Somoza period is based on three factors: the power and visibility of Nicolasa Sevilla under the dictatorship, the state's support of prostitution for the National Guard's economic gain, and the rape of numerous anti-Somocista women. Anti-Somocistas' anxieties about the Somozas' sexual legacy are also rooted in early and mid-twentieth-century preoccupations over the effects of modernization and U.S. intervention on women.

This chapter deals with sexual politics under the Somozas and with how the Somoza period is remembered in contemporary Nicaragua. The first section addresses early twentieth-century concerns over modernization and women's sexuality; the second considers the experiences of women rightly and wrongly accused of prostitution; the third discusses the history of prostitution in Nicaragua; the fourth and fifth examine the rape of anti-Somocista women under the dictatorship; the sixth deals with the intersections between maternalism and clientelism; the seventh addresses the concepts of both sexual order and disorder used to characterize the regime and the ways in which Somocista women's discourse may reveal elements of resistance; and the eighth section discusses contemporary memory, the masculinization of Nicaragua's "new" Right in the 1990s, and the "Righting" of Nicaragua's Left after 2007.

"They Learned the Diabolic Art of Seducing Men": Women, U.S. Intervention, and Modernization

In the 1920s and 1930s, U.S. intervention in Nicaragua and Nicaraguan women's entry into the labor force in the decades that followed provoked concerns over women and their sexuality. During the 1920s, many Conservatives deplored the supposed end of "the old patriarchal customs," considered to be "gone forever."[3] In the 1940s, intellectuals like Francisco Palma Martínez (1892–1950?) worried about the sexual and class disorder created by the emergence of the "modern woman," which they blamed, at least in part, on the U.S. Marines. U.S. imperialism, wrote Palma Martínez, had familiarized women of all social classes with the devil: "We have seen how makeup started. . . . The occupying Marines brought it to Nicaragua in 1926, to dominate working-class women, who up until then had been reluctant to wear it. Those of the middle class had learned the new fashion from the movies, and society [ladies] who had gone to the United States, it was there that they learned the diabolic art of seducing men."[4]

Makeup "made in U.S.A." was the symbol of modernism in Palma Martínez's eyes, a great evil that plagued feminine sexuality: "More than industrialization, more than her economic independence, more than the last two World Wars, what has caused the current state of woman's immorality is something that appears to be . . . innocent: lipstick."[5]

Believing the "modern woman" to be sexually and morally corrupt, Palma Martínez launched a campaign against her in his book *El siglo de los topos*. Not only had modernity provoked the sexual liberation of women in the United States, with disastrous results: "a terrible wave of disorders, kidnappings, elopements, divorces, adulteries, abortions, assassinations, and sexual crimes," but it had done so in Nicaragua as well, where, he feared, women had been "Yanqui-ized."[6] Palma Martínez saw a direct correlation between the employment of women and prostitution:

> Now woman looks for a job and finds one, and she becomes economically independent. By doing this, she goes against natural law:

woman was not made to work, she was made for the home, and to procreate. Whether you like it or not; and don't blame me for it, for I did not make her that way. Work is a disgrace for women. When she works, she rebels against her parents. . . . As a laborer, she would have obtained a husband of her own social class; now she is admired and wooed by her employers, office workers, elegant men. . . . She goes through all kind of excesses, all types of prostitution and freedoms, and she thinks she has reached the pinnacle of her happiness.[7]

Anxiety over the "modernization" of women spread throughout Latin America. In Brazil, as in many other countries, this anxiety was tied to industrialization, European immigration, and the development of the Left and the feminist movement.[8] In Nicaragua, it was linked to U.S. imperialism and the development of a feminist movement in the 1920s, and, after the 1930s, to the incorporation of urban women into the labor force as a result of the Somocista state's expansion.

Palma Martínez was not wrong when he observed that working for wages outside the home, in whatever occupation, made women sexually vulnerable.[9] Employment also introduced them to a wider group of men than they normally would have encountered, while also providing them with a certain degree of economic independence, which did indeed help workingwomen break some of the long-established patterns of class segregation. Nonetheless, in Nicaragua, as elsewhere, short-term economic opportunities or openings for women of different social classes did not bring about long-term economic independence, possibly because so many workingwomen were single parents, and the wages they received were lower than men's wages.

The Somocista Era: "Ladies Versus Prostitutes"

Political participation for women and prostitution were [considered] one and the same thing.
—*Sandinista Comandante Doris María Tijerino*

A prostitute is not only the woman who sells herself in exchange for money, but also the woman who seeks husbands or men for pleasure.
—*Aura Lila Lacayo*[10]

Women's political and economic participation has often been associated with prostitution. In the case of the Somocista regime, Nicolasa Sevilla, the founder of the Somocista Popular Fronts, was not the only one accused of prostitution, although she was particularly vulnerable due to her working-class origins. The professional middle-class leaders of the Ala Femenina, the Women's Wing of the Liberal Party, were accused of being mistresses to the Somozas. And Liberal women of advanced age such as the feminist Josefa Toledo de Aguerri (1866–1962) were accused of promoting the prostitution of their young female students.

Three unrelated informants, one female and two male, volunteered the same information to me, revealed as rumor: "You do know what they say about your doña Chepita, don't you? She wasn't such a saint, you know." Specifically, my informants told me that Josefa Toledo de Aguerri presented virgin teenage students as "gifts" to Presidents José Santos Zelaya (1893–1909) and Anastasio Somoza García (1937–47; 1950–56). Some of these students then went on to become prominent leaders of the Ala Femenina.

When I asked my informants whether they personally believed these rumors were true, the Somocista female informant dismissed them as gossip and made me promise that I would not tell anyone she had repeated such stories. By contrast, the two male informants (one Somocista and one anti-Somocista) appeared to believe they might be true or, at the very least, were unwilling to tell me what they really thought about the accusations against doña Chepita.

To assess how widespread these unlikely rumors about Toledo de Aguerri and Ala leaders were, I asked Isabel Domínguez (pseudonym), a Liberal teacher, whether she knew about them. Domínguez's response was brief and filled with disgust toward me: "Yes, that is what some people say." My question appeared to have angered her; she seemed to think I was a pervert and, as a result, became very reserved during the rest of the interview. In view of her reaction, I did not ask any other informants this question.

Whether based on rumors or "facts," the figure of the prostitute came to symbolize the moral corruption of the regime. The Conservative anti-Somocista leader and eventual martyr Pedro Joaquín Chamorro (1924–1978) made a moral distinction between Somocista and anti-Somocista women. Although women from both groups have told me that they were considered sexually suspect by their enemies simply because of their participation in public life, Chamorro labeled the Somocistas "prostitutes" and the anti-Somocistas "ladies." Recalling a time when he and other anti-Somocista activists were arrested in the 1950s, Chamorro noted:

> We were turned over to . . . a gang paid by the Somozas to spit at us and throw rocks at us.

The crowd was led by a woman called "Nicolasa Sevilla," whose history has stained Nicaraguan politics. She was furious and shouted the most obscene utterances imaginable.

She had really been sent to "block" our relatives [from entering the prison]. . . . It was the old trick used by Somoza [García] since 1944, when he paid a large number of prostitutes to throw themselves at the mothers and wives of those who were imprisoned at the time, as they walked clad in black through the streets of Managua. In [Somoza's] attitude then, and in his sons' attitude now, there was a dichotomy upon which the regime established itself: immorality on the one hand, and terror on the other. It was the total inversion of the moral values of Nicaraguan life: prostitutes against mothers, alcohol against civic duty, blackmail against honesty, lowlifes against citizens.[11]

The dichotomy described by Chamorro is the main theme of *De Mrs. Hanna a la Dinorah*, in which Viktor Morales Henríquez argues that sexual corruption brought the first Somoza to power and the last dictator to ruin. According to Morales, the wife of Matthew Hanna, the U.S. ambassador to Nicaragua from 1930 to 1933, fell in love with Somoza García and helped him climb to power. Decades later, according to Morales, Anastasio Somoza Debayle would lose his head over his mistress, Dinorah Sampson, forgetting all about the country's welfare: "We must not remain indifferent to the fact that the most disgraceful dictatorship in the Americas, born from a delinquent act such as the betrayal of a wife against her husband, concluded with the most scandalous betrayal of a husband against his wife. Between the Germanic Mrs. Hanna, who crowned the founder of the dynasty in her passionate and sinful bed, and the provincial Nicaraguan Dinorah Sampson, last mistress of the Somozas who hurried . . . the fall of the empire, there flows a river of decay, which contaminated the nation for almost half a century."[12] Even today, the Somoza period is remembered as one filled with sexual excesses of all kinds. Moral and sexual corruption, however, were symbolized by the body of a woman or prostitute, not of a Somoza male.

But what were the experiences of prostitutes under the dictatorship? To answer this question, we must rescue the voices of those women accused of prostituting themselves or others and analyze their situation in a political and economic context. In a letter written by Sonia Rocha (pseudonym), from the province of León, to the secretary of the presidency in 1962, we can appreciate the complexity that existed in the lives of these Somocista women:

Honorable Dr. Ramiro Sacasa Guerrero,
From the beginning I have been a Liberal and a fervent Somocista
and I have even had fights defending the cause. I am a poor woman
who receives assistance from no one and with my sewing, washing
and ironing I manage through life. To make matters worse, I had
two operations three months ago and due to this I am now in debt;
but what has aggravated my situation the most is the following:
[Fernando] Agüero supporters, to damage me, have bad-mouthed
me to the Departmental Commander of the [National Guard] and
even over the radio, saying that I have commerce with women of
bad conduct in my home. The National Guard has arrested me
three times and I have had to spend on an attorney and fines almost
four hundred córdobas, which I am paying in installments. What
really happened is that sometimes society [male] friends, among
them doctors, have begged me to let them meet with young women
in my home and I have agreed to such pleas; but in light of what has
happened, I no longer allow such visits.

Now that I have explained what has occurred, I beg you to talk to
the appropriate person, so that I will not be bothered again. . . . I
hope you are kind enough to respond to me by telegram.[13]

Without a doubt, women like Rocha occupied an extremely vulnerable position in society and were victims of their political enemies and
the National Guard of their own party. But, as this letter demonstrates,
they also had a voice and believed they had rights. This means that
working-class Somocista women rightly or wrongly accused of involvement in prostitution were not simply victims or accomplices of the
regime's immorality. Their situation was quite complex and must be
documented as such.

Of course, not all actual prostitutes and madams were Somocistas.
Margaret Randall interviewed a Sandinista woman in 1981 who had been
a prostitute under the Somozas:

My real name is Melania Dávila, but I used "Maribel" on the street.
We'd change our names not realizing that people would recognize
us anyway. My family comes from San Miguelito de Chontales, in
Río San Juan. My parents separated when I was six months old and
I was left with my mother. But she was very poor and in the end was
forced to send me to my aunts. They treated me like dirt and continually humiliated me. I grew up feeling like I was nobody. To get
away from them I went off with a man who worked in the capital.

I married that man just after I turned thirteen. I had two children with him, Silvia and Francisco. I left my husband when he joined the National Guard. I never wanted to have anything to do with anyone in the military. When I left him, Silvia came with me, and he took Francisco. I never saw my son again; he'd be twenty-three now. After that, I started living with another man. He was no better. He beat me terribly. I stayed with him three long bitter years. We had two children—Delimo, who was killed last year, and María de los Angeles. But finally I couldn't stand it any longer and had to leave.

That's when I began working the streets to support myself and my children. One of my neighbors offered me a job as a waitress and I took it to earn some extra money. It turned out that it wasn't a waitress they wanted. That's how I got into that kind of work. After I left home, it was the only way I could support us. I went to Granada and worked out of a house run by a very wicked woman they called "la China." She beat me all the time and rigged things so that none of us got paid. There were about fifteen of us in the house. They'd dress us in secondhand clothes, and if we complained they'd let us have it. They tried to make us completely submissive. They'd lock us in when we weren't working so we couldn't get away. Finally, I was able to escape. I went to Managua and started working in the Campo Bruce district. At least I got paid there, and so was able to send my oldest daughter to live with my mother. Neither of them had the slightest idea where my money came from.

The FSLN changed my life. That was seven years ago, here in León. I met comrades Azida and Abel, who is dead now, and through them I started working with the Organization. . . .

I look older than thirty-nine because I've worked hard all my life and have suffered a lot. I'm tired of washing and ironing—I want to live a different life. Despite my age, I want something new.[14]

Melania Dávila's circumstances were very similar to those of other women who worked as prostitutes in the 1960s and early 1970s. According to Juan Navas Barraza, in 1966, "four out of every 130 women in Managua [were] prostitutes."[15] Interviews with twenty-four of these prostitutes revealed that "none of these women received sexual education. The majority was thrown into prostitution due to poverty. Almost all came from poor and large families. . . . The vast majority did not have a happy childhood. All were very young. Twelve and a half percent had already suffered from a venereal disease. They began to prostitute themselves between the ages of twelve and fifteen."[16]

In addition to providing a general picture of prostitution, Navas Barraza treats the economic aspect of prostitution in greater depth: "The worst-paid prostitute [had] an income four to five times larger than the best-paid male laborer [*operario*]; nonetheless, her economic situation, [was], in many cases, inferior."[17] This was because prostitutes needed to pay a percentage of their earnings to their madams and fines or bribes to the National Guard. As we saw in the letter quoted earlier, madams were often fined by the National Guard, decreasing in this way not only their own incomes but the earnings of the prostitutes themselves.

A Brief History of Prostitution in Nicaragua: 1880s–1980s

Legally, between 1880 and 1927, prostitutes, madams, and pimps were punished for vagrancy rather than prostitution, not only in Nicaragua but in other Latin American countries as well. Sandra Lauderdale Graham notes that in Brazil in the late 1880s, "despite repeated attempts to prohibit prostitution, no law specifically forbade it. Instead, women suspected of being prostitutes were charged as vagabonds and with provoking disorder."[18]

After being treated as vagrancy for almost fifty years, prostitution was legalized and regulated in Nicaragua between April 18, 1927, and August 1955. Prostitutes were required to register and to report every week for gynecological exams. Women who did not were to be arrested and fined by the Preventive Police, the National Police, or, after 1933, by the U.S.–created National Guard.[19]

Legislation on prostitution was also passed in other Latin American countries under U.S. occupation in the twentieth century, presumably for the protection of U.S. Army personnel.[20] Nor was the United States the first imperialist power to protect its troops from sexually transmitted diseases by requiring local women to obtain gynecological exams. England during the late nineteenth century subjected women in its colonies to physical examinations. According to Cynthia Enloe, "the Cantonment Acts overseas permitted colonial police authorities to conduct compulsory genital examinations on women around imperial military bases for the sake of allowing British soldiers overseas to have sexual relations with colonial women without fear of venereal disease."[21]

After August 1955, Nicaraguan law called for madams and others who promoted prostitution to be fined and jailed.[22] But, by then, the National Guard had taken firm control of the prostitution business and fined and jailed only those independent operators who did not pay the necessary bribes. E. Mendieta, a scholar who traced the development of prostitution legislation in Nicaragua, noted that, after 1955, "from a legal perspective, prostitution [was] prohibited; from a sanitary perspective, there [was] no control of prostitution, and from a policing point of view, there [was] no persecution of prostitution."[23]

In many ways, Nicaragua's treatment of prostitution was typical for Latin America, where most countries first treated prostitution as vagrancy and then went back and forth between regulation and prohibition, varying only in the degree to which they enforced the laws of the time. In Argentina, for instance, prostitution was legalized in 1875, later prohibited, then legalized again, first for the military in 1944 and then also for civilians in 1954, when Juan Domingo Perón reopened the municipal bordellos.[24] In Costa Rica, prostitution was first regulated by law in 1894, though the law was not strictly enforced, then prohibited altogether in 1943.[25] By contrast, in Guatemala and Puerto Rico, regulatory laws passed in 1887 and 1894, respectively, were more strictly enforced.[26]

Regulating prostitution was considered a step toward becoming a modernized nation because it involved the medical profession in the path toward progress. For this reason, it tended to be favored by Liberals. But because Liberals came to power rather late in Nicaragua, a prophylaxis law was not debated until 1904, during the Liberal Zelaya administration.[27]

The interest in regulation was a trait of Catholic nations, according to Donna Guy, since Catholics were more likely than Protestants to view prostitution (i.e., licensed brothels) as a necessary evil, following the Augustinian and Thomist traditions.[28] Ironically, in the case of Nicaragua, regulation appears to have been backed by a Protestant country, the United States. But the United States did not embark on a campaign of sexual repression in Nicaragua, however, as it had done in Puerto Rico in the 1890s and the late 1910s.[29] This was probably at least in part because the United States had greater military control of Puerto Rico than it did of Nicaragua. Moreover, until the creation of the National Guard by the United States in the 1930s, there was no modern military force in Nicaragua and therefore there was little capability of enforcement, even if there had been interest in crackdowns against sex workers. Extreme repression of prostitutes did not take place in Nicaragua until after the Sandinista revolution, when prostitutes' homes were destroyed and hundreds of prostitutes were jailed, to be "rehabilitated" by the revolutionary state.[30]

During the Somoza period, women who were arrested for prostitution or accused of being involved in it had a difficult time finding gainful employment outside the trade. In recognition of this fact, during the early 1950s, the Committee for the Regeneration of the Fallen Woman, led by

Haydeé Espinoza vda de Solorzano, gave women wishing to leave the trade the chance to have their names "erased from the 'list'" and offered them "opportunities to work" in other occupations.[31] Even with these incentives, however, the achievements of the organization were limited: "Yesterday they were successful; eight accepted, with tears, the offer they were made, even though some of their colleagues laughed at them and the [Committee members]. A total of twenty have [left prostitution] thanks to the work of this Committee."[32]

Charitable efforts to rehabilitate prostitutes continued into the 1960s and 1970s. In 1975, in commemoration of the International Women's Year, Josefina Pérezalonso, the vice president of the Nicaraguan chapter of the World Association of Women Journalists and Writers (Asociación Mundial de Mujeres Periodistas y Escritoras), praised Haydee Espinoza's work and held it up as an example to follow. Although second-wave international feminist perspectives on prostitution would not gain much ground in Nicaragua until the reemergence of feminism there in the 1980s, it is important to note that Somocista women were discussing prostitution in the mid-1970s. Although Pérezalonso called for a nationwide charitable crusade to save prostitutes from their way of life, she also had some radical things to say. She was familiar with U.S. feminist Kate Millet's writings on prostitution and thus noted that "leaders of the feminist movement view 'the oldest profession in the world' from a completely new angle. . . . They point out that prostitution is a matter of concern for all women without exception because, in the eyes of men, women belong to the sex that prostitutes itself, that is, the sex that traditionally sells its body in exchange for money."[33]

Pérezalonso also emphasized Millet's treatment of prostitution as a problem of consciousness whereby women who were not prostitutes believed prostitutes to be totally different from them.[34] Although the economic roots of prostitution were obvious to everybody, some Somocista women, like feminists, saw prostitution as a more complicated phenomenon.

For the Sandinista leadership, on the other hand, prostitution was exclusively about class oppression and Nicaraguan women's victimization by Somocista men. Thus, in the aftermath of the Somozas' defeat in 1979, the FSLN benefited from publicizing how rampant prostitution had been under the Somoza dictatorship and how important the revolutionary 1980 police operations against prostitution were, until it became clear that jailing prostitutes in a revolutionary society was undermining the class-based argument about the causes of prostitution. Why, if prostitution was a by-product of capitalist Somocismo, had it not disappeared

with the Somozas? Most important perhaps, police raids were not eliminating prostitution, the original goal of the repressive measures enacted
by the FSLN, and there was disagreement between social service agencies
and the police on how to best treat the problem.[35] The raids eventually
diminished in importance as the nation turned its attention in 1982 to
the Contra war and to other internal enemies of the state.

Prostitution and the National Guard

As Helen Collinson and colleagues explain, "prostitution flourished under
the patronage of the [Somozas]. . ; [the] National Guard were also deeply
implicated. 'The brothel owners used to give the Guardia a cut,' explains
an ex-prostitute from the port of Corinto. 'If the prostitutes managed
to escape, the Guardia would seek them out and return them to the
owners.'"[36] Sometimes the administration of the brothels was even more
direct: some members of the National Guard were owners of their own
centers of prostitution.[37] According to Gregorio Selser, "General Gustavo
Montiel, with the participation of high-ranking National Guard officials, retired and active, administer[ed] high-class prostitution motels
(pushbuttons) in the outskirts of Managua in association with pro-Batista
Cubans."[38] Jeffrey Gould, in his study on Chinandega, notes that Alejandro Acevedo, "an outsider connected to the Guardia and to some hacen-
dados, had become the informal but absolute political boss of Tonala. His
wealth and power emanated from his control over the prostitution racket
and the local Guardia. Many villagers were offended by Acevedo's disregard for public morality: thirty prostitutes, under his command, walked
right through town every Saturday and Monday. This weekly parade of
prostitutes symbolized Acevedo's particular brand of power. Acevedo
projected a crude *machista* vision of an amoral world."[39]

Amalia Chamorro also stresses the importance prostitution had in
Somocismo and how the population reacted: "In the 1960s, Somoza
took advantage of his personal friendship with Howard Hughes and the
exiled Cubans, incorporating into the sphere of his business sectors like
prostitution, gambling houses, and the illegal export of blood (trafficking
in blood), all of which contributed to create an atmosphere of corruption, particularly in urban zones, and [led to] a widespread rejection of
Somocismo."[40]

In effect, the dictatorship's promotion of prostitution increased disapproval toward the Somozas, especially among Sandinistas, who associated
the sale of sex with capitalist oppression. According to FSLN co-founder

Tomás Borge, prostitution was "a war of prejudice, discrimination, a war in which capitalism tries to turn women into trash, buying and selling them like merchandise, like a luxury item or cheap vegetable, depending on the quality of the merchandise."[41] As noted earlier, the FSLN's ideological opposition to prostitution was so great that, according to a study conducted by the Nicaraguan Institute of Social Security and Welfare (INSSBI) on this topic, "the first actions taken by the Sandinistas with regard to prostitution" were the destruction and burning of "a great number of brothels, bars, and gambling houses, places typified by the new revolutionary moral to be foci of corruption maintained by the Somocista Guard."[42] The destruction of brothels in 1979 is not surprising since the FSLN had proposed the elimination of prostitution ten years earlier, in its 1969 political statement.[43]

The income generated from prostitution was an integral part of the dictatorship's inner workings. Gregorio Selser contends that

> the highest officials were implicated in the business of prostitution motels. . . . Through this web they had indirect access to income, and they were supported by the tolerance and the authorizing wink that emanated from the supreme power. . . . National Guard members stole and extorted because the government paid them poorly; the government underpaid Guards in order to induce them to criminal activities. [Crime] automatically associated thieves and extortionists with their tolerating superiors. Therefore, Guards had to be the first defenders of the system through which they obtained their pitiful legal salaries and their extra income, which was not legal, but was accepted at all levels.[44]

For their part, contemporary Nicaraguans remember the relationship between prostitution and the National Guard in two separate, seemingly contradictory ways. The first way is best expressed by Viktor Morales Henríquez, who proclaims that "plunder, death, and sex" was the magical formula through which the Somozas remained in power.[45] Morales Henríquez sums up what he perceives as the inevitability of the Somozas' involvement in prostitution and sexual depravity with the proverb "a hen that eats eggs will do so even if its beak is burned [*gallina que come huevo, aunque le quemen el pico*]."[46] In other words, the Somozas were involved in the prostitution industry because it was in their nature.

The second way Nicaraguans remember the link between prostitution and the National Guard is through "María de los guardias" (The National Guard's María), a song written and popularized by world-renowned

Nicaraguan musician Carlos Mejía Godoy in the 1970s but still widely popular today. In it, María tells the story of her lifelong association with the National Guard:

> Dejenme que me presente, yo soy la María del Raso Potosme.
> En antes perdí la inocencia por las inquirencias del Teniente
>   Cosme.
> Tambien quiero paladrearles que fuí medio novia del Sargento
>   Guido.
> Lo que pasa es que ese jaño ya hace quince días que fué
>   transferido.
>
> Yo soy la María, María es mi gracia, pero a mi me dicen
> María de los guardias.
> Yo soy la María, María
> No ando con razones, razones.
> Yo llevo en mi cuenta, por cuenta, cinco batallones.
>
> Yo nací ahí en el comando.
> Mi mamá cuidaba al Capitán Juan Dique . . .
> No es cosa que me la pique
> de ser de la guardia
> la reina y señora
> pero mi primera pacha la chupe chigüina
> de una cantinflora . . .
>
> Ajustaba los quince años
> cuando me mataron al primer marido.
> Fué durante un tiroteo contra un hombre arrecho llamado
>   Sandino.
> A mi varón lo encontraron
> de viaje tilinte . . .
> Yo lo vide al pobrecito todo pasconeado como un colador . . .
>
> Tanto me quiso un tal Mingo
> que en mi propia casa me puso un estanco . . .
> Mingo lo tengo patente
> nunca me decía
> mi nombre de pila
>
> Como te decía María?

Como el era medio pueta [*sic*]
solo me decía "flor de bartolina . . ."

In English, the song is as follows:

Let me introduce myself, I am Private Potosme's María.
I lost my innocence due to Lieutenant Cosme's "inquirencias."
I also wish to tell you that I was Sergeant Guido's semi-girlfriend.
What happened is that that guy was transferred fifteen days ago.

I am María, María is my name, but they call me
the National Guard's María.
I am María, María
I have no reasons, reasons.
It seems I have five battalions in my account.

I was born in the Command Center.
My mother took care of Captain Juan Dique . . .
It's not like I'm bragging of being
the National Guard's queen and lady
but the first bottle I had as a baby
was a canteen.

I was almost fifteen
when my first husband was killed.
It happened during a skirmish against a brave man named
    Sandino.
They found my man
completely stiff . . .
I saw the poor thing, full of holes like a sieve . . .

A man called Mingo [Domingo] loved me so much
he put a government store in my home . . .
I remember Mingo clearly
he never called me
by my baptismal name.

What did he call you María?

Since he was kind of a poet
he would call me a "flower of the barracks" . . .[47]

If "María" had been a true historical figure and she had lived to be eighty years old, her adult life would have spanned the entire existence of the National Guard, for she would have been fifteen sometime in the late 1920s and early 1930s, the years during which the U.S. Marines and Anastasio Somoza García fought against Augusto C. Sandino. What is most important about this song, however, is that, although it was written by a man, and sung by a group of men, the protagonist is a working-class woman. Moreover, although the incredibly naive María is ridiculed in the song for being so promiscuous—a prostitute according to Aura Lila Lacayo's definition—she is proud of her association with the National Guard, proud of being called "flor de bartolina" by a loving, poetic partner.

Although the song highlights her poverty and the sexual abuse (statutory rape) she was subjected to, María is not portrayed as a victim of men or of the Somozas' manipulative ways, as Somocista women often are in the writings of anti-Somocistas such as Viktor Morales Henríquez. Perhaps it is this complexity in María's life that made the song enormously popular among Somocistas in Nicaragua and apolitical audiences throughout Latin America. Carlos Mejía Godoy—himself an anti-Somocista—was able to reveal in this song, as in many others of his songs, the everyday realities of working-class Nicaraguans, regardless of their political affiliations.

Rape and Prostitution

Although we do not know the exact number of women who were raped by the National Guard, or even by the Somozas themselves, between 1936 and 1979, and even though not all women taken into custody were raped, we know that state-sponsored rape of anti-Somocista women was a common practice under the Somozas. Four cases provoked widespread international public outcry and are still remembered today as some of the most horrific examples of violence under the dictatorship. These are the rape of Amada Pineda, the rape of Doris Tijerino, the rape of the women of El Cua, and the rape of a U.S. Peace Corps volunteer (whose name was never disclosed), in 1979, by a National Guard member.[48]

Amada Pineda (b. 1943), a peasant woman jailed and raped by the National Guard in 1974 for revolutionary activity, told her story to writer Margaret Randall in 1980: "That night, several of them came to where they were holding me. They raped me. I struggled and they began to beat me and that's when they did all those terrible things to me. My legs were black and blue, my thighs, my arms. I had bruises all over me. That's the way they treated all the peasant women they picked up; they raped them and tortured them and committed atrocities. It was just three days, but those three days were like three years to me—three years of being raped by those animals."[49]

Amada Pineda had married at eighteen and had nine children, of whom only four survived childhood. Like her husband, she became a socialist in the early 1960s, and both then became FSLN supporters. In 1974, she was raped seventeen times by National Guardsmen. The seven male peasants who were imprisoned with her were also severely tortured, as was her husband soon after her release.[50] Her abuse received world-wide attention and her story continues to be remembered in the Nica-raguan press.

The experiences of Comandante Doris Tijerino Haslam, a Sandinista who continues to play a role in Nicaraguan politics, were also publicized outside Nicaragua by Margaret Randall and other foreign journalists; they were similar to those of Pineda. Tijerino was arrested four times between 1967 and 1978:

> The third time the [National Guard] captured me was after a battle. By then, the persecution was ferocious, and I was, of course, clan-destine. They had orders to kill me, and had decided to do away with me slowly so that I would suffer more, and they began with brutal beatings. They even sent out an international cable saying that I had been captured in combat, wounded and taken to the military hos-pital where I had died in surgery. But they did not realize that a journalist had been there when I was captured, that he had taken some photos and recorded a brief conversation with me, in which I had said that I was not wounded. . . . After the notice came out about my supposed death, this recording began circulating in all the churches and schools, because, of course, the media were censored. And that's what saved my life. But they had already tortured me hor-ribly, inflicting bruises and wounds in the genital area from forcing me to open my legs, and injuries on my face from the beatings. . . .
>
> They kept telling me grotesque things that they were going to do to me, all related to sex, because that was the way to torture me. . . . I spent sixteen days like that, thirteen of which they gave me abso-lutely nothing to eat, but after a while I felt no hunger. They kept me naked and without bathing for the full time. . . .
>
> One of [Anastasio Somoza Debayle]'s sons would come and watch when they tortured me; I think it was Julio. He also brought guests. When he arrived, the attitude of all those who were torturing

me changed, and they would say "señor" to him. During one of these visits, a torturer violently forced his hand inside my vagina, inflicting deep cuts and causing me to hemorrhage. They gave me sanitary [napkins] to staunch the flow, and Somoza's son ordered me to stand there naked while they began to throw me from one to the other, like a ball. One would grab me by the breast, another by the buttocks, and so on, and then pass me on to the next one.

I thought I was going to die, but first I was going to put up a fight. When Julio Somoza saw me bleeding, he said that I made him sick; and I asked him why, when he was the one who had ordered that all these things be done to me. I also told him I knew who he was. . . . After that, he left and he stopped coming to the torture sessions. . . .

I have had many physical problems as a result of the tortures. I suffer from a neurological disorder, a kind of stroke, brought on by the trauma of the beatings, and I am permanently under a doctor's care.[51]

The rape of Doris Tijerino, an urban, middle-class woman, hit close to home for many Ala members, especially those who knew her family in Matagalpa. However, some Ala leaders were able to justify the abuse by arguing that she was a documented Sandinista and she deserved to be punished.[52]

The 1968 collective rape of the peasant women of El Cua, in the north central region of Nicaragua, was immortalized in poetry by the anti-Somocista priest Ernesto Cardenal and in song by Carlos Mejía Godoy. It is perhaps the best-known instance of sexual abuse under the Somozas. Nineteen women and many men were arrested and imprisoned for months by the National Guard for supporting the Sandinista guerrillas. The following women were among those arrested: Amanda Aguilar, María González Hernández, Facunda Catalina González Díaz, Angela Díaz, Luz Marina Hernández, Apolonia González Romero, Candida María González Donaire, Esperanza Hernández García, María Venancia, Candida Martínez, and Natividad Martínez. All nineteen women were tortured and raped; many of the men were killed, thrown out of planes, or never seen again.

"Amanda Aguilar" was a pseudonym for María de la Cruz, also known as "Petrona Hernández López," a woman who, along with her mother, had collaborated with Sandino in the 1920s during his fight against the U.S. Marine occupation. A Sandinista to the end, Amanda Aguilar was the oldest Nicaraguan on record at the time of her death at the age of 116 in February 2007. She would have turned 117 on May 3.[53]

What follows is the beginning of Carlos Mejía Godoy's song about the women of El Cua, a song most adult Nicaraguans know by heart:

Voy a hablarles compañeros, de las mujeres del Cua,
que bajaron de los cerros
por orden del general,
de la María Venancia y de la Amanda Aguilar,
dos hijas de la montaña
que no quisieron hablar.

Ay! Ay! A nadie vimos pasar.
La noche negra se traga aquel llanto torrencial.
Ay! Ay! La patria llorando está.
Parecen gritos de parto
los que se oyen por allá . . .

A la Candida Martínez
un guardia la convidó
"vení chavala," le dijo, "lavame este pantalón."
La cipota campesina
fué mancillada ahí nomás.
Y Tacho desde un afiche
reía.

These are the lyrics in English:

Compañeros, I am going to tell you about the women of El Cua
who came down from the mountains
following the General's orders,
[I'll tell you] about María Venancia and Amanda Aguilar,
two of the mountain's daughters
who were not willing to speak.

Ay! Ay! We saw no one go by.
The dark night swallows that torrential flood of tears.
Ay! Ay! The homeland is crying.
The cries that can be heard
sound like those of a woman in labor . . .

A Guard member invited
Candida Martínez

"come, kid," he told her "wash these pants for me."
The peasant child
was raped right there
as Tacho [Anastasio Somoza Debayle]
laughed from a poster.[54]

Somocistas responded to the rapes of anti-Somocista women in two ways. Most appeared to doubt the veracity of the rape accusations, believing instead that they were lies meant to demonize the dictatorship. Predictably, the rest tended to believe that the women deserved to be raped as punishment for getting involved with the Sandinistas.

Some Somocista women actually wrote letters of support for the Somozas and against Doris Tijerino in the aftermath of the abuse she suffered in 1969. In response to anti-Somocista protests in the Tijerino case, which included hundreds of women marching as mothers, one Somocista female leader wrote to *Novedades*, the Somocista newspaper, demanding even stronger measures than rape against "extremists" like Tijerino: "I support the termination of extremists who wish to disturb order in Nicaragua and I ask for punishment for those who remain alive. I am a mother and do not want a bad example [for my children]."[55]

Some Somocista women, however, appeared to have supported Doris Tijerino, at least privately. One of my Somocista informants was shocked when I told her that I had found her name listed along with dozens of others attached to a letter published in *Novedades* against Tijerino. She claimed that her name was written down without her permission. Perhaps because she was personally acquainted with the Tijerino family, this Somocista woman told me, "No, I would not have signed my name to a letter against Doris." On the other hand, the letter in *Novedades* included the names of all her co-workers at a state-run institution. Asking that her name be removed from the letter might have cost this woman her job.

Although, as can be expected, Sandinistas reacted to the rape of their female constituents with outrage, this outrage did not lead the FSLN to alter rape laws immediately after the triumph of the revolution in 1979. As noted in chapter 2, these laws were not changed until 1992, well after the Sandinistas were out of power. Why did rape under the Somozas not provoke immediate legal change under the Sandinistas, as prostitution did? This question leads us to examine gender ideologies and their intersection with class politics, enabling us to better understand sexual politics in twentieth-century Nicaragua.

Although the threat of sexual violence against anti-Somocista female prisoners was always present, the fact that not all anti-Somocista female prisoners were raped is perhaps one reason why antirape sentiment did not become widespread within anti-Somocismo. Moreover, in the context of censorship, it was difficult to obtain information on what exactly happened to prisoners—both male and female. Once the atrocities committed by the Somozas were publicized, rape tended to be categorized with other types of torture and violations of human rights, not as a specific crime against women, making it hard to organize specifically against rape, except in well-publicized specific cases.

Other factors might have also affected the different treatment of rape and prostitution. Before 1992, rape was a private crime in Nicaragua, and many cases resulted in the marriage of the survivor and the perpetrator, the solution encouraged by the state to resolve rape cases. The rape of female prisoners by National Guard members was very different from the type of rape cases that ended in marriage, making it easier to characterize the former as human rights violations.

Unlike rape, prostitution involved the exchange of money, constituting a for-profit transaction, an obvious expression of capitalist oppression that was criticized by the Left throughout the world. Thus the Cuban Communist newspaper *Hoy* declared in 1952: "Prostitution is a consequence of class differences, of capitalist exploitation, of the backwardness and enslavement of women in bourgeois society."[56] Prostitution was also more visible to the population at large than rapes committed by the National Guard, and it affected more women. Perhaps because prostitution under the Somozas seemed more widespread and less arbitrary than rape and because Sandinista men were not involved in the administration of Somocista brothels, it was much easier for the FSLN to link prostitution to a system of oppression—capitalism—than it would have been to link rape, or even prostitution, to a patriarchal society in which Sandinista men participated (or could potentially participate) and benefited.

In other words, prostitution caused outrage among anti-Somocistas both because it was in fact reprehensible, widespread, and systemic and because it also fit well into revolutionary critiques of capitalism. A more serious discussion of prostitution would have led to a discussion of sexism. On the other hand, even a superficial discussion of rape would have led to a debate on male dominance. Therefore no official discussion took place on either subject under the Sandinistas.[57]

There is another reason why Sandinista men may have been unwilling to talk openly about rape. In the Somozas' jails, men were sometimes hanged by their testicles; they were often kicked in the groin, threatened with castration, and given electric shocks to their genitals.[58] Many were subjected to sexual violence, including rape. It is hard to know whether the survivors of this type of torture would have been able, much less willing, to talk about something so close to what they had experienced.

Maternalism and Clientelism

As noted earlier, the Somoza regime did not emphasize motherhood as the only appropriate role for women, unlike other right-wing regimes. Even though, as Suzanne Baker writes, "motherhood [and] its attendant attributes of morality and self-sacrifice are praised and heralded in Nicaraguan society (during Mother's Day celebrations, in poetry and song, and in church sermons), prior to 1979 this value was really not made manifest in everyday practice."[59] On the other hand, Somocista women did sometimes mobilize as mothers, especially in their fight against Communism, suggesting that maternalism acquires greater importance in the context of war or when there is a possibility of war, as reflected in a telegram sent by nine women from Diriamba to Anastasio Somoza Debayle in 1969: "Recognizing that it is our obligation to defend our interests, we are sending to you our message of solidarity. We are simply MOTHERS. . . . We have observed how other countries in the Americas have fallen under the yoke of Communism, but we feel sure and confident as Nicaraguans that we have a firm government that will help us to unmask [Communism's] skillful costumes and lies. As mothers, we thank you for your effort and work."[60]

Maternalism also prevailed in the discourse of individual working-women looking for jobs or economic assistance within the Somozas' clientelistic system. One such woman wrote to Anastasio Somoza Debayle in 1962:

> Very esteemed Sir:
> I am a humble woman who earns a living with a small clothing store on the sidewalk of the Central Market. I ardently ask for your help . . . because you truly have a good heart toward poor people, for my poverty is due to my husband's illness and at the same time to a robbery. . . . I am in a very sorry economic state, I have to feed four children and buy medicines for my husband. . . .
> I wish to inform you that I am the daughter of . . . an Eastern Market Somocista Committee President and I am a Somocista Liberal. . . . I also cooperate with the Ala Femenina in the propaganda for my party.[61]

It was precisely to fulfill their *economic* roles as female heads of household that most working-class women supported the dictatorship, hoping to advance economically in exchange for their pro-Somoza votes. This situation, in which favors are exchanged between unequal individuals, creating an asymmetrical power relationship, constitutes the essence of clientelism.[62] Although women in general have had less access than men to clientelistic pyramids of command,[63] in the case of Nicaragua under the Somozas, women occupied a crucial place in the system, but they rarely bargained collectively as mothers.

Middle-class women, even if they were mothers, tended not to participate in Somocismo to better fulfill their economic roles as mothers. The regime's main attraction for them was their new political identity as citizens and their new economic identity as state employees, although they used the maternalist discourse to obtain the support of working-women and to mobilize them politically. As Marta García (pseudonym), a middle-class co-founder of the Ala Femenina, recalled, "we would tell [poor women] that they should vote for their future and for the future of their children; we especially lifted up the hopes single mothers had for their children."[64]

Typical of the maternalist language Somocista female leaders used to inspire women to vote for the Liberal Party are the words of Cecilia de Argüello in her 1969 article "El Triunfo de Somoza":

> Nicaraguan women, women of all social classes, fight for your husbands, for your children, for your parents, for your siblings, and for all the inhabitants of Nicaragua . . . and that fight is actualized . . . in one [political] bloc: LONG LIVE THE NATIONALIST LIBERAL PARTY . . . LONG LIVE TACHO. LONG LIVE GENERAL ANASTASIO SOMOZA DEBAYLE, our hope in the future . . . the man who . . . will rebuild Managua, will give a roof and shelter to all our brothers [and sisters] in pain, opening new sources of employment and driving away the ghost of misery and hunger from our children's side. Women of Nicaragua, we must fight united, let us not support strikes that are a trick aimed at retarding progress.[65]

In general, Somocista female leaders, no matter what their class background, did not personally subscribe to maternalism, even though they resorted to maternalist discourse to strike a chord among their followers and society at large. For the most part, women leaders saw themselves as genderless and believed they had earned their leadership role through hard work that went beyond voting and marching in the streets. Like some men, some female Somocista leaders seemed to look down upon women who identified primarily as mothers or who used motherhood as a springboard for political activism. I found no prominent Somocista mother's groups within the Somocista women's movement, although poor women did use the language of motherhood to bargain, individually, with the dictators for their share of the spoils. On the other hand, women who won the title of "Humanist Mother of the Year" were praised for their "charitable virtues" and for their work in favor of "the development of culture and progress in Nicaraguan society."[66] And the Officers' Wives Social Committee (fig. 16), a prominent charitable society founded by First Lady Hope Portocarrero, Anastasio Somoza Debayle's wife, provided prenatal care for the wives of National Guard soldiers as well as schooling for their children.[67]

Somocista women's relationship to maternalism and clientelism appears unique when compared to that of women in other parts of the world. Javier Auyero's research on women's participation in clientelistic networks is one of the few studies on the subject, and what he describes as the case for Peronist women is far removed from the political realities of Somocista women in Nicaragua:

> Women brokers see their public role as based on "traditional" roles: taking care of the household. They legitimize their role in politics by conceiving of it as that of the mother in a house larger than their own: the municipal building. They are supermadres. . . . They become so in order to function publicly as Peronists. . . .
>
> Being a Peronist woman in politics "naturally" implies taking care of or mothering the poor, doing social (as opposed to political) work, and collaborating with the man who makes the decisions. . . . Taking care of [or] mothering the poor is thus constructed as part of women's identity, something for which they are perceived by men as well as by they themselves to have a natural propensity. Without a doubt, this is a source of power for these women. By claiming not just the right but the duty to do social work, they carve out one of the few—albeit limited—spaces in which they have autonomy.[68]

None of the Somocista female leaders I interviewed ever described her participation in politics as an extension of her household duties. None was a "supermadre," and none portrayed her explicitly political activities as social work. Working-class clients came the closest to understanding their participation in Somocismo as an extension of their motherly duties, but these duties were understood in economic terms and were normally related to employment opportunities.

We already have the terms "female heads of household," "female breadwinners," "working mothers," and "single mothers" (among others) to underscore the reality that many single women who are mothers work for wages outside the home out of financial necessity and that some women parent alone. I use the term "maternal breadwinners" to emphasize the connection both between mothers and breadwinning and between mothering and the financial sustenance of a home. And I use it to stress how, for many Somocista women, working for a living was both their maternal responsibility and their duty in the absence of responsible fathers and a welfare state. Linda J. Seligmann, among others, has noted that "in many societies [women's] work is not conceptualized as physical caretaking, but rather as the economic maintenance of children."[69] The idea that mothering is providing financially for one's family has rarely, if ever, been applied to Nicaragua in scholarly works. This is unfortunate, given its usefulness in understanding political developments under Somocismo.

It is urban women's status as maternal breadwinners that largely explains working-class Nicaraguan women's economic and political mobilization on behalf of the Somozas. To Somocista maternal breadwinners, working for wages outside the home in jobs obtained through their political participation in Somocismo was not "like" mothering, it *was* mothering. And, necessary as it was to obtain employment, even women's political participation could arguably be considered mothering by maternal breadwinners.

The Nicaraguan case not only challenges our understanding of women's participation in right-wing politics. It also challenges our understanding of motherhood and women's political participation in Latin America. Asunción Lavrin argues that, in the Southern Cone (Argentina, Chile, and Uruguay), between 1890 and 1940, "motherhood eventually redefined the relationship between women and the state, which would owe women protection for their nurturing of new lives. Motherhood was a key asset in supporting women's claims for empowerment."[70]

Motherhood did eventually "redefine the relationship between women and the state" in Nicaragua, but not because the state owed women *protection* for their nurturing of new lives. Instead, the Somocista state offered mothers *employment,* reflecting a radically different understanding of the "nurturing" that mothers must provide to their young.

The tension on the personal and national level between women's reproductive and physical roles as mothers, on the one hand, and their need to sustain their families economically, on the other, created a fertile ground for the Somozas' clientelistic populism to develop and flourish. Given the high percentage of households headed by women in Nicaragua and many men's lack of financial support for their children, it seems only logical that a government would want to encourage paternal responsibility through marriage, to incorporate women into the workforce, or both.[71] The Somozas had no success with the first goal (one they did not actively pursue), but they had great success with the second one, in part because it was propelled by women's own economic needs and the ways in which working-class women themselves understood mothering. Maternal breadwinners thus became the backbone of the Somozas' working-class support and an important prototype of working-class female Somocista citizens. In short, working-class female citizenship itself came to rest on the economic necessity of employment outside the home, channeled through women's political participation in Somocismo.

In her 1953 Juris Doctorate thesis, Ala leader Amelia Borge de Sotomayor suggests that even lower-middle-class married women understood working outside the home as mothering:

> The saying that "woman is for the home and only for the home" is today truer than ever because in these times woman has to work in the home and for the home [por y para el hogar], both in and out of it. . . . The vast majority of women, if they do not have to meet all the expenses of the home, at least have to address some. Modern life does not permit the housewife of a middle-class type of home the luxury of idleness . . . because she has to share with her husband the [economic] burden that raising and educating a child entail. Because of this, she finds that she has to work, not only . . . [in] taking care of her family, but [also] in such a way that her work produces cash, so necessary to meet the exigencies of the home.[72]

Regardless of their social and political position, all Nicaraguans understood that both getting a job and keeping one were necessarily linked to taking a pro-Somoza stand. Indeed, those who did not support the Somozas frequently lost their jobs, as was the case of the well-known opposition figure Saturnina Guillén, a Conservative leader and suffragist who lost her job as the director of a school when the Somozas came to power.[73] But how exactly did the Somozas provide employment opportunities to Somocista women, and what did these opportunities mean in the lives of these women? The case of Antonia Rodríguez (pseudonym) clearly demonstrates this process. When she arrived in Managua from her province in central Nicaragua, an acquaintance was able to obtain a letter of recommendation on her behalf from Luis Somoza. With that letter, Rodríguez secured the job she wanted. Decades later, she still remembers with gratitude Somoza's gesture. Moreover, in 2009, she still had in her possession the note that allowed her "admission" to Luis Somoza's office.[74] Communication through letters, telegrams, or in person with the Somozas—especially with Luis—was a common experience among Somocista women of different social classes. It was also their common practice to solicit employment or letters of recommendation from the Somozas, often with a high degree of success.

Once they were employed, Nicaraguan women inevitably experienced salary discrimination, the main type of discrimination the Somocista women I interviewed remember. According to statistics compiled by the U.S. Agency for International Development (AID) in 1975, not only did Nicaraguan women normally earn less than men for performing the same job, those employed as professionals and technicians also occupied the lowest ranks in their respective fields.[75] For example, in 1974, 81 percent of primary school teachers were women, whereas only 40 percent of secondary school teachers were female. Not surprisingly, fifteen out of sixteen province inspectors at the Ministry of Education were men.[76]

Although statistics vary depending on the study, there was a gradual increase in the percentage of women employed outside the home between the 1950s and the 1970s. According to Gary Ruchwarger, in 1950, women constituted 14 percent of the economically active population. This percentage climbed to nearly 22 percent in 1970,[77] reflecting a great increase in the number of professional women. A study conducted by the business school INCAE in 1974 revealed that women represented 39 percent of the employers and administrators, 47 percent of the professional/technical sector, and 70 percent of the workers in commerce and sales in the urban zones of Masaya and León.[78] Women made up 43 percent of the economically active population both in these two cities and among the urban population nationwide.[79] This increase in women's labor force participation—primarily in the professional and technical fields—was related to the increase of the Nicaraguan middle class, which went from being 11 percent of the population in 1960 to 15 percent in 1975.[80]

Like society at large, Somocista women were affected by the highs and lows of the Nicaraguan economy, by the 1972 earthquake, and by the high levels of unemployment at the end of the 1970s. Although there are discrepancies in the figures, urban unemployment appears to have been higher among women than men during the last years of the Somoza dictatorship: 7.2 percent for women as compared to 6.4 percent for men according to the 1974 census.[81] Neither rising unemployment nor the general economic crisis that engulfed the country in 1978 and 1979 diminished the faith of those women who even today claim to be Somocistas and who, with pride, proclaimed that, under the Somozas, "we all were the Liberal Party."[82] But it did make even the staunchest supporters of the regime admit that the last Somoza "might have gone too far."[83]

Sexual Order, Sexual Disorder, and Resistance

During the Somoza years, where anti-Somocistas saw sexual and familial disorder, some Somocista women saw a source of order in their lives, even though the Somozas did not proclaim that they were upholding a strict moral code, as other right-wing movements have done. Some Somocista women attributed a paternal role to the Somozas, and some even asked the Somozas to personally intervene in their marital disputes.

Indeed, the portrayal of the Somozas as "fathers of the poor"—a portrayal they embraced and promoted—was quite popular. Yolanda Herrera (pseudonym) wrote in a letter to Luis Somoza: "When your dear father died [in 1956] I went to visit you at the Workers' Hall [Casa del Obrero] and at the [National] Palace. His death pained me as if he had been my father."[84] In another letter to Luis Somoza, Mercedes Sotelo (pseudonym) declared: "Sir, you are my refuge and my father. I have no one else to confide in, please forgive this trouble I am causing you. I hope to be consoled by you."[85] On another occasion, Carmen Salazar (pseudonym) wrote: "You are like a father to me and that is why I feel a need to tell you what is happening to me."[86] Sometimes the Somozas were praised in highly exaggerated terms and even compared to a heavenly father, as in the following letter written by Eva Telica (pseudonym) to Luis Somoza in 1957:

> Today and always it is our duty to be all together, all of us women, so that the fruit of General Somoza's loins can be blessed among all of us women, we must go forward with our triumphant march and shout Long Live God our Father in heaven and General Somoza look after his angels, who left us the angel of peace, and the guardian angel for the happiness and tranquility of our Nicaragua.
>
> (Hoy y siempre nuestro deber es estar juntitas, todas las mujeres, para que sea bendito el fruto del General Somoza entre todas las mujeres tenemos que cumplir nuestra marcha triunfal y gritar Viva Dios nuestro señor en el cielo y el general Somoza vele por sus

angeles, que nos dejó el angel de la paz y el angel de la guarda para la dicha y tranquilidad de nuestra Nicaragua.)[87]

As Sandra McGee Deutsch has noted for Juan Domingo Perón, the emphasis on a dictator's paternal qualities limits the autonomy and power of the working classes.[88] But excessive deference might instead be a sign of resistance, as James Scott argues:

> I shall use the term *public transcript* as a shorthand way of describing the open interaction between subordinates and those who dominate. The public transcript, where it is not positively misleading, is unlikely to tell the whole story about power relations. It is frequently in the interest of both parties to tacitly conspire in misrepresentation. . . . [T]he greater the disparity in power between dominant and subordinate and the more arbitrarily it is exercised, the more the public transcript of subordinates will take on a stereotyped, ritualistic cast. In other words, the more menacing the power, the thicker the mask. . . . [A]n assessment of power relations read directly off the public transcript between the powerful and the weak may portray a deference and consent that are possibly only a tactic.[89]

To what extent women's praise of the Somozas was only a tactic for obtaining assistance is hard to know. What we do know is that some women were genuinely interested in receiving help from the Somozas to deal with all sorts of problems, including marital problems. In particular, wives of military men appealed to the Somozas to regulate their sexual lives and punish their cheating husbands, but the end results were not always completely satisfactory.

In the case of Aurora Balladares (pseudonym), the Somozas gave her wayward husband an ultimatum. To Balladares's dismay, her high-ranking military husband chose his lover over her. A Somocista political leader in her own right who never remarried, Balladares nevertheless is still grateful to the Somozas for their emotional support during such difficult times. Most important, she feels she received fair treatment in Somocista politics even though she was divorced.[90]

On another occasion, Nadia Otero (pseudonym) wrote to the secretary of the presidency asking for help with regard to her husband's infidelity:

> Dear Dr. [Ramiro Sacasa Guerrero]:
> David has become involved with a bad woman . . . who has almost succeeded in destroying my home, after taking what he could be

giving to us. I have terrible reports about her and I am desperate, for she gets him drunk and takes his money and then he has none left for us.

I write all of this to you because I know how good you are and how Catholic and as a result you will understand that the destruction of a marriage where there are children is a crime. I don't understand what has happened to David, I think that woman has given him something to forget his obligations as a father, not to mention those of a husband. . . . In short, I cannot force him to love me, only to give me child support.[91]

Ramiro Sacasa Guerrero, secretary of the presidency, answered Otero's letter, but this was probably not the response she had hoped for:

Since you tell me you do not want David to know that you told me about the situation you are in, I am unable to help you with this matter, for any action on my part would enable him to know that you have told me, since he knows I am not a psychic and have no other way of finding out about these things.

I think you and your children are the ones who, proceeding with skill and tactfulness, can win David back. The woman you mentioned has no moral authority to come between you and David, and I do not think that David would ever allow her to occupy that position, nor do I think she would seek it, for the information I have reveals that she is not satisfied with the patronage of only one [male] friend.

Wishing that the light of harmony, which is the basis for happiness, shine again soon in your home . . . I greet you with affection.[92]

The Somocista government represented a last resort for women like Nadia Otero who were desperate because of their poverty and because of the abuse and neglect they received at the hands of their husbands. Women appealed to right-wing movements to solve marital problems in other countries besides Nicaragua. Historian Nancy MacLean found that, in the United States during the 1920s, female members of the Ku Klux Klan appealed to the Klan "for aid against their male relatives or neighbors. . . . In verbal and written requests they asked the Klan for help. In effect they drew it in to offset the power imbalance placing them at a disadvantage vis-à-vis the men in their lives. . . . The Georgia realm office . . . reported receiving an average of twenty letters *each week* from women inviting the order to threaten or use violence against people whose conduct they disapproved of."[93]

Obviously, that extremist movements and dictatorial regimes provided hope and comfort to some women in no way diminishes their terrible legacies. But this dynamic does help explain the complex relationship between women's sexuality, politics, and work, leaving aside, once and for all, simplistic explications that blame the devil and women's sexual deviance for the many troubles the Nicaraguan nation has seen.

Nicaragua's "New Right" and the "Righting" of the Sandinista Left

The right-wing politics and culture of the Somozas did not fit the popular stereotype of what the Right is supposed to stand for when it comes to women, perhaps because the Catholic Church played a somewhat limited role in designing Somocista social policy. Whereas the Conservative Party traditionally promoted conservative views on women and the family, under the Somozas, the Liberal Party had generally emphasized women's political and economic participation, de-emphasized women's roles as mothers and wives, and stayed silent on abortion and homosexuality. But that would change radically when Arnoldo Alemán gained control of the Nicaraguan Liberal Right in the 1990s, leading me to make a distinction between the "old" Somocista Liberal Right and the "new" socially and politically conservative Liberal Right, strongly allied with the hierarchy of the Catholic Church and its Nicaraguan representative, Cardinal Miguel Obando y Bravo.

In a completely unpredictable turn of events in 2006, Arnoldo Alemán, who had served as Nicaragua's president from 1997 to 2002 (and been convicted of stealing millions of dollars from state coffers in 2003), reached a power-sharing agreement with his political enemy, Daniel Ortega, dividing government posts, and thus political power, between the FSLN and Alemán's Constitutional Liberal Party (PLC), the heir of Somocista Liberalism.[94] The changes in Nicaragua's constitution and electoral law resulting from the deal struck by the two leaders made it possible for Ortega to win the 2006 elections with only 38 percent of the popular vote. Against this backdrop, Cardinal Miguel Obando y Bravo, previously an enemy of the Sandinistas, became an ally of Daniel Ortega and his wife, Rosario Murillo (who are now what might be considered "born again" Catholics).

The current emphasis on the nuclear family, procreation, marriage, and Catholicism made by Nicaragua's "new Right" is one that has been strengthened by the pact between Daniel Ortega and Arnoldo Alemán. Indeed, with the full backing of the Catholic Church, the new Right, in collusion with Daniel Ortega's Sandinista Party, was able to pass a law in 2006 that, for the first time in Nicaraguan history, prohibits abortion under all circumstances, even to save the life of the mother. Although it is doubtful that FSLN rank-and-file members find the new Right's cultural values embraced by their party to be the most important issues in their everyday lives, the harassment of feminist organizations and the prohibition against abortion have made many Nicaraguan women's lives (and some men's lives) more difficult. Moreover, the new abortion law has already resulted in the death of several women, leading to a great deal of consternation nationally and internationally. The law was the last straw for some in the international solidarity movement, who withdrew their support from the FSLN in favor of the Sandinista Renovation Movement (Movimiento de Renovación Sandinista).

Daniel Ortega's acceptance of Alemán's and Obando y Bravo's cultural values—his embrace of Catholicism, his support of the antiabortion law, and his persecution of feminist groups—constitutes a monumental break not only with the Left, and with its own political trajectory, but with Somocista practices. Ortega, in effect, has helped the Liberal Right usher Nicaragua into a brand-new world of right-wing cultural politics. Where this will lead the country remains to be seen.

Although the Somozas benefited from often cordial relations with the Catholic Church, they and their female supporters fully accepted the secular Liberal state they had inherited. As we enter the second decade of the twenty-first century, however, the Church holds great power within the Nicaraguan Liberal Right and within Nicaraguan politics in general. The Catholic hierarchy (albeit specific sectors of that hierarchy) plays a central role in Liberal, Conservative, and FSLN politics. This type of ideological homogeneity in relation to "family values" and Catholicism has never been seen in Nicaragua. Today the Liberal Right led by Arnoldo Alemán looks very much like the Conservative Right *and* the FSLN when it comes to policies on women, sexuality, and the family.[95]

Pending further research into the respective positions of the Somoza, Alemán, and Ortega administrations on "the family," let me make some preliminary arguments. From my research thus far, I attribute the shift in gender policies within Nicaraguan Liberalism to four main factors, in addition to the role of the Church discussed above. First, charged with dismantling the state in furtherance of neoliberal global economic policies that produced high levels of unemployment, Alemán had no need for women to become involved in formal sectors of the economy and thus also had no economic incentives to offer them. Second, during the last twenty years, the Nicaraguan Liberal Right was heavily influenced by socially conservative (and Catholic fundamentalist) groups headquartered in the United States, groups that placed great importance on the family and "family values."[96] The Somozas had also been influenced by the U.S. Right, but they had adopted its anti-Communism, not its views on women and the family. Third, the militarization of Nicaraguan politics during the revolutionary war of the 1970s and the Contra war of the 1980s diminished the role women played within the Nicaraguan Liberal Right. In exile during the 1980s, many Somocista women raised funds for the counterrevolutionary (Contra) forces but otherwise retreated into the world of nonpolitical employment,[97] while Somocista men took over the task of planning what type of government would eventually replace the Sandinistas.[98] And, fourth, Alemán had to contend with a politically and economically strong feminist movement, whereas the Somozas were able to co-opt and weaken the early twentieth-century feminist movement that existed in Nicaragua when they came to power in 1937.

It is important to repeat that the resurgence of the Liberal Party—and neo-Somocismo—in Nicaragua during the 1990s did not include an embrace of the Somozas' Liberal clientelistic populism, which had brought political and economic gains to some urban women in exchange for their political support. Unlike the Somozas, and like their Conservative rivals, the new Liberals emphasized conservative family values. Liberals at the end of the twentieth century made only veiled references to the Somozas' policies toward women, usually by praising the adoption of women's suffrage in 1955.[99]

It is my contention, based on my fieldwork, that Liberals were too embarrassed by and ashamed of the mobilization of prostitutes, the support for prostitution, and the rape of political prisoners under the Somoza regime to dare speak of a Somocista gender heritage. This is one of the many reasons why no one (to my knowledge) in the Alemán administration dared to claim the Somocista vision on gender as their own, even though the Liberal women's movement in the late 1990s used some of the same tactics to mobilize women that the Somozas had used.[100]

The presence of shame in Somocista—particularly Somocista women's—collective memories of the dictatorship might help explain why the official Somocista position, which proclaimed that sexual order existed during the 1936–79 period, did not prevail. Jeffrey L. Gould, building on Ann Norton's work, notes that "shame must be absent from local memory for the memory to be absorbed into a national narrative."[101] As noted earlier, Somocista women had good reason to feel shame. Some were specifically accused of being sexually suspect and morally corrupt while others were considered guilty by association. Moreover, they had to

justify their support for a regime that sexually tortured its female prisoners, sponsored prostitution, and gave power and visibility to someone like
Nicolasa Sevilla.

Whether or not Somocista women believed that the Somozas engaged
in sexual violence against anti-Somocista women, and whether or not Nicolasa Sevilla was actually a prostitute, Sevilla's role in the dictatorship was
a constant reminder to other Somocista women of the Somozas' support
for prostitution and for the public humiliation of anti-Somocista women.[102]
Nicolasa Sevilla's role in Somocismo, in and of itself, was a great embarrassment and a source of shame for some of the Somocista women I
interviewed. On the other hand, even the most ardent Somocista women
I spoke with admitted that, in certain areas, the last Somoza (Anastasio
Somoza Debayle) "went too far [se le pasó la mano]." Presumably, they
were talking about the human rights abuses committed by Somoza and
the National Guard. None of them, however, said, "We went too far."

Inevitably, given the polarized and complicated nature of politics in
Nicaragua, the complexity of Somocista women's support for the regime
is hard to grasp. It is much easier to dismiss Somocista women by label-
ing them "mujeres públicas," to pity them for having been manipulated
by the dictatorship, or to blame them for the sexual corruption of the
nation than it is to weave their complicated stories into Nicaragua's
already complicated history.

Conclusion

The subordination and underestimation of women is at the core of
Nicaragua's popular imaginary and body politic. This observation, however, does not explain the concrete manifestations of inequality between
men and women, nor does it reveal why anti-Somocistas saw the figure
of the female prostitute as a metaphor for the Somoza dictatorship. In
addition to capturing the national anxiety over female prostitution and
the exploitation of women, the metaphor of the prostitute who sells
her body in exchange for a few dollars appears to be a frank reading of
unequal international power relations between the United States and the
Third World.[103] Indeed, for many Nicaraguans, the metaphor symbolizes
their nation's history during the last hundred and fifty years. But what
effect has anxiety associated with this metaphor had on Nicaraguans'
attitudes toward women and their bodies? In the mid-1990s, Katherine
Hoyt, a U.S. American woman observing an FSLN Party Congress in
Managua, asked the Nicaraguan man seated next to her the name of

the fiery female speaker. The man responded, "I think her name is Nico-lasa."[104] Of course, the Sandinista speaker's name was not Nicolasa. Hardly anyone was named "Nicolasa" in Nicaragua at that time. But in this man's subconscious, it appeared that all women in public were Nico-lasas, that is, "mujeres públicas" (prostitutes). Unfortunately, this is the legacy not only of Somocismo, but also of the way anti-Somocistas have incorporated the dictatorship into the Nicaraguan popular imaginary.

Ironically, the popular political culture that anti-Somocistas drew upon to construct their moralistic critique of Somocista gender policies and attitudes toward women was the same sexist popular culture that Liberals relied on to advance their more inclusive yet "degenerate" agenda. This underscores two common insights about sexual politics. First, that popular cultures comprise competing models of sexuality. And second, that dominant regimes have to take the sexual attitudes of popular culture into account if they are to rule effectively. What is possibly unique about the Somozas is that their version of Nicaragua's modernization opened up a social and political space for some sexually marginalized women, causing an uproar among the regimes' opponents.

Two rather specific questions remain in relation to this discussion of prostitution and sexual politics under the Somozas. The first question is: To what extent did the Somozas finance the National Guard through the sale and degradation of women's bodies? Although fines and bribes derived from the sale of sex supplemented the meager salaries of individual guardsmen, so did their involvement in other activities like gambling. Far more important to the National Guard's survival, however, was the economic assistance it received from the U.S. government, which totaled more than 20 million dollars between 1941 and 1976.[105] The second question—To what extent did the Somoza regime use and manipulate women sexually and politically?—is in many respects a question about women's agency and the political uses of history. It demands an examination of the contradictions within the dictatorship. It also requires an acknowledgment that some women were victims or unwilling accomplices of the Somozas, some stood by and watched, while others actively participated in the dictatorship, benefited from it, or both.

We might also ask a third question: Why did the Somozas allow alleged prostitutes to play a highly visible role in their regime? The Somozas presided over a rather inclusive and elastic nation-building project, one that incorporated "colorful personalities" as local caudillos and caudillas into Somocismo. Because the Somozas did not subscribe to a moralistic discourse or agenda, the presence of prostitutes was not a moral problem for them.

Conservatives and Sandinistas claimed to occupy a higher moral ground than Somocistas, turning sexuality into "a convenient boundary between 'us' and 'them.'"[106] But, even as anti-Somocistas criticized the dictatorship for promoting degeneracy and for encouraging women's subordination, they "relied on traditional notions of women as victims and women as susceptible to immoral behavior"[107] in order to "save" them.

Moralistic discourses like those used by anti-Somocistas have tended to be simplistic discourses, which is why they can work so well as propaganda in political mobilizations. But their simplicity—"We are good; they are bad"—is what can cause moralistic discourses to backfire. Moralistic discourses only work if "we" are able to maintain a morally untarnished image. Once images are tarnished, moral movements tend to fall apart.

One of the principal legacies of the Somocista years is the politicization of sex. Between 1936 and 1979, anti-Somocistas emphasized that different types of governments promoted different types of sexual policies and practices, a point not lost on the Nicaraguan population. It was during the dictatorship that discussions of sex came to be inextricably tied to the capitalist/socialist (right-wing/left-wing) dichotomy, a dichotomy that is still the reference point in contemporary debates over sexual issues in Nicaragua, as exemplified by the 1998 Zoilamérica Narváez case.

In March 1998, Narváez publicly accused her stepfather, Daniel Ortega, of repeated rape and sexual abuse from 1979, when she was eleven, to 1990. Ortega and his wife, Rosario Murillo, Narváez's mother, promptly and publicly pronounced Narváez's accusation a lie. Narváez's legal case was supported by feminists but dismissed in 2001 by Nicaraguan courts, which ruled that the statute of limitations had expired. In 2008, Narváez withdrew her case still pending before the Inter-American Commission on Human Rights, stating that the case had been manipulated by different political groups and that she would seek resolution at the personal level.[108]

Cultural theorist Laura Kipnis argues that "Narváez's decision to tell the nation, and indeed the world, her sexual abuse story was not the only or most obvious way of proceeding. . . . But for that choice to be made, narrative structures had to preexist into which her particular story could be inserted." She further argues that "[international] feminism . . . provided that narrative structure."[109] Though I agree with Kipnis's first point, I must take issue with her second. My examination of Nicaraguan sexual politics in historical perspective leads me to conclude that it was the Sandinistas themselves who originally crafted "the sexual abuse narrative" in Nicaragua, only to have it boomerang decades later against their party leader, albeit in a reconstituted feminist form.

CONCLUSION

The twentieth century was marked by four major women's movements in Nicaragua: first-wave feminism, a Somocista women's movement, a Sandinista women's movement, and second-wave feminism. *Before the Revolution* deals with the first two—and most misunderstood—of these movements.

First-wave feminism had its origins in the nineteenth century. After independence, some elite men and women became interested in ending women's subordination, particularly in the educational arena. It was not until the second half of the nineteenth century, however, that there were significant changes in women's status. Feminists like Josefa Toledo de Aguerri (1866–1962) began actively working toward girls' and women's secular public education at the primary and secondary or normal levels, expanding their demands as the years progressed. By 1893, the arguments for women's suffrage had become commonplace within progressive circles; by 1913, the Nationalist Liberal Party (PLN) had promised to endorse the vote for women.

Education and suffrage were the two primary feminist demands during the nineteenth and early twentieth centuries. In support of these goals, feminists gathered in a wide range of organizations between the 1910s and the 1940s: the Nicaraguan Feminist League, the International

League of Iberian and Hispanic American Women and Nicaraguan Women's Crusade (LIMDI y Cruzada), the Inter-American Commission of Women (IACW), the Workingwomen's Cultural Center, the First Pan-American Women's Education League, the Nicaraguan chapter of the International League for Peace and Freedom (WILFP), and female teacher organizations, among others. These groups were independent of the state, political parties, and the Catholic Church, although many had structural ties to international feminist organizations (such as the WILPF and IACW), ideological links to Liberalism and socialism, or both.

In the 1940s, a new generation of women's rights activists arose in Nicaragua. This group actively mobilized on behalf of women's suffrage as part of a Central Women's Committee. Although the committee was nonpartisan, many of its members, often former pupils of Toledo de Aguerri, were affiliated with partisan women's groups. Suffragists' embrace of partisan politics signaled the end of first-wave feminism in Nicaragua.

The transition from feminism to Somocismo was not a smooth one, controlled from above by the Somoza family. It was a complicated process in which women of different political persuasions actively participated. The Somozas did not pull all the strings, although they did have the coercive power of the state at their disposal.

Contemporary Nicaraguans generally understand that the Somozas governed by terror. As historian Jeffrey L. Gould notes, scholars and laypeople tend to "agree that the . . . regime ruled through repression and to a lesser degree, co-optation."[1] Gould's study goes beyond these views, however, to suggest a more complex interpretation of the period. My research results support his contention that during the early and middle years of the dictatorship, the Somozas experimented with populism. For a time, independent nonpartisan feminists were able to participate in the populist project. By 1955, however, the year women won the vote, they were no longer admitted as players within the dictatorship.

Once women's suffrage was achieved, the Somozas ushered in a new era of women's involvement in politics. The Somozas' male-dominated Nationalist Liberal Party sought direct control over women's political participation through its partisan, nonfeminist women's organization, the Ala Femenina. The Ala's existence significantly altered the decades-old relationship between autonomous Liberal-leaning feminists and the PLN. For almost one hundred years, feminists had tended to agree with Liberals ideologically but had retained their organizational autonomy. After women won the vote, however, the Nationalist Liberal Party, under the guidance of the Somoza dictatorship, moved to exert ideological as well as organizational control over women who espoused Liberal ideas.

Through the Ala Femenina, the PLN succeeded in shutting independent feminists out of the political process. Originally made up of the nation's first generation of university-educated Liberal women, the Ala expanded its membership to include urban working-class women from different walks of life, bringing hundreds of thousands of women to the polls over the years. By voting for the Somozas between 1957 and 1979, these women sought to retain the rights Toledo de Aguerri and other early twentieth-century feminists had fought hard and long to achieve: secular education, the right to "be able to live independently of [men], if [they] so desired, and earn [their] own living," and women's suffrage. Through the vote, Ala members had a chance to influence politics in a way feminists were denied during the dictatorship. By successfully fostering women's support for the Somoza regime, this wing of the Liberal Party turned into its "backbone."[2]

Participating in Somocismo was an empowering experience for many women. It is my contention that Somocista women supported the dictatorship because they understood its clientelistic populism as an intimate reciprocity that met their psychological, political, and economic needs. And, indeed, once Somocismo stopped functioning as a system of intimate reciprocity, women stopped supporting the Somozas. The clear expectation of *reciprocity* in Somocismo is evident in Faustina Castro Palacio's 1978 statement to human rights authorities after the Sabogales Massacre (quoted in the introduction): "I never expected my services to the government and the Liberal Party to be repaid in this way."[3] The *intimate* aspect of this reciprocity was the personal relationship Somocista women felt they had with the Somozas. The possibility of speaking directly to Anastasio Somoza Debayle was a very real one for Castro Palacio: "If I could at this moment speak to General Somoza, I would tell him that. . . ." What Castro Palacio wanted to tell Somoza was that she had met her end of the bargain but he had not. Since the death of her neighbors and the destruction of her home were not acceptable to her, the only solution was for Somoza to "give up power."[4]

My research findings about the first generation of feminism in Nicaragua and women's support for the Somoza dictatorship challenge past interpretations of Nicaraguan women's history, which generally held that women's mobilization began in 1979. These findings not only serve to revise the chronology of Nicaraguan women's history; they also add to our understanding of the development of the Somocista state.

In relation to the development of the Nicaraguan state under the Somozas, Knut Walter writes:

> The question that must be asked is, What difference would a democracy have made? What would have an elected government headed, for example, by General [Emiliano] Chamorro have done differently . . . ?
>
> The answers to these questions hinge on a proper understanding of the Nicaraguan state. Things probably would not have developed much differently if Somoza had not come to power or if he had not remained as head of the Guardia Nacional for so long. This is so because the Nicaraguan state during the Somoza regime represented an overall consensus among the politically dominant groups on the desirability of export-oriented, capitalist economic growth and the need to guarantee the institutional and coercive powers of the state to foster and assure such growth. . . .
>
> The only significant aspect of Nicaraguan political development and of the Nicaraguan state that would have been different in the absence of a Somoza in power was the Somoza business empire. . . . If Somoza had not been around to take advantage of the opportunities that political power offered to enlarge his businesses, others would have taken his place, although economic power might not have been so centralized and concentrated as it was under Somoza.[5]

My research results suggest that the Nicaraguan state might have developed in quite a different manner if someone like General Chamorro had presided over its modernization. For one thing, since incorporating women into the modern state was a Liberal, not a Conservative, goal, women's mobilization might not have taken place to the extent or in the way that it did.

But what impact, in the end, did women's inclusion have on the state and on Nicaragua? Women's support for the dictatorship most likely lengthened the Somozas' stay in power; it also helped shape the type of Liberal clientelistic populism the Somozas instituted during their reign. Meanwhile, women provided a vast supply of low-paid workers to drive the urban economy.

The long-term effects of women's massive entry into the workforce and their participation in clientelistic politics under the Somozas are less clear. Certainly, such mobilization did not bring about women's emancipation. What it might have accomplished, however, was the legitimization of a significant group of women: female heads of households, a group I call "maternal breadwinners."

It is fairly easy to understand why urban, middle-class, Liberal professional women supported the Somoza dictatorship. Of all women, they benefited the most from Somocismo. The support offered by urban working-class Somocistas is harder to understand, until we remember that a large percentage of them were female heads of households.

That women were often the only source of financial, emotional, and educational support for their families was obvious to the Somozas. In a 1966 speech to the town of Masaya, Anastasio Somoza Debayle addressed the problem as he saw it: "There are approximately fifteen thousand married people in Masaya and the rest live in free [common-law] unions. I would like them to achieve the definitive family union so that women do not end up with the children and alone have to take on the burden of educating them. Our nation should be characterized by family unity, and fathers should have the responsibility toward their children who are the citizens who will forge Nicaragua's future."[6]

This statement could have been followed by specific suggestions on how to collect child support from "deadbeat dads" or how to encourage higher marriage rates. Or it could have been followed by a diatribe against women's promiscuity. Instead, Somoza went on to say: "There are more women than men and my purpose here in Masaya and Nicaragua is to see how we can bring woman to a dignified and productive state. I am determined to . . . assist [women] so that they can work and help sustain their homes economically, and in that way help lift up [both] home and homeland."[7]

Statements like this one led me to conclude that the Somozas understood that vast numbers of Nicaraguan women needed to work outside the home for financial reasons. Therefore, unlike Joaquín Balaguer in the Dominican Republic, who was also campaigning for president in the mid-1960s, Anastasio Somoza Debayle did not call upon women's "reserves of maternal sentiment."[8] Instead, he promised them employment and a "more active participation, with more responsibilities, in the direction of public affairs."[9] Like the Somozas, Somocista working-class maternal breadwinners understood working outside the home itself to be good mothering, and Ala leaders promoted this perspective.

As noted in the introduction, *Before the Revolution* is not meant to legitimize the Somoza dictatorship or broaden its appeal. The regime's relative "openness" toward some women should not lead us to forget the Somozas' legacy of terror or to question the right-wing status of the dictatorship. Somocistas—women and men alike—considered themselves to be on the right of the political spectrum. They were anti-Communists, opposed class struggle, and favored hierarchical survival strategies such as patron-clientelism. Moreover, they were generally opposed to the imposition of economic equality by the state.[10]

Throughout the preceding chapters, I have made a special effort to portray Somocista women's support for the Somoza dictatorship in a manner consistent with the available sources. To clear up any remaining confusion, I feel it is important to reiterate that, although they claimed to have pursued gender equality, for the most part, Somocista women did not seek to alter traditional gender relations, making it difficult to speak of them as "feminists." Nonetheless, a handful of Somocista women, such as Amelia Borge de Sotomayor and Olga Núñez de Saballos, wrote extensively about feminism and toiled for decades on behalf of women's rights. Women like them tended to believe the Somozas were feminists.

In closing, I wish to note that this study is only a first step toward gaining a clearer understanding of the role women have played in Nicaraguan history. Indeed, it is meant to invite further research and dialogue not only on the subject itself but also on the broader issues of feminism, maternalism, dictatorship, populism, and clientelism. It is my hope that Somocista women's experiences will help us better understand the role that gender plays in right-wing politics and will encourage scholars to undertake comparative analyses of women's political activism. The Nicaraguan case can also help us understand postsuffrage politics in a broader perspective and lead us to reflect more extensively on the writing of women's history. Undoubtedly, the study of Somocista women complicates one of the primary goals of both feminist activism and women's history, which is to give women a voice. Listening to right-wing women's stories challenges historians to expand the boundaries of women's history while forcing all of us to recognize the nuances of human experience.

APPENDIX A:
UNION DE MUJERES AMERICANAS (UMA)
FOUNDING MEMBERS

This list is drawn from a one-page document given me by one of my informants, who wishes to remain anonymous. The document states that the founding members signed the original statutes on January 30, 1942, at the home of Josefa T[oledo] de Aguerri. (This appears to contradict the 1939 founding date given by Margarita López Miranda, or it could be that the organization was started informally in 1939 and formally in 1942.)

Rosibel Aguilar, Soledad de Arriola, Yolanda Caligaris, Mary Coco de Callejas, Esperanza Centeno, Ana M. de Cortés, Justina de Espinoza, Leonor de Estrada, Carmela de Flores, Isaura de Flores, Angela de Fox, María de Frawley, M[aría] Luisa de Gertsch, Estela Herrera, Inés de Hurtado, Mercedes de Hurtado, Coco de Knoepffler, Isabel de Maltez, Ana de Mendieta, Julieta de Miranda, Anita Mora, Olga Núñez Abaunza, Sofía de Ocón, Carlota de Pereira, Julia de Pereira, Soledad de Pérez, Elena de Picasso, Margot de Ré, Carmen de Recalde, Amalia de Reyes, Elena de Riguero, Marta de Rodríguez, Pina de Romero Rojas, Tryni de Rosales, Emigdia de Salomón, Polina de Salomón, Berta de Solís, Celina de Tellería, Josefa T[oledo] de Aguerri, Joaquina Vega, Arcadia de Vijil, Carlota de Vijil, Isabel de Westtein, and Leonor de Wheelock.

APPENDIX B:
CENTRAL WOMEN'S COMMITTEE MEMBERS

From *Exposición del Comité Central Femenino Pro-Voto de la Mujer de Nicaragua (Adscrito a la Federación de Mujeres de América) a la Asamblea Nacional Constituyente. Presentado por la Doctora Infieri Srita. Joaquina Vega* (Managua: Imprenta Democrática, n.d.), 9, 10. Since this is one of the few surviving documents that contain the names of Nicaraguan suffragists, I find it important to list their names here. Whenever possible, I have included biographical information (which journalist Helena Ramos kindly shared with me) on these seventy-two activists.

Ninfa Aburto, Evangelina [Argüello] de Sansón (died in 1974, mother of writer Mariana Sansón), Nieve Andina Arnesto (painter from city of Matagalpa), Laura B. Báez, Irma Balladares, Anita de Barahona, Ernestina Barberena S., Olimpia Barboza Rosales, Yelba Bermúdez, Carmen R. de Caldera, Yolanda Caligaris (poet, 1910–1964), Lucrecia Castellón, Rosalina Castillo, Magda Chamorro M. (Conservative activist jailed by Somozas in mid-1950s), María de Conrado Vado, Emma Delgadillo, Sylvia de Delgadillo, Noelia S. de Olivas, Margarita H. de Ré, Ilse Egner, Gladys R. de Espinosa S., Bertha Fernández, Margarita Fiallos, Josefina González T., Mercedes de González, Stela Guerrero Rivas, Saturnina Guillén (Conservative journalist), Celina de Hammer, Vilma Hammer V., Matilde Haydée Díaz [Landeros] (radio announcer, journalist, and Catholic activist, 1918–1997), Justina Huezo [Ortega] de Espinosa (writer), Aminta de Lanzas, Salvadora Latino, Margarita Leal, María A. v. de Leal, Carmen de Llanes, María C. López, Pina de Luna, Nelly Marín A., María Hilda Martínez, Concepción Mayorga, Daisy Mayorga, Evelina Mayorga, Ramona Mayorga, Dolores de Mayorga Rivas, Alicia Miller, Bertha de Miranda, Ada de Mondragón, María Argentina Mondragón, Sofía Montiel, María Fidelia de Navarro, Lola de Ortega, Isabel Palacio, Inés de Palma M., Cony Peña, Sylvia Quintana O., Nena de Reyes, Elena de Riguero, Elida Genie v. de Sánchez, Esperanza Sansón A., Camila Solórzano C., Rosa Solórzano C., Juana Helena Soriano, Paquita Soriano, Emma Sotomayor de Valenzuela, Mélida Terán H., Francisca de Torres, Haydée de Ulloa, Josefina de Valladares, Celia Valle de Lola, Lidya G.Walsh, and Karem Weelock.

NOTES

PREFACE

1. For an example of how my research findings (although not cited and slightly mangled) inform mainstream interpretations, see the *Wikipedia* entry "Ala Femenina del Partido Liberal Nacionalista," accessed September 13, 2009, http://es.wikipedia.org/wiki /Ala_Femenina_del_Partido_Liberal_Nacionalista. For an example of how my research results have been adopted in mainstream textbooks, see Clemente Guido Martínez, *Nueva historia de Nicaragua* (Managua: Alba Editores, 2008), 173.

2. The term "mestizo/a" has a complicated history. It was first used to refer to the mixed-race children born to the Spanish conquistadors and indigenous women after the Spanish conquest of the Americas. It was then applied to all Indian-Spanish mixed-race peoples who were "half" Spanish and "half" Indian. As the colonial period progressed, it became harder and harder to tell who was a biological mestizo/a and who a cultural one. Eventually, countries such as Nicaragua and Mexico embraced the idea that their entire population was made up of mestizos/as, bringing about the erasure, in the national imaginaries, of the many indigenous peoples who continued to live there, a trend reversed only in the recent past. Meanwhile, in the 1980s, the term "mestiza" was given a new life, and a positive spin, by Latina feminist activists in the United States. Gloria Anzaldua, in particular, theorized that "la nueva mestiza" (the new mestiza) consciousness represented a new way of identifying that could empower women of color. When I say I am "twice mestiza," I mean that I am the product of two specific historical moments that brought about the blending of distinct cultures/"races."

The literature on *mestizaje* is extensive. See Gloria Anzaldua, *Borderlands/La Frontera: The New Mestiza* (San Francisco: Aunt Lute Books, 1987). For mestizaje in Nicaragua, see Jeffrey L. Gould, *To Die in This Way: Nicaraguan Indians and the Myth of Mestizaje, 1880–1965* (Durham: Duke University Press, 1998).

For more on Carlos Fonseca Amador and the Matagalpa he grew up in, see Matilde Zimmermann, *Sandinista: Carlos Fonseca and the Nicaraguan Revolution* (Durham: Duke University Press, 2000). For more on Tomás Borge and his views on Matagalpa, see his autobiography, *The Patient Impatience: From Boyhood to Guerrilla; A Personal Narrative of Nicaragua's Struggle for Liberation* (Willimantic, Conn.: Curbstone Press, 1992).

3. See Gould, *To Die in This Way.*

4. For more on Nicaragua's nineteenth- and twentieth-century immigrants, see Eddy Kühl Arauz, *Nicaragua: Historia de inmigrantes* (Managua: Hispamer, 2007).

5. One of my father's grandfathers had been a lawyer, however; one of his aunts was the first young woman from Matagalpa to graduate from high school, and one of his cousins became the first woman from our town to complete a doctorate.

6. For more on Ben Linder, see Joan Kruckewitt, *The Death of Ben Linder: The Story of a North American in Sandinista Nicaragua* (New York: Seven Story Press, 1999).

7. See Barack Obama's *Dreams From My Father: A Story of Race and Inheritance* (New York: Three Rivers Press, 2004).

8. The People's Cultural Centers were created by the revolution in an attempt to democratize access to training in the arts. The harassment of young girls in the streets of Nicaragua is not as severe as it used to be, in part because of feminist activism.

9. I had only been in the United States for two and a half years when I entered Oberlin, not long enough to get a nuanced feel for the ways in which sexism operates in this country. My experiences as a student activist in college, however, would reinforce my decision to embrace feminism as a political ideology.

10. One well-known exception is Luis Alfonso Velasquez Flores, a child martyr of the revolution, born, as I was, in 1969. Although not a combatant, he died at the hands of the Somozas' National Guard in 1979.

11. Without delving into the merits of national histories, I do wish to point out that most historians have mixed feelings about nationalism and the ways it continues to shape our field despite the realities of transnationalism and globalization.

INTRODUCTION

1. Instituto de Estudios Interdisciplinarios (IEI), *El voto ciudadano: Una perspectiva desde adentro; Significados, memoria, y participación en Granada, Nicaragua* (Granada: Editorial Casa Tres Mundos, 2007), 15. Unless otherwise noted, translations from Spanish-language sources throughout volume are my own.

2. Ibid., 87.

3. Ibid., 13–15.

4. See "Latin America's Richest and Poorest," *Latin Business Chronicle*, April 27, 2009, http://www.latinbusinesschronicle.com/app/article.aspx?id=3356.

5. IEI, *El voto ciudadano*, 13–15.

6. Ibid., 87.

7. Ibid., 37, 42.

8. Ibid., 40, 41.

9. Comité Permanente de Derechos Humanos (CPDH), *Los derechos humanos en Nicaragua: Segundo informe* (Managua: Comité Permanente de Derechos Humanos, 1978), 106, 107.

10. On the "Sabogales Massacre," see Juanita, Testimonios, "Se siente, se siente, Monimbó está caliente. Se siente, se siente, Monimbó aguerrido y valiente," *Casa de las Américas* (Havana) 20, no. 117 (1979): 171.

11. CPDH, *Los derechos humanos en Nicaragua*, 107.

12. Ibid., 123.

13. Ibid.

14. Ibid., 124, 125.

15. Ibid., 137.

16. Margaret Randall, *Sandino's Daughters: Testimonies of Nicaraguan Women in Struggle*, ed. Lynda Yanz (Vancouver: New Star Books, 1981), 216, 217.

17. Ibid., 218, 219.

18. Ibid., iv; Helen Collinson et al., *Women and Revolution in Nicaragua*, ed. Helen Collinson (London: Zed Books, 1990), 154.

19. Carlos M. Vilas, *The Sandinista Revolution: National Liberation and Social Transformation in Central America* (New York: Monthly Review Press, 1986), 108.

20. Collinson et al., *Women and Revolution*, 140.

21. John A. Booth, *The End and the Beginning: The Nicaraguan Revolution*, 2nd ed. (Boulder: Westview Press, 1985), 98, 102.

22. Ibid., 102.

23. Ibid., 104, 113.

24. Ibid.

25. Ibid., 114.

26. Ibid., 114, 115.

27. Karen Kampwirth, "Women in the Armed Struggles in Nicaragua: Sandinistas and Contras Compared," in *Radical Women in Latin America: Left and Right*, ed. Victoria González and Karen Kampwirth (University Park: Pennsylvania State University Press, 2001), 82–83.

28. Ibid., 84.

29. Ana Isabel García and Enrique Gomariz, *Mujeres centroamericanas ante la crisis: La guerra y el proceso de paz*, vol. 1, *Tendencias estructurales: Información estadística por sexo* (San José: FLACSO, 1999), 360.

30. Roser Solà i Montserrat, *Geografía y estructura económicas de Nicaragua en el contexto centromericano y de América Latina* (Managua: UCA, 1990), 59.

31. Vilas, *The Sandinista Revolution*, 101.

32. Ibid., 103.

33. Solà i Montserrat, *Geografía y estructura económicas*, 54.

34. U.S. Comptroller General, *Nicaragua: An Assessment of Earthquake Relief and Reconstruction Assistance* (Washington, D.C.: U.S. General Accounting Office, March 1977), 1.

35. Vilas, *The Sandinista Revolution*, 102.

36. Solà i Montserrat, *Geografía y estructura económicas*, 56.

37. For more on Nicaragua's political and economic crisis in the late 1970s, see Roser Solà i Montserrat, *Un siglo y medio de economía nicaragüense: Las raíces del presente* (Managua: IHNCA, 2007). See also Frances Kinloch Tijerino, *Historia de Nicaragua*, 3rd ed. (Managua: IHNCA, 2008).

38. Booth, *The End and the Beginning*, 129, 134, 136, 145.

39. Ibid., 145.

40. Benjamin Keen, *A History of Latin America*, 5th ed. (Boston: Houghton Mifflin, 1996), 567.

41. Anna Fernández Poncela, "Nicaraguan Women: Legal, Political, and Social Spaces," in *Gender Politics in Latin America: Debates in Theory and Practice*, ed. Elizabeth Dore (New York: Monthly Review Press, 1997), 37.

42. See, for example, Collinson et al., *Women and Revolution*, 137, 138; Ileana Rodríguez, *Registradas en la historia: 10 años del quehacer feminista en Nicaragua* (Managua: CIAM, 1990), 13.

43. For more on Liberal reforms affecting women in Nicaragua, see Teresa Cobo del Arco, *Políticas de género durante el liberalismo: Nicaragua, 1893–1909* (Managua: UCA, 2000), 65–180. See also Elizabeth Dore, "The Holy Family: Imagined Households in Latin America," in Dore, *Gender Politics*, 110, 111. For more on Liberalism and gender throughout Latin America, see Elizabeth Dore, "One Step Forward, Two Steps Back: Gender and the State in the Long Nineteenth Century," in *Hidden Histories of Gender and the State in Latin America*, ed. Elizabeth Dore and Maxine Molyneux (Durham: Duke University Press, 2000), 22, 23. See also Maxine Molyneux, "Twentieth-Century State Formation in Latin America," in Dore and Molyneux, *Hidden Histories*, 42–50.

44. For more on Sandinista women's lack of autonomy during the 1980s, see Fernández Poncela, "Nicaraguan Women," 45. See also Randall, *Sandino's Daughters*, 23–30,

and Lorraine Bayard de Volo, *Mothers of Heroes and Martyrs: Gender Identity Politics in Nicaragua, 1979–1999* (Baltimore: Johns Hopkins University Press, 2001), 88.

45. See Suzanne Baker, "Gender Ideologies and Social Change in Revolutionary Nicaragua" (Ph.D. diss., Boston University, 1995), 60, 61; and Bayard de Volo, *Mothers of Heroes and Martyrs*, 23.

46. For more on right-wing regimes and maternalism in Argentina, Brazil, and Chile, see Sandra McGee Deutsch, "Spreading Right-Wing Patriotism, Femininity, and Morality: Women in Argentina, Brazil, and Chile, 1900–1940," 223–48; and Margaret Power "Defending Dictatorship: Conservative Women in Pinochet's Chile and the 1988 Plebiscite," 299–324, both in González and Kampwirth, *Radical Women*. On right-wing regimes and maternalism in Europe, see Claudia Koonz, *Mothers in the Fatherland: Women, the Family, and Nazi Politics* (New York: St. Martin's Press, 1987), 5, 6, 14, 17. See also Victoria de Grazia, *How Fascism Ruled Women: Italy, 1922–1945* (Berkeley and Los Angeles: University of California Press, 1992), 41–76; and Daniele Bussy Genevois, "Mujeres de España: De la República al franquismo," in *Historia de las mujeres en occidente*, ed. Georges Duby and Michelle Perrot (Madrid: Santillana, 1993), 228.

47. Margaret Power, "Defending Dictatorship: Conservative Women in Pinochet's Chile and the 1988 Plebiscite," in González and Kampwirth, *Radical Women*, 306.

48. Bayard de Volo, *Mothers of Heroes and Martyrs*.

49. Roser Solà [i Montserrat] and María Pau Trayner, *Ser madre en Nicaragua: Testimonios de una historia no escrita* (Barcelona: Icaria Editorial, 1988), 14.

50. García and Gomariz, *Mujeres centroamericanas*, 329.

51. Lorraine Bayard de Volo, in her study of the mothers of heroes and martyrs of Matagalpa, notes that "over 70 percent of those interviewed did not live with a male companion." Bayard de Volo, *Mothers of Heroes and Martyrs*, 124.

52. Ibid., 128.

53. García and Gomariz, *Mujeres centroamericanas*, 392.

54. Some women lost their children *and* husbands. For example, María Eugenia Vargas lost two sons and her husband. Esmeralda Noguera lost six sons, her husband, and a brother. Solà [i Montserrat] and Pau Trayner, *Ser madre*, 49, 85.

55. Vilas, *The Sandinista Revolution*, 109.

56. The average member of the Matagalpa Committee of Mothers of Heroes and Martyrs was in her fifties, according to Bayard de Volo, *Mothers of Heroes and Martyrs*, 124.

57. Gary Ruchwarger, *People in Power: Forging a Grassroots Democracy in Nicaragua* (South Hadley, Mass.: Bergin and Garvey, 1987), 199.

58. Knut Walter, *The Regime of Anastasio Somoza, 1936–1956* (Chapel Hill: University of North Carolina Press, 1993), xvii.

59. Molyneux, "Twentieth-Century State Formations in Latin America," 47.

60. Ibid., 67.

61. Ibid., 56.

62. Ibid., 57, 56.

63. Javier Auyero, "The Logic of Clientelism in Argentina: An Ethnographic Account," *Latin American Research Review* 35, no. 3 (2000), 58.

64. Ibid., 75.

65. Jeffrey L. Gould. *To Lead as Equals: Rural Protest and Political Consciousness in Chinandega, Nicaragua, 1912–1979* (Chapel Hill: University of North Carolina Press, 1990), 15, 45.

66. Many of my Somocista informants used this expression. They also added: "No se puede ser bueno todo el tiempo, ni con todo el mundo. Hay que ser bueno con los

buenos y malo con los malos" (One cannot be good all the time, or with everyone. One must be good to those who are good, and bad to those who are bad).

67. See Instituto Nicaragüense de Seguridad Social y Bienestar (INSSBI), *La prostitución en Nicaragua* (Managua: Programa de Rehabilitación del INSSBI, 1980), 60.

68. Ibid. See also Collinson et al., *Women and Revolution*, 69; Amalia Chamorro, "Estado y hegemonía durante el somocismo," in *Economía y sociedad en la construcción del estado en Nicaragua*, ed. Alberto Lanuza et al. (San José: ICAP, 1983), 271; and Gould, *To Lead as Equals*, 169.

The assertion that anti-Somocistas equated Somocista women's activism with prostitution is based on dozens of interviews and conversations with Sandinista and Somocista activists. See also Pedro Joaquín Chamorro, *Estirpe sangrienta: Los Somoza* (Managua: Ediciones el Pez y la Serpiente, 1978), 160, and Viktor Morales Henríquez, *De Mrs. Hanna a la Dinorah: Principio y fin de la dictadura somocista; Historia de medio siglo de corrupción* ([Managua?]: [1980?]), 39, 40, 57.

69. See Denis Lynn Daly Heyck, *Life Stories of the Nicaraguan Revolution* (London: Routledge, 1990), 64–67.

70. P. J. Chamorro, *Estirpe sangrienta*, 163.

71. For more on Barrios de Chamorro's maternal image, see Karen Kampwirth, "The Mother of the Nicaraguans: Doña Violeta and the UNO's Gender Agenda," *Latin American Perspectives* 23, no. 1 (Winter 1996): 69.

72. Collinson et al., *Women and Revolution*, 69.

73. Walter, *The Regime of Anastasio Somoza*, xvii.

74. Ibid.

75. I assume that male informants did not ask about my mother for traditionally sexist reasons. Middle-class female Somocista informants, however, appear to have asked about my father for a different reason. Since I was not the daughter of a Somocista female leader, they seemed to think I might have been the daughter of a high-ranking Somocista man, someone they might have known. They clearly assumed that I came from a Somocista family.

76. Francisco Obando Somarriba, *Doña Angélica Balladares de Argüello: La primera dama del liberalismo; Su vida, sus hechos, episodios de la historia de Nicaragua* (Managua: Tipografía Comercial, 1969), 77–79.

77. Modesto Armijo, *Derechos políticos de la mujer* (León: Tipografía Progreso, de Sofonías Salvatierra, 1912), 60.

CHAPTER I

1. Josefa Toledo de Aguerri, *Educación y feminismo: Sobre enseñanza; Artículos varios (reproducciones)* (Managua: Talleres Nacionales de Imprenta y Encuadernación, 1940), 17.

2. Ibid., 20.

3. For earlier use of "feminism" in Nicaragua, see Benjamín Cuadra's antifeminist thesis *Situación jurídica de la mujer nicaragüense* (Granada: Tipografía de El Centro-Americano, 1905), 16, 18. For earlier use of the term in the Southern Cone, see Asunción Lavrín, *Women, Feminism, and Social Change in Argentina, Chile, and Uruguay, 1890–1940* (Lincoln: University of Nebraska Press, 1995), 15, 16. For a discussion of the debates over historians' use of the term for the nineteenth century, see Judith Allen, *Rose Scott: Vision and Revision in Feminism* (Melbourne: Oxford University Press, 1994), 1–32.

4. By "autonomous," "independent," or "nonpartisan," I mean that feminists were not directly tied to Nicaraguan political parties, the Nicaraguan state, or the Catholic Church.

5. The names in Spanish of these five organizations are, respectively, Liga Feminista de Nicaragua, Liga Internacional de Mujeres Ibéricas e Hispanoamericanas y Cruzada de Mujeres Nicaragüenses (LIMDI y Cruzada), Primera Liga Panamericana Femenina de Educación, Comisión Interamericana de Mujeres (CIM), and the Centro Femenino de Cultura Obrera.

6. June E. Hahner, *Emancipating the Female Sex: The Struggle for Women's Rights in Brazil, 1850–1940* (Durham: Duke University Press, 1990), xiii.

7. Nancy F. Cott, *The Grounding of Modern Feminism* (New Haven: Yale University Press, 1987), 9.

8. Ibid., 9, 37.

9. That giving gender issues top priority distinguishes feminists from nonfeminists is a distinction also made by K. Lynn Stoner, *From the House to the Streets: The Cuban Woman's Movement for Legal Reform, 1898–1940* (Durham: Duke University Press, 1991), 3.

10. Margarita López Miranda, *Una chontaleña en la educación nacional: Biografía de Josefa Toledo de Aguerri* (Juigalpa: Asociación de Ganaderos de Chontales [ASOGACHO], 1988), 143.

11. "Instrucción pública," *Aurora de Nicaragua*, no. 2 (1837): 2.

12. Mauricio Pallais Lacayo, *El periodismo en Nicaragua, 1826–1876* (Managua: Banco Central de Nicaragua, 1982), 1:24. Gregorio Juárez went on to serve as foreign minister in the late 1850s. See José Dolores Gámez, *Historia de Nicaragua desde los tiempos prehistoricos hasta 1860, en sus relaciones con España, México, y Centro-América* (Managua: Tipografía de El País, 1889), 699. See also Michel Gobat, *Confronting the American Dream: Nicaragua Under U.S. Imperial Rule* (Durham: Duke University Press, 2005), 45. Frances Kinloch Tijerino considers Gregorio Juárez "one of the main intellectuals of the period." See Kinloch Tijerino, "El primer encuentro con los filibusteros en Nicaragua: Antecendes y contextos," *Boletín AFEHC*, no. 36 (June 2008), http://afehc-historiacentroamericana.org/index.php?action=fi_aff&id=1925.

13. Lucrecia Noguera Carazo, *Evolución cultural y política de la mujer nicaragüense* (Managua: n.p., 1974), 6.

14. According to Julián N. Guerrero and Lola Soriano de Guerrero, de la Cerda "possessed and cultivated the ideals of independence, liberty and autonomy for the people, as he demonstrated . . . when he led the first rebel movement against Spain in the city of Granada, becoming a martyr for his ideals when he was sent to suffer prison . . . in Spain for over four years. [Moreover, d]uring his tenure as Subdelegate of Matagalpa [in the colonial period] his ideals led him to adopt a moderate policy towards the indigenous residents of the region. . . . Prudently and shrewdly, he propagated his ideal of respecting citizens' right and the need for them to be free to govern themselves." Guerrero and Soriano de Guerrero, *Matagalpa* ([Managua?]: n.p., 1967), 74, 75.

For a sampling of works on the relationship between men and women in postindependence Latin America, see Dore and Molyneux, *Hidden Histories*.

15. Cobo del Arco, *Políticas de género*, 41.

16. Noguera Carazo, *Evolución cultural*, 5.

17. Josefa Vega's father was General Fulgencio Vega, who, as director of state, signed the decree that turned Managua into Nicaragua's capital in 1852, thus ending the yearslong conflict between Granada and León, the two cities vying for that title. Fulgencio Vega died in 1868. According to Roberto Sánchez Ramírez, Vega enrolled not only

his daughter Josefa but also his other daughter, Mercedes, at the University of Granada. Moreover, he supported women's right to obtain a university degree. See Sánchez Ramírez, *El recuerdo de Managua en la memoria de un poblano* (Managua: Dirección de Patrimonio Historico Municipal Alcaldía de Managua, 2008), 42, 43.

18. Alejandro Barberena Pérez, *Estampas de Granada y sus 450 años de fundación* (Managua: Imprenta Nacional, 1974), 110, 111.

19. Ibid., 111, 112.

20. Ibid. For more on the history of Josefa Chamorro, see Ignacio Briones, "La nicaragüense y su evolución cultural y política," *Bolsa de Noticias,* March 8, 2000, http://www.grupoese.com.ni/2000/bn/03/08/ibMM0308.htm.

21. Francesca Miller, *Latin American Women and the Search for Social Justice* (Hanover, N.H.: University Press of New England), 71.

22. Justin Wolfe cautions us on the issue of anarchy during this period: "I want to suggest that we focus, instead, on the relationship between state formation and what we might term 'social anarchy.' This is an effort to see the conflicts between elites and the population at large not merely as resulting from social transformations (which undoubtedly were occurring) but as responses to state formation." See Wolfe, *The Everyday Nation State: Community and Ethnicity in Nineteenth-Century Nicaragua* (Lincoln: University of Nebraska Press, 2007), 26.

23. Donald C. Hodges, *Intellectual Foundations of the Nicaraguan Revolution* (Austin: University of Texas Press, 1986), 8.

24. Ciro F. S. Cardoso, "The Liberal Era, c. 1870–1930," in *Central America Since Independence,* ed. Leslie Bethell (Cambridge: Cambridge University Press, 1991), 56.

25. Ibid., 62.

26. For a Conservative perspective on women's situation in society, see the autobiography of Emiliano Chamorro Vargas (1871–1966), who twice served as president of Nicaragua (1917–21; March–November 1926), *El último caudillo* (Managua: Ediciones del Partido Conservador, 1983), 258, reprinted from *Revista Conservadora,* edición extraordinaria, no. 67 (1966).

27. "Instrucción pública," *Aurora de Nicaragua,* no. 2 (1837), 2.

28. E. Chamorro, *El último caudillo,* 258.

29. R. L. Woodward Jr., "The Aftermath of Independence," in Bethell, *Central America Since Independence,* 32.

30. Walter, *The Regime of Anastasio Somoza,* 20.

31. Ibid., 21. For more on Cuadra Pasos's Catholic corporatist views, see Gobat, *Confronting the American Dream,* 224–26.

32. "La grandeza de la mujer," *El Reflector,* April 13, 1926, 1, cited and translated by David Whisnant in *Rascally Signs in Sacred Places: The Politics of Culture in Nicaragua* (Chapel Hill: University of North Carolina Press, 1995), 393.

33. Armijo, *Derechos políticos,* 61, 63. Modesto Armijo went on to become a close economic adviser to Somoza in the 1950s. See Walter, *The Regime of Anastasio Somoza,* 192.

34. Florencia Mallon, *Peasant and Nation: The Making of Post-Colonial Mexico and Peru* (Berkeley and Los Angeles: University of California Press, 1995), 161. Armijo was not the only one to defend feminism in 1912, however. That same year, another attorney, Bernardo Sotomayor, wrote a profeminist thesis: "Civil Capacity with Respect to Sex." See also Amelia Borge de Sotomayor, *La mujer y el derecho* (León: Editorial San José, 1953), 61.

35. Cobo del Arco, *Políticas de género,* 42.

36. Catholic doctrine holds that adultery, whether by wife or husband, is a sin, whereas secular Liberal law, on the other hand, punished a husband's adultery only under certain circumstances. Ibid., 111–15.

37. Enrique Guzmán, as quoted in ibid., 87, 173.

38. José Madríz, as quoted in ibid., 172–73.

39. Ibid., 75.

40. Josefa Toledo de Aguerri, *Educación y feminismo*, 19.

41. Based on the sources, I cannot tell if the *Ateneo* group was made up of men or women or both.

42. *El Ateneo*, September 1, 1881.

43. Ibid.

44. *El 93: Diario Político y de Variedades*, September 1, 1916.

45. Ibid. Teresa Cobo del Arco, citing Silvio Morales-Ettienne, notes that the PLN officially endorsed women's suffrage at its convention in August 1913. See Cobo del Arco, "Populismo, somocismo, y el voto femenino: Nicaragua, 1936–1955," in *Poder local, poder global en America Latina*, ed. Gabriela Dalla Corte et al. (Barcelona: Universitat de Barcelona, 2008) 155.

46. *El 93: Diario Político y de Variedades*, September 1, 1916.

47. Ibid.

48. Noguera Carazo, *Evolución cultural*, 11.

49. Ibid.

50. Jorge Rodríguez, *Elena Arellano, los salesianos en Centroamérica, y la casa de Granada, Nicaragua* (Managua: Ministerio de Educación, 1992), 58.

51. Noguera Carazo, *Evolución cultural*, 10. Julia de Rivera Castro is also remembered as "Julia de Pereira Castro." See Instituto Nicaragüense de Cultura (INC), *Catálogo de periódicos y revistas de Nicaragua, 1830–1930* (Managua: Instituto Nicaragüense de Cultura, 1992), 157.

52. Whisnant, *Rascally Signs*, 409.

53. Ibid.

54. Ibid.

55. An orphan, Umaña suffered from tuberculosis and died poor and alone. See Helena Ramos, "Colectiva: La mujer en la literatura nicaragüense," accessed July 25, 2009, http://www.escritorasnicaragua.org/critica?idcritica=23.

56. *El 93: Diario Político y de Variedades*, September 1, 1916.

57. Ibid.

58. Gobat, *Confronting the American Dream*, 189.

59. Luis Manuel Debayle, "The Status of Women in Nicaragua," *Mid-Pacific Magazine* (Honolulu) 45, no. 3 (1933): 238.

60. Ibid. For more on Aura Rostand (María Selva Escoto de Ibarra), see Erin S. Finzer, "Poetisa Chic: Fashioning the Modern Female Poet in Central America" (Ph.D. diss., University of Kansas, 2008), 279–85.

61. Gunnar Fromen to Doris Stevens, December 22, 1934, Doris Stevens Papers, MC 546, Box 83.

62. Gobat, *Confronting the American Dream*, 189.

63. López Miranda, *Una chontaleña*, 108, 109.

64. "Biography of Mrs. Florence Terry Griswold," accessed September 13, 2009, http://www.partt.org/marchbanks_ftg_bio.html.

65. Josefa Toledo de Aguerri, *Al correr de la pluma: Crónicas de viajes, escritas para "Revista Femenina Ilustrada" (de agosto a diciembre de 1920) desde Costa Rica y Estados Unidos de América, pasando por Panamá y la Habana* (Managua: Tipografiá Nacional, 1924), 65–68.

66. López Miranda, *Una chontaleña*, 109, 116.

67. Ibid. See also Gabriela Cano, *Se llamaba Elena Arizmendi* (Mexico City: Tusquets Editores, 2010).

68. López Miranda, *Una chontaleña*, 108.

69. *Boletín de la Unión Panamericana* 55 (1922): 105, 135.

70. Ibid., 131, 132.

71. Antonia Rodríguez [pseud.], interview by author. As noted in the preface, I conducted most interviews with Somocista women in confidentiality. To preserve their anonymity and that of certain others I interviewed, spoke with, or quoted, I have used pseudonyms and withheld information about place and date.

72. Carlos M. Vilas, "Family Affairs: Class, Lineage, and Politics in Contemporary Nicaragua," *Journal of Latin American Studies* 24, no. 2 (May 1992): 317.

73. Ibid., 315, 316.

74. Molina de Fromen suffered from postpartum depression and, after two serious appendix operations, had a nervous breakdown. In the midst of her breakdown, she killed her eleven-month-old son and committed suicide in her New York City apartment a few days before Christmas 1934. She had no other children. Gunnar Fromen to Doris Stevens, December 22, 1934, Doris Stevens Papers, MC 546, Box 83.

75. Gunnar Fromen to Doris Stevens, December 22, 1934, Doris Stevens Papers, MC 546, Box 83.

76. Emilie Bergmann, *Women, Culture, and Politics in Latin America: Seminar on Feminism and Culture in Latin America* (Berkeley and Los Angeles: University of California Press, 1990), 17.

77. Miller, *Latin American Women*, 105.

78. Ibid.

79. *CIM Inter-American Commission of Women, 1928–1973* (Washington, D.C.: General Secretariat, Organization of American States, 1974), 1, as quoted in Bergmann, *Women, Culture, and Politics*, 16.

80. Bergmann, *Women, Culture, and Politics*, 16.

81. Juanita Molina de Fromen to Doris Stevens, February 12, 1931; Gunnar Fromen to Doris Stevens, February 1933, both in Doris Stevens Papers, MC 546, Box 83.

82. Juanita Molina de Fromen to Doris Stevens, October 27, 1933, Doris Stevens Papers, MC 546, Box 83.

83. Wallace Thompson, *Rainbow Countries of Central America* (New York: E. P. Dutton, 1926), 234.

CHAPTER 2

1. Juanita Molina de Fromen to Alice Paul, March 21, 1930, Alice Paul Papers, MC 399, Box 102, Folder 1337.

2. Ibid.

3. "Nicaraguan Women Lose," *New York Times*, September 27, 1932, 12. Journalist Helena Ramos first suggested to me that "María Gomez" was really María Gámez, daughter of Nicaragua's pioneer historian José D. Gámez. She was, of course, correct. According to Thomas Dodd, Woodward had had extensive experience in Latin America: "A veteran of the Spanish American War and with service experience in the Philippines, he served in Brazil and Peru in the early 1920s as head of the United States naval mission in both countries. . . . From 1928 to 1931, he was acting governor of the Canal Zone in Panama. Many U.S. officials considered him the most qualified officer on active service who could handle the delicate and sensitive Nicaraguan assignment." Dodd,

Managing Democracy in Central America: A Case Study; United States Election Supervision in Nicaragua, 1927–1933 (New Brunswick: Transaction, 1992), 128. On the virtually unlimited powers of the Election Mission, see Gobat, *Confronting the American Dream*, 205–16, esp. 209–10.

4. María Gámez to Doris Stevens, June 17, 1932, and June 27, 1932. The second letter had the bill in favor of women's suffrage as an attachment. Doris Stevens Papers, MC 546, Box 83.

5. Ibid.

6. Ibid.

7. Rodolfo Espinosa R., as quoted in Borge de Sotomayor, *La mujer y el derecho*, 62.

8. Cobo del Arco, "Populismo, somocismo," 156.

9. "Nicaragua Bars Vote for Women," *New York Times*, January 8, 1933, 3.

10. Borge de Sotomayor, *La mujer y el derecho*, 62.

11. Gobat, *Confronting the American Dream*, 209.

12. María Gámez to Doris Stevens, June 17, 1932, Doris Stevens Papers, MC 546, Box 83.

13. Ibid.

14. Allan Reed Millet, *Semper Fidelis: The History of the United States Marine Corps* (New York: Free Press, 1991), 248, accessed September 13, 2009, http://books.google.com/books?id=sgkbAbwcLfAC&pg=PA248&dq=alan+Reed+Millet+Semper+Fidelis+McCoy#v=onepage&q=&f=false.

15. Carleton Beals, as quoted in "U.S. Intervention and Elections in Nicaragua," *Envío*, no. 32 (February 1984), http://www.envio.org.ni/articulo/3961.

16. Ellen [Carol] DuBois and Lauren Derby, "The Strange Case of Minerva Bernardino: Pan American and United Nations Women's Right Activist," *Women's Studies International Forum* 32 (2009): 44.

17. See, for instance, Francisco Palma Martínez, *El siglo de los topos: Crítica y enseñanza en plan de ciencia; Filosofía del sexo, psicología, sociología, eugenesia, religión, y arte* (León: Editorial La Patria, [1949?]), 66.

18. Gobat, *Confronting the American Dream*, 192.

19. María Gámez to Doris Stevens, June 17, 1932, Doris Stevens Papers, MC 546, Box 83.

20. Josefa Toledo de Aguerri, "Apreciaciones sobre la mujer nicaragüense." Helena Ramos, personal communication with author, September 4, 2009. See Toledo de Aguerri, *Anhelos y esfuerzos: Reproducciones* (Managua, Imprenta Nacional, 1935).

21. María Gámez to Doris Stevens, June 17, 1932, Doris Stevens Papers, MC 546, Box 83.

22. INC, *Catálogo de periódicos y revistas de Nicaragua*, 39.

23. López Miranda, *Una chontaleña*, 105.

24. Juanita Molina de Fromen to Alice Paul, March 21, 1930, Alice Paul Papers, MC 399, Box 102, Folder 1337.

25. Toledo de Aguerri, *Educación y feminismo*, 57–62. See also Jorge Eduardo Arellano, *Héroes sin fusil: 140 nicaragüenses sobresalientes* (Managua: Editorial Hispamer, 1998), 267, 268.

26. The National Woman's Party had been founded in 1917 by Alice Paul, one of the U.S. feminists in touch with María Gámez and Juanita Molina de Fromen. Doris Stevens was also a leader in the NWP until she parted ways with Alice Paul and the organization in 1947. Debayle, "The Status of Women in Nicaragua."

27. Gunnar Fromen to Doris Stevens, December 22, 1934, Doris Stevens Papers, MC 546, Box 83.

28. Debayle, "The Status of Women in Nicaragua," 238.

29. Ibid., 237.

30. Doris Stevens to Mr. and Mrs. Debayle, telegram, May 6, 1939, Doris Stevens Papers, MC 546, Box 63. Luis Manuel Debayle would go on to become a colonel in the Somozas' National Guard, Nicaragua's minister of health, and head of the state-run electric company Empresa Nacional de Luz y Fuerza (ENALUF). This last job earned him the nickname of "Tío Luz." He died in exile in Miami in 1984. See *La Estrella de Nicaragua* 16, no. 382 (July 1–15, 2008), http://www.estrelladenicaragua.com/382-EDICION/382-fotohistorica.html.

31. Toledo de Aguerri, *Educación y feminismo*, 27–30.

32. Ibid., 28–29.

33. Alejandro Cole Chamorro, *145 años de historia política: Nicaragua* (Managua: Editora Nicaragüense, 1967), 122, 123.

34. Toledo de Aguerri, *Educación y feminismo*, 25.

35. Ibid., 21, 24.

36. Ibid., 25.

37. "Nicaraguan Women Plan a Drive for Suffrage," *New York Times*, December 4, 1938, 51.

38. Josefina Arnesto, interview by author, Matagalpa, July 29, 1995.

39. Guillermo Sevilla Sacasa, *La mujer nicaragüense ante el derecho de sufragar: Por que me opuse a que se le concediera; La verdad sobre mi actitud en la Constituyente* (Managua: Talleres Gráficos Pérez, 1939), 5, 6.

40. Ignacio Briones, "Las mujeres nicaragüenses ayer y hoy," *Bolsa de Noticias*, March 20, 2007, http://www.grupoese.com.ni/2007/mar/20/nacho.htm.

41. Cobo del Arco, "Populismo, somocismo," 157.

42. "Ask Vote for Nicaraguan Women," *New York Times*, January 20, 1939, 9.

43. Miller, *Latin American Women*, 112.

44. See Woodward, "The Aftermath of Independence," 58; Toledo de Aguerri, *Educación y feminismo*, 27.

45. Borge de Sotomayor, *La mujer y el derecho*, 75–77.

46. Ibid.

47. Fray Felipe Muñoz, as quoted in ibid., 76.

48. Borge de Sotomayor, *La mujer y el derecho*, 76, 77.

49. Ibid., 77.

50. 1826 Constitution, as quoted in Antonio Esgueva, "El derecho al voto femenino en la legislación de Nicaragua," *Encuentro: Revista de la Universidad Centroamericana*, no. 43 (January 1997): 112.

51. Esgueva, "El derecho al voto femenino," 112.

52. 1939 Constitution, as quoted in ibid.

53. 1950 Constitution, as quoted in ibid., 113.

54. Ibid.

55. Esgueva, "El derecho al voto femenino," 113; *La Gaceta*, April 21, 1955, 795.

56. "Nicaragua Liberals Act: Convention Favors Presidential Re-Election and Woman Suffrage," *New York Times*, January 11, 1944, 5.

57. "Women's Vote Bill in Nicaragua," *New York Times*, May 9, 1945, 14; see Cobo del Arco, "Populismo, somocismo," 157.

58. As quoted in Cobo del Arco, "Populismo, somocismo," 157, 158.

59. Juanita Molina de Fromen died in 1934, as noted above. María Gámez died sometime between 1935 and 1945; we do not know exactly when. Helena Ramos alerted me to Gratus Halftermeyer's having stated, in his *Diccionario biográfico-histórico de Managua*

(1945), that Gámez had "died in Managua with clouded reasoning." She had a son, Chester M. Gámez, who lived in Washington, D.C., in the 1930s. See letter from María Gámez to Doris Stevens, June 17, 1932, Doris Stevens Papers, MC 546, Box 83.

60. Esgueva, "El derecho al voto femenino," 111.

61. "Nicaraguan Women Seek Vote," *New York Times*, August 17, 1950, 17.

62. *Exposición del Comité Central Femenino Pro-Voto de la Mujer de Nicaragua (Adscrito a la Federación de Mujeres de América) a la Asamblea Nacional Constituyente: Presentado por la Doctora Infieri Srita. Joaquina Vega* (Managua: Imprenta Democrática, n.d.), 6, 7.

63. Cobo del Arco, "Populismo, somocismo," 159.

64. Manuel Rubio Sánchez, *Status de la mujer en Centroamérica, 1503–1821* (Guatemala City: Editorial José de Pineda Ibarra, 1976), 231, 232; Collinson et al., *Women and Revolution*, 19. Rape was made a public crime in Nicaragua in 1992, which meant that, once accused, a rapist would be prosecuted even if the victim married the rapist or the victim's family was given money or goods by the rapist. For coverage of the debates over the 1992 changes to the rape laws, see Luis Sánchez Sancho, "Se casa el médico que violó a joven: Ella lo perdonó en el juzgado," *Barricada*, June 24, 1992; Sofía Montenegro, "La perversión del Parlamento. El Estado como violador," Opiniones, *Barricada*, June 16, 1992; Irene Pineda Ferman, "La mujer violada ante el Artículo 208," Opiniones, *Barricada*, June 27,1992; Noel Irías, "El código penal es del siglo pasado," *Gente*, August 17, 1992.

65. *Exposición del Comité Central Femenino*, 5.

66. "Nicaraguan Women Seek Vote," *New York Times*, August 17, 1950, 17.

67. "Nicaraguan Women Not to Vote," *New York Times*, September 2, 1950, 6.

68. María Gámez to Doris Stevens, June 27, 1932. Doris Stevens Papers, MC 546, Box 83.

69. María Gámez to Doris Stevens, June 17, 1932, Doris Stevens Papers, MC 546, Box 83.

70. "Proyecto de ley del voto femenino en Nicaragua," attached to note from María Gámez to Doris Stevens, June 27, 1932, Doris Stevens Papers, MC 546, Box 83.

71. María Gámez to Doris Stevens, June 27, 1932, Doris Stevens Papers, MC 546, Box 83.

72. "No solo el hogar y el hilo dicen las mujeres: Lideresas conservadoras se reunen," *La Prensa*, April 26, 1950, 1.

73. Margarita Cole Zavala, as quoted in ibid.

74. Margarita Cole Zavala, as quoted in "Mujeres marchan sobre Managua: 'El factor femenino derroca las dictaduras,'" *La Prensa*, April 30, 1950, 1, 2.

75. Ibid.

76. Saturnina Guillén, as quoted in "El voto no puede ser burlado dice Srita. Saturnina Guillen," *La Prensa*, August 15, 1950, 1, 4.

77. Ibid.

78. Rosa Gutiérrez, as quoted in "No solo el hogar y el hilo dicen las mujeres: Lideresas conservadoras se reunen," *La Prensa*, April 26, 1950, 1.

79. Saturnina Guillén, as quoted in "El voto no puede ser burlado," *La Prensa*, August 15, 1950, 1, 4.

80. Amelia Borge de Sotomayor, "Nicaragua: La condición legal de la mujer y su situación de hecho; Compilación y análisis de leyes que discriminan a la mujer" (unpublished manuscript, Tufts University, 1975), 5.

81. Booth, *The End and the Beginning*, 89, 90.

82. Unlabeled document, January 31, 1957, Año 1957, Fondo: Presidencial, Sección: Partido Liberal Secretaría Privada, Referencia: Partido Liberal (Ala Femenina), Signatura 295, Archivo General de la Nación.

83. Matilde Haydée Díaz, "La mujer ante las urnas electorales: ¡Por primera vez . . . !," February 3, 1957, Año 1957, Fondo: Presidencial, Sección: Partido Liberal, Secretaría: Privada, Referencia: Partido Liberal (Ala Femenina), Signatura 295, Archivo General de la Nación.

84. *Exposición del Comité Central Femenino*, 5, 6.

85. Ibid., 6.

86. For more on María Teresa Sánchez, see Helena Ramos, "Escritoras nicaragüenses: Ilustres desconocidas," accessed September 14, 2009, http://www.dariana.com/dic cionario/maria_teresa_sanchez2.htm#ramos.

87. "Feministas en pleito por lugar prominente," *La Prensa*, August 26, 1950, 1, 4.

88. Ibid.

89. "El voto femenino se decidirá hoy: Estarán presentes en el Congreso representativas del bello sexo," *La Prensa*, August 29, 1950, 1, 4.

90. Borge de Sotomayor, *La mujer y el derecho*, 75.

91. Obando Somarriba, *Doña Angelica Balladares*, 84. Some people have told me that this sort of emotional display was uncharacteristic of Toledo de Aguerri and was unlikely to have occurred.

92. Esgueva, "El derecho al voto femenino," 111, 112.

93. Cobo del Arco, "Populismo, somocismo," 160.

94. Ibid., 161.

95. See Victoria González, "Josefa Toledo de Aguerri and the Forgotten History of Nicaraguan Feminism" (master's thesis, University of New Mexico, 1996).

96. Ignacio Briones, "Las mujeres nicaragüenses ayer y hoy," *Bolsa de Noticias*, March 20, 2007, http://www.grupoese.com.ni/2007/mar/20/nacho.htm.

CHAPTER 3

1. Antonia Rodríguez [pseud.], interview by author. According to an anti-Somocista factbook published in 1967 by the U.S. Institute for Comparative Study of Political Systems, "few persons outside government circles bothered to register [for these elections], election day went almost unnoticed, and Somoza defeated his opponent by an 8 to 1 ratio and a 300,000-vote majority." Institute for the Comparative Study of Political Systems (ICSPS), *Nicaragua Election Factbook* (Washington, D.C.: Operations and Policy Research Inc.; Institute for the Comparative Study of Political Systems, 1967), 30.

2. "Nicaraguans Register," *New York Times*, November 6, 1956, 19.

3. As early as 1935, the Nicaraguan Workers Party (Partido Trabajador Nicaragüense) had organized socialist women in the Workingwomen's Front (Frente Obrero Femenino). See Armando Amador, *Un siglo de lucha de los trabajadores de Nicaragua* (Managua: UCA, 1992), 94. During the 1950s, 1960s, and 1970s, Conservative women were organized in the Women's Conservative Front (Frente Femenino Conservador). See Borge de Sotomayor, *Nicaragua*, 15. Sandinista women were organized in the Luisa Amanda Espinoza Association of Nicaraguan Women (AMNLAE) from the 1980s onward.

4. John Bodnar, *Remaking America: Public Memory, Commemoration, and Patriotism in the Twentieth Century* (Princeton: Princeton University Press, 1992), 15.

5. William H. Beezley, Cheryl English Martin, and William E. French, "Introduction: Constructing Consent, Inciting Conflict," in *Rituals of Rule, Rituals of Resistance: Public Celebrations and Popular Culture in Mexico*, ed. William H. Beezley, Cheryl English Martin, and William E. French (Wilmington, Del.: Scholarly Resources, 1994), xiii.

6. Ibid.

7. Ibid.

8. Mary Kay Vaughan, "The Construction of the Patriotic Festival in Tecamachalco, Puebla, 1900–1946," in Beezley, English Martin, and French, *Rituals of Rule*, 232.

9. Ibid.

10. "Dice que le rajaron la cabeza porque votó," *La Noticia,* February 5, 1957, 1.

11. "Una lectora hace un pregunta electoral . . . ," *La Prensa,* Sección Voz del Pueblo, January 3, 1957, 2.

12. "Votación fué desanimada y sin lucha," *La Prensa,* February 5, 1957, 1.

13. Dora Ubeda, interview by author, Matagalpa, May 12, 1998.

14. Nemesio Hernández, interview by author, Matazano, May 14, 1998.

15. "No hubo coacción ni halago en votaciones: Carta de Salvador Castillo en respuesta a *La Prensa,*" *Novedades,* September 4, 1974, 28.

16. Isidro Sequeira to President Luis Somoza, March 10, 1962, Años 1960–62, Fondo: Presidencial, Sección: Secretaría Privada, Referencia: Misceláneos Correspondencia, Caja 773, Archivo General de la Nación.

17. Nicolas Artola Zamora to President Anastasio Somoza García, February 15, 1956, Años 1956–57, Fondo: Presidencial, Sección: Partido Liberal, Autor: Liberales del Dept. de Granada, Signatura 295, Archivo General de la Nación.

18. Eduardo Presentación Reyes Robles, José Angel García Díaz, Felix Pedro Mena Alemán, and José Cupertino Mena Alemán to President Anastasio Somoza García, January 14, 1956, Años 1956–57, Fondo: Presidencial, Sección: Partido Liberal, Autor: Liberales del Dept. de Granada, Signatura 295, Archivo General de la Nación.

19. Letter to President Anastasio Somoza Debayle, January 15, 1972, Fondo: Presidencial, Sección: Partidos Políticos, Caja 306, Relación: Junta Nacional y Legal del PLN, Código 1.5, Archivo General de la Nación.

20. Letter to President Luis Somoza Debayle, May 27, 1958, Fondo: Presidencial, Sección: Partido Liberal, Signatura 296, Archivo General de la Nación.

21. *La Noticia,* February 5, 1957, 1.

22. Presupuesto de gastos para proyectado mitín liberal en Boaco, May 30, 1958, Fondo: Presidencial, Sección: Partido Liberal, Signatura 296, Archivo General de la Nación.

23. George A. Bowdler and Patric Cotter, *Voter Participation in Central America, 1954–1981: An Exploration* (Washington, D.C.: University Press of America, 1982), 64.

24. Iván Hernández to President Anastasio Somoza Debayle, November 14, 1971, Telegram, Fólder: Juventud Liberal Somocista, Caja 306, Relación: Juntas Directivas PLN, Código 1.5, Archivo General de la Nación.

25. Antonia Rodríguez [pseud.], interview by author.

26. Maritza Zeledón [pseud.], interview by author.

27. Ibid.

28. Other ANMU members in 1968 were pharmacist Elba Ochomogo de Gutierrez, attorney Gloria Zeledón de Sanchez (president), attorney Evelina Mayorga de Henríquez, and M. D. Haydee Ramírez de Ulloa. On ANMU's 1968 revision to its statutes, see *La Gaceta,* October 15, 1968.

29. "Brillante embajada cultural guatemalteca visita Nicaragua," *Ala Femenina de Juventud Liberal Nicaragüense* 1, no. 2 (September 1955): 43.

30. Marta García [pseud.], interview by author.

31. "The Nicaraguan Woman Speaks," 1958, Fondo: Presidencial, Signatura 296, Sección: Partido Liberal, Archivo General de la Nación.

32. Ibid.

33. Alejandra Flores [pseud.], interview by author.

34. Maritza Zeledón [pseud.], interview by author.

35. Marta García [pseud.] and Eugenia Robleto [pseud.], interviews by author.

36. Josefa Toledo de Aguerri, "Divagaciones sobre patriotismo," *Ala Femenina de Juventud Liberal Nicaragüense* 1, no. 2 (September 1955): 35, 36.

37. "Brillante embajada cultural guatemalteca visita Nicaragua," *Ala Femenina de Juventud Liberal Nicaragüense* 1, no. 2 (September 1955): 41, 43.

38. Gladys Bonilla Muñoz, "Preparación política de la mujer nicaragüense," *Ala Femenina de Juventud Liberal Nicaragüense* 1, no. 2 (September 1955): 22.

39. Marta García [pseud.], interview by author.

40. Borge de Sotomayor, *La mujer y el derecho*, 51.

41. "Brillante conferencista," *Ala Femenina de Juventud Liberal Nicaragüense* 1, no. 2 (September 1955): 33.

42. Antonia Rodríguez [pseud.], interview by author.

43. Shirley Hayes, "Women Seek Power Throughout Americas," *Boca Raton News*, August 16, 1976, 4.

44. Comisión Interamericana de Mujeres, accessed September 13, 2009, http://portal.oas.org/Portals/7/CIM/documentos/CD-doc.25.esp.doc.

45. Ignacio Briones, "Las mujeres nicaragüenses ayer y hoy," *Bolsa de Noticias*, March 29, 2007, http://www.grupoese.com.ni/2007/mar/29/nacho.htm.

46. Antonia Rodríguez [pseud.], interview by author.

47. Ibid.

48. Ibid.

49. Borge de Sotomayor, "Nicaragua," 14.

50. Antonia Rodríguez [pseud.], interview by author.

51. Marta García [pseud.], interview by author.

52. Antonia Rodríguez [pseud.], interview by author

53. Maritza Zeledón [pseud.], interview by author.

54. Alejandra Flores [pseud.], interview by author.

55. Gould, *To Lead as Equals*, 293; but see also Booth, *The End and the Beginning*, 65.

56. Sandy Johnson [pseud.], letter to President Luis Somoza Debayle, [n.d.], Año 1957, Fondo: Presidencial, Sección: Partido Liberal Secretaría Privada, Referencia: Liberal (Ala Femenina), Signatura 295, Archivo General de la Nación.

57. Alan Knight, "Populism and Neo-Populism in Latin America, Especially Mexico," *Journal of Latin American Studies* 30, no. 2 (1998): 226.

58. Ibid., 231.

59. Ibid., 226 and 232.

60. Rocío Cruz [pseud.], interview by author.

61. Clara Benavides [pseud.], letter to President Luis Somoza Debayle, January 28, 1957, Año 1957, Fondo: Presidencial, Sección: Partido Liberal, Secretaría Privada, Referencia: Partido Liberal (Ala Femenina), Signatura 295, Archivo General de la Nación.

62. Marta García [pseud.], interview by author.

63. Ara Wilson, *The Intimate Economies of Bangkok: Tomboys, Tycoons, and Avon Ladies in the Global City* (Berkeley and Los Angeles: University of California Press, 2004), 100.

64. Anastasio Somoza Debayle, *Hacia la meta . . . : Mensajes políticos del Gral. Anastasio Somoza Debayle, Presidente Constitucional de Nicaragua 1967–1972 ante la Gran Convención del Partido Liberal Nacionalista, durante su campaña electoral y toma de posesión* (Managua: Imprenta Nacional, 1968), 14.

65. Ibid., 145.

66. Noguera Carazo, *Evolución cultural*, 14. At the time that Noguera Carazo delivered these remarks, she was also president of the Nicaraguan chapter of the World Association of Women Journalists and Writers (Asociación Mundial de Mujeres Periodistas y Escritoras).

67. Ibid., 7.

68. Somoza Debayle, *Hacia la meta* . . . , 145.

69. Ibid.

70. Noguera Carazo, *Evolución cultural*, 15.

71. Ibid., 15, 16.

72. Bernard Diederich, *Somoza and the Legacy of U.S. Involvement in Central America* (New York: E. P. Dutton, 1981), 82.

73. "Boogie-Woogie Somoza," *Nicaragua: Patria Arte Cultura*, no. 9 (February 1956).

74. Unlabeled document, January 28, 1957, Año 1957, Fondo: Presidencial, Sección: Partido Liberal Secretaría Privada, Referencia: Partido Liberal (Ala Femenina), Signatura 295, Archivo General de la Nación.

75. Unlabeled document, January 1957, Año 1957, Fondo: Presidencial, Sección: Partido Liberal Secretaría Privada, Referencia: Partido Liberal (Ala Femenina), Signatura 295, Archivo General de la Nación.

76. Borge de Sotomayor, "Nicaragua," 3.

77. Ibid. See pp. 16, 17 for a longer list of women who occupied positions in government in 1975.

78. Antonia Rodríguez [pseud.], interview by author.

79. "Una desengañada del Ala Femenina," *La Prensa*, August 21, 1956, 2.

80. Maritza Zeledón [pseud.], interview by author.

81. Antonia Rodríguez [pseud.], interview by author.

82. Rosa Alvarez [pseud.], interview by author.

CHAPTER 4

1. Kathleen Blee, *Women of the Klan: Racism and Gender in the 1920s* (Berkeley and Los Angeles: University of California Press, 1991); Nancy MacLean, "White Women and Klan Violence in the 1920s: Agency, Complicity, and the Politics of Women's History," *Gender and History* 3, no. 3 (Autumn 1991); Glen Jeansomme, *Women of the Far Right: The Mother's Movement and World War II* (Chicago: University of Chicago Press, 1996).

2. Rebecca Klatch, *Women of the New Right* (Philadelphia: Temple University Press, 1987), 18.

3. Kathleen Blee, "Evidence, Empathy, and Ethics: Lessons from Oral Histories of the Klan," *Journal of American History* 80, no. 2 (1993): 606.

4. The Somocista women leaders I interviewed often asked about other Somocista women leaders, wanting to know if I had interviewed their former colleagues and how they were doing. Indeed, two former Ala leaders conducted research on Somocista women at the National Archive soon after I interviewed them, according to an employee at the National Palace, where the archive is located.

5. See, for example, Justiniano Pérez, *Los mitos de la Guardia Nacional de Nicaragua* (Miami: Orbis Products and Services, 2007).

6. Schick served as president just after Luis Somoza Debayle and just before Anastasio Somoza Debayle, the last of the Somozas; he was widely thought to have been the puppet of both Luis and Anastasio.

7. Marta García [pseud.], interview by author.

8. Maritza Zeledón [pseud.], interview by author.

9. A city of approximately 10,000, Chinandega was air-bombed in February 1927, leaving "more than ten blocks of the town" in "smoldering ruins." "Says Chinandega Has Been Retaken," *New York Times*, February 8, 1927, 25.

10. Somoza Debayle, *Hacia la meta . . .* , 88.

11. Ibid.

12. Sergio Gutiérrez [pseud.], interview by author.

13. Kampwirth, "Women in the Armed Struggles," in González and Kampwirth, *Radical Women*, 93.

14. Javier Auyero, *Poor People's Politics: Peronist Survival Networks and the Legacy of Evita* (Durham: Duke University Press, 2000), 186–87.

15. Somoza Debayle, *Hacia la meta . . .* , 97–98.

16. These were the same themes mentioned by the participants in the 2006 Granada study discussed in the introduction.

17. Lucrecia Noguera Carazo, "¿Hasta cuando se convencerán los comunistas?," *Novedades*, August 6, 1969, 6.

18. John D. French and Daniel James, "Oral History, Identity Formation, and Working-Class Mobilization," in *The Gendered Worlds of Latin American Women Workers: From Household and Factory to the Union Hall and Ballot Box,* ed. John D. French and Daniel James (Durham: Duke University Press, 1997), 299, quoting Ann Farnsworth-Alvear.

19. Popular Memory Group, "Popular Memory: Theory, Politics, Method," in *The Oral History Reader*, ed. Robert Perks and Alistair Thomson (London: Routledge, 1998), 76–77.

20. McGee Deutsch, "Spreading Right-Wing Patriotism," 224.

21. Power, "Defending Dictatorship," 302.

22. de Grazia, *How Fascism Ruled Women*, 43.

23. Ibid., 44.

24. Koonz, *Mothers in the Fatherland*, 5, 6.

25. Gilberto Cuadra, as quoted in Heyck, *Life Stories*, 129, 130.

26. Kathleen M. Blee, "Reading Racism: Women in the Modern Hate Movement," in *No Middle Ground: Women and Radical Protest*, ed. Kathleen M. Blee (New York: New York University Press, 1998), 196.

CHAPTER 5

1. Telegram, Managua, March 20, 1962, Año 1962, Caja 09, Signatura 306, Fólder 06, 1.5.6, Invitaciones, Telegramas, Archivo General de la Nación.

2. Antonia Rodríguez [pseud.], interview by author.

3. Rafael Suárez [pseud.], interview by author.

4. Tomás Borge, interview by author, New York City, March 18, 1997. See also Roberto Escobedo Caicedo, "Los pandilleros son los 'Tonton Macoutes' de los Ortega-Murillo," *Nicaragua Hoy*, accessed September 13, 2009, http://www.nicaraguahoy.info /dir_cgi/topics.cgi?op=print_topic;cat=Opinion;id=56750.

5. Luis E. Duarte, "Las hordas de la Nicolasa Sevilla," *La Prensa* magazine, August 10, 2008, 17.

6. Ibid.

7. Morales Henríquez, *De Mrs. Hanna*, 74; Josefa Ortega [pseud.], interview by author.

8. Josefa Ortega [pseud.], interview by author.

9. Antonia Rodríguez [pseud.], interview by author.

10. Ibid.

11. Duarte, "Las hordas de la Nicolasa Sevilla," 15.

12. Ibid., 16.

13. Ibid.

14. Joaquín Absalom Pastora, as quoted in ibid.

15. Rafael Suárez [pseud.], interview by author; Mario Vega [pseud.], personal conversation with author.

16. "Luctuosa," *Ala Femenina de Juventud Liberal Nicaragüense* 1, no. 2 (September 1955): 47.

17. "Comité Departamental de Propaganda Pro-Candidatura Coronel Luis A. Somoza D. Ocotal, Nueva Segovia," Años 1956–57, Fondo: Presidencial, Sección: Secretaría Privada, Referencia: Partido Liberal, Signatura 295, Archivo General de la Nación.

18. See ICSPS, *Nicaragua Election Factbook*, 16.

19. Rafael Suárez [pseud.], interview by author.

20. Antonia Rodríguez [pseud.], interview by author.

21. William Krehm, "Call All Trulls," *Time*, August 7, 1944, 38.

22. Antonia Rodríguez [pseud.], interview by author.

23. Rafael Suárez [pseud.], interview by author.

24. Krehm, "Call All Trulls," 38.

25. William Krehm, as quoted in Gregorio Selser, *Nicaragua de Walker a Somoza* (Mexico City: Mex Sur Editorial, 1984), 250.

26. Antonia Rodríguez [pseud.], interview by author.

27. Reina Zambrano [pseud.], interview by author.

28. Interview and correspondence with relatives of Nicolasa Sevilla.

29. "Luctuosa," *Ala Femenina de Juventud Liberal Nicaragüense* 1, no. 2 (September 1955): 47.

30. Antonia Rodríguez [pseud.], interview by author. See also Diederich, *Somoza;* Selser, *Nicaragua;* and Krehm, "Call All Trulls."

31. *La Prensa*, June 29, 1944, as quoted in Walter, *The Regime of Anastasio Somoza*, 131.

32. Krehm, "Call All Trulls," 38.

33. Diederich, *Somoza*, 71.

34. Miriam Argüello, interview by author, Managua, November 29, 1997.

35. Luciano Cuadra Vega, as quoted in Helena Ramos, "Luciano Cuadra Vega: Un siglo de amor y de Guerra," *El Nuevo Diario*, September 14, 2001, http://archivo.elnuevodiario.com.ni/2001/septiembre/14-septiembre-2001/variedades/variedades1.html.

36. *La Prensa*, August 21, 1969, 1, and *La Prensa*, August 22, 1969, 1.

37. Dionisio Herrera y Canales, "A 31 años del asalto a la Casa del Maestro," *El Nuevo Diario*, August 20, 2000, http://archivo.elnuevodiario.com.ni/2000/agosto/20-agosto-2000/nacional/nacional6.html.

38. Edgard Barberena, "Un viejo luchador aspira al PARLACEN," *El Nuevo Diario*, January 2, 2001, http://archivo.elnuevodiario.com.ni/2001/enero/02-enero-2001/nacional/nacional7.html.

39. Onofre Guevara López, *Cien años de movimiento social en Nicaragua* (Managua, IHCN, 2008), 133.

40. Evelia Matamoros [pseud.], interview by author.

41. Guillermo Rothschuh, "Una radio en la historia," *Confidencial* 12, no. 602 (September 21–27, 2008), http://www.confidencial.com.ni/archivo/2008-602/medioySociedad_602.html.

42. Rafael Suárez [pseud.], interview by author.

43. Antonia Rodríguez [pseud.], interview by author.

44. Duarte, "Las hordas de la Nicolasa Sevilla," 17.

45. Interview with Sevilla family member, 2004.

46. "La Nicolasa Sevilla pintó otra vez el alma del regimen," *La Prensa*, December 13, 1962, 14.

47. Roberto Collado Narváez, "Herty Lewites: Fiallos sustituye a la Nicolasa," *El Nuevo Diario*, March 12, 2001, http://archivo.elnuevodiario.com.ni/2001/marzo/12-marzo-2001/nacional/nacional21.html.

48. Morales Henríquez, *De Mrs. Hanna*, 74.

49. Marta García [pseud.], interview by author.

50. "Patriotic prostitute" is a term Donna Guy uses in *Sex and Danger in Buenos Aires: Prostitution, Family and Nation in Argentina* (Lincoln: University of Nebraska Press, 1990), 207.

51. Xavier Campos Ponce, *Sandino: Biografía de un héroe* (Mexico City: EDAMEX, 1979), 38–39.

52. Evelia Matamoros [pseud.], interview by author.

53. The term "niñas" refers to unmarried, presumably virgin, women of any age. "La Nicolasa Sevilla es la mejor propaganda para la oposición," *La Prensa*, July 11, 1944, 1, 4.

54. Milagros Palma, *Por los senderos míticos de Nicaragua* (Managua: Editorial Nueva Nicaragua, 1984), 26, 160.

55. Ibid., 160.

56. Rubén Darío, *Poesías completas* (Madrid: Aguilar, 1952), 243–44.

57. Rolando Hernández Aburto, "La destrucción de *La Nueva Prensa* y el boicot de *El Nuevo Diario*," *El Nuevo Diario*, July 20, 2001, http://archivo.elnuevodiario.com.ni/2001/julio/20-julio-2001/opinion/opinion2.html.

58. Collado Narváez, "Herty Lewites."

59. Consuelo Cruz Sequeira, "Mistrust and Violence in Nicaragua: Ideology and Politics," *Latin American Research Review* 30, no. 1 (1995): 218.

60. Herty Lewites, as quoted in Collado Narváez, "Herty Lewites."

61. See, for instance, Duarte, "Las hordas de la Nicolasa Sevilla," 10.

62. Roger Miranda and William Ratliff, *The Civil War in Nicaragua: Inside the Sandinistas* (New Brunswick: Transaction, 1993), 167, 168. These authors even make the argument that members of Sevilla's gangs ended up participating in the "turbas divinas" of the 1980s, presumably due to political opportunism and financial need.

63. José Luis Rocha, "Ten Photos That Shook the Eighties," *Revista Envío*, no. 336 (July 2009), http://www.envio.org.ni/articulo/4029.

64. Guillermo Cortés Domínguez, "Periodistas 'sandinistas'?," *Nicaragua Hoy*, September 6, 2009, http://www.nicaraguahoy.info/dir_cgi/topics.cgi?op=view_topic;cat=Opinion;id=57563.

CHAPTER 6

1. Roger Lancaster, *Life Is Hard: Machismo, Danger, and the Intimacy of Power in Nicaragua* (Berkeley and Los Angeles: University of California Press, 1992), 124–25.

2. The textbook cited, *Educación moral, cívica, y social*, was used for fourth, fifth, and sixth graders. Karen Kampwirth, "Democratizing the Nicaraguan Family: Struggles over the State, Households, and Civil Society" (Ph.D. diss., University of California at Berkeley, 1993), 55.

3. Nicaraguan Conservatives speaking in 1928, as quoted and translated in Whisnant, *Rascally Signs*, 397.

4. Palma Martínez, *El siglo de los topos*, 66.

5. Ibid., 61.

6. Ibid., 65.

7. Ibid., 66, 67.

8. Susan K. Besse, *Restructuring Patriarchy: The Modernization of Gender Inequality in Brazil, 1914–1940* (Chapel Hill: University of North Carolina Press, 1996), 2. See also Dore and Molyneux, *Hidden Histories*; Eileen J. Suárez Findlay, *Imposing Decency: The Politics of Sexuality and Race in Puerto Rico, 1870–1920* (Durham: Duke University Press, 1999); Ann Farnsworth-Alvear, *Dulcinea in the Factory: Myths, Morals, Men, and Women in Colombia's Industrial Experiment, 1905–1960* (Durham: Duke University Press, 2000); and SueAnn Caulfield, *In Defense of Honor: Sexual Morality, Modernity, and Nation in Early Twentieth-Century Brazil* (Durham: Duke University Press, 2000).

9. This was the case of Sergio Gutiérrez's mother, as noted in chapter 4. Sergio Gutiérrez [pseud.], interview by author.

10. The subtitle for this section of the text derives from P. J. Chamorro, *Estirpe sangrienta*, 160. The first epigraph, from Doris María Tijerino, is quoted in Heyck, *Life Stories*, 64. The second, from Aura Lila Lacayo, is quoted in Ada Julia Brenes et al., *La mujer nicaragüense en los años 80* (Managua: Ediciones Nicarao, 1991), 79. Lacayo was a member of the Democratic Party of National Confidence (Partido Demócrata de Confianza Nacional), one of the many parties that made up the anti-Sandinista National Opposition Union (Unión Nacional Opositora or UNO) in the late 1980s.

11. P. J. Chamorro, *Estirpe sangrienta*, 162, 163.

12. Morales Henríquez, *De Mrs. Hanna*, 15.

13. Sonia Rocha [pseud.], letter to Secretary to the Presidency Ramiro Sacasa Guerrero, [n.d.], Año 1962, Fondo: Presidencial, Sección: Secretaría Presidencial, Referencia: Misceláneo, Caja 773, Archivo General de la Nación.

14. Melania Dávila, as quoted in Randall, *Sandino's Daughters*, 205–8.

15. Juan M. Navas y Barraza, *La educación sexual y su estado actual en Nicaragua* (Managua: UNAN, 1966), 202.

16. Juan M. Navas y Barraza, *Educación sexual: Estudio de la sexualidad en Nicaragua, Centroamérica, y Rubén Darío* (Managua: Editorial Hospicio, 1967), 98.

17. Ibid., 98.

18. Sandra Lauderdale Graham, *House and Street: The Domestic World of Servants and Masters in Nineteenth-Century Rio de Janeiro* (Cambridge: Cambridge University Press, 1988), 132.

19. E. Mendieta, "Evolución de la legislación nicaragüense sobre la prostitución," in *Pensamiento y sociedad* (Managua: n.p., n.d.), 23–35.

20. Lara Elizabeth Putnam, "The Work and Lives of Prostitutes During Costa Rica's Early Twentieth-Century Banana Booms," 4, paper presented at the Twenty-Second Annual Meeting of the Latin American Studies Association (LASA), Miami, March 2000.

21. Cynthia Enloe, *Bananas, Beaches, and Bases: Making Feminist Sense of International Politics* (Berkeley and Los Angeles: University of California Press, 1989), 82.

22. Mendieta, "Evolución de la legislación."

23. Ibid., 20.

24. Guy, *Sex and Danger*, 38, 180–94.

25. Putnam, "The Work and Lives of Prostitutes," 14, 15; Juan José Marín Hernández, "Prostitución y pecado en la bella y próspera ciudad de San José, 1850–1930," in *El*

paso del cometa: Estado, política social, y culturas populares en Costa Rica, 1800–1950, ed. Iván Molina and Steven Palmer (San José: Editorial Porvenir, 1994), 74.

26. Putnam, "The Work and Lives of Prostitutes," 14, 15; Findlay, *Imposing Decency,* 89.

27. Cobo del Arco, *Políticas de género,* 121.

28. Guy, *Sex and Danger,* 13.

29. On U.S. efforts to repress prostitution in Puerto Rico in the 1890s and late 1910s, see Findlay, *Imposing Decency,* chaps. 3 and 6.

30. INSSBI, *La prostitución en Nicaragua,* 60.

31. "Redención de la mujer caída," *La Prensa,* January 11, 1955, 1.

32. Ibid.

33. Josefina Perezalonso, *Evolución física y espiritual de la mujer* (Managua: Imprenta Nacional, 1975), 10.

34. Ibid., 11.

35. INSSBI, *La prostitución en Nicaragua,* 61, 76.

36. Collinson et al., *Women and Revolution,* 69.

37. Ibid., 70.

38. Gregorio Selser, *Nicaragua de Walker a Somoza* (Mexico City: Mex Sur Editorial, 1984), 267.

39. Gould, *To Lead as Equals,* 169, 170.

40. A. Chamorro, "Estado y hegemonía durante el somocismo," 271.

41. Tomás Borge, as quoted in Collinson et al., *Women and Revolution,* 69.

42. INSSBI, *La prostitución en Nicaragua,* 59.

43. Baker, "Gender Ideologies," 156.

44. Selser, *Nicaragua,* 269.

45. Morales Henríquez, *De Mrs. Hanna,* 45.

46. Ibid., 55.

47. Any mistakes in the Spanish transcription or the English translation are my own.

48. Katherine Hoyt, *Thirty Years of Memories: Dictatorship, Revolution and Nicaragua Solidarity* (Washington, D.C.: Nicaragua Network Education Fund, 1996), 62.

49. Amada Pineda, as quoted in Margaret Randall, *Sandino's Daughters,* 80.

50. Ibid.

51. Doris Tijerino Haslam, as quoted in Heyck, *Life Stories,* 64–67.

52. Interviews with Ala leaders.

53. "Murió Amanda Aguilar, una de las heroicas mujeres del Cuá," Radio la Primerísima, February 14, 2007, http://www.radiolaprimerisima.com/noticias/9834. See also Mayra Pardillo Gómez, "¡Ay!, ¡Ay! la patria llorando esta: Parecen gritos de parto los que se oyen por allá," written on September 22, 2005, and reproduced by Radio la Primerísima, February 14, 2007, http://www.radiolaprimerisima.com/noticias/9836. The names in *Wikipedia*'s entry "Las mujeres del Cuá" are as follows: María Venancia, Angelina Díaz Aguilar, Candida Martínez, Martina González Hernández, Aurelia Hernández, Facunda Catalina González, Natividad Martínez Sánchez, and Amanda Aguilar [María de la Cruz], accessed August 28, 2010, http://es.wikipedia.org/wiki/Las_muje res_del_Cua.

54. Any errors in the Spanish transcription or the English translation are mine.

55. Letter written by Tomasa Calderón [pseud.], *Novedades,* August 20, 1969, 2.

56. *Hoy* (Havana), January 11, 1952, as cited in Tomás Fernández Robaina, *Historia de mujeres públicas* (Havana: Editorial Letras Cubanas, 1998), 71.

57. Randall, *Sandino's Daughters,* 28, 250.

58. Amnesty International, *Informe de Amnistía Internacional: Incluyendo las recomendaciones de una misión enviada a Nicaragua entre el 10 y el 15 de mayo de 1976* (London: Amnesty International, 1978), 42, 43, 80.

59. Baker, "Gender Ideologies," 148.

60. *Novedades*, August 18, 1969, 7.

61. Letter to President Anastasio Somoza Debayle, [n.d.], Años 1961–62, Fondo: Presidencial, Sección: Secretaría Privada, Referencia: Correspondencia Particular, Caja 772, Archivo General de la Nación.

62. Nikki Craske, *Women and Politics in Latin America* (New Brunswick: Rutgers University Press, 1999), 29.

63. Ibid.

64. Marta García [pseud.], interview by author.

65. Cecilia de Argüello, "El Triunfo de Somoza," *Novedades*, September 4, 1969, 4. On January 4, 1968, a 4.6-point magnitude earthquake damaged buildings on the southeast outskirts of Managua; no deaths or serious injuries were reported.

66. Graciela Lara de Delgado, *Hacia la superación* (Managua: Imprenta Nacional, 1975), 49.

67. Antonia Rodríguez [pseud.], interview by author.

68. Auyero, *Poor People's Politics*, 139, 148, 150.

69. Linda J. Seligmann, "Introduction," in *Women Traders in Cross-Cultural Perspectives: Mediating Identities, Marketing Wares*, ed. Linda J. Seligmann (Stanford: Stanford University Press, 2001), 3.

70. Lavrín, *Women, Feminism*, 38.

71. Another way to assist single mothers, of course, would be through child support, but paternity tests did not exist at the time. Even if they had existed, poor women would not have been able to afford them.

72. Borge de Sotomayor, *La mujer y el derecho*, 51–52.

73. *La Prensa*, August 28, 1960, 1, 5.

74. Antonia Rodríguez [pseud.], interview by author.

75. Paula Diebold de Cruz and Mayra Pasos de Rappacioli, *Report on the Role of Women in the Economic Development of Nicaragua* (Managua: U.S. AID, 1975), 68.

76. Ibid., 28.

77. Ruchwarger, *People in Power*, 199.

78. Diebold de Cruz and Pasos de Rappacioli, *Report on the Role*, 66.

79. Ibid., 65, 66.

80. A. Chamorro, "Estado y hegemonía," 254.

81. Diebold de Cruz and Pasos de Rappacioli, *Report on the Role*, 66.

82. Antonia Rodríguez [pseud.], interview by author.

83. Interviews with several Somocista women, 1994–99.

84. Yolanda Herrera [pseud.], letter to President Luis Somoza Debayle, [n.d.], Años 1961–62, Fondo: Presidencial, Sección: Secretaría Privada, Referencia: Correspondencia Particular, Caja 772, Archivo General de la Nación.

85. Mercedes Sotelo [pseud.], letter to President Luis Somoza Debayle, [n.d.], Años 1960–62, Fondo: Presidencial, Sección: Secretaría Privada, Referencia: Correspondencia Particular, Caja 773, Archivo General de la Nación.

86. Carmen Salazar, [pseud.], letter to President Luis Somoza Debayle, [n.d.], Años 1960–62, Fondo: Presidencial, Sección: Secretaría Privada, Referencia: Misceláneos Correspondencia, Caja 773, Archivo General de la Nación.

87. Eva Telica [pseud.], letter to President Luis Somoza Debayle, [n.d.], Año 1957, Fondo: Presidencial, Sección: Partido Liberal Secretaría Privada, Referencia: Liberal (Ala

Femenina), Signatura 295, Archivo General de la Nación. I have included the Spanish version so that Spanish-speaking readers may get a better appreciation for the religious language.

88. Sandra McGee Deutsch, "Gender and Sociopolitical Change in Twentieth-Century Latin America," *Hispanic American Historical Review* 71, no. 2 (1991): 279.

89. James Scott, *Domination and the Arts of Resistance: The Hidden Transcripts* (New Haven: Yale University Press, 1990), 2, 3.

90. Aurora Balladares [pseud.], interview by author.

91. Nadia Otero [pseud.], letter to Secretary of the Presidency Ramiro Sacasa Guerrero, [n.d.], Año 1962, Fondo: Presidencial, Sección: Secretaría Privada, Referencia: Miscelaneo, Caja 773, Archivo General de la Nación.

92. Ibid.

93. Nancy MacLean, *Behind the Mask of Chivalry: The Making of the Second Ku Klux Klan* (Oxford: Oxford University Press, 1994), 121.

94. Katherine Hoyt, "Parties and Pacts in Contemporary Nicaragua," in *Undoing Democracy: The Politics of Electoral Caudillismo*, ed. David Close and Kalowatie Deonandan (Lanham, Md.: Lexington Books, 2004).

95. For a brief discussion of Alemán's policies on women and the family, see Margaret Randall, *Las hijas de Sandino: Una historia abierta* (Managua: Anama Ediciones, 1999) 37. See also Karen Kampwirth, "Arnoldo Alemán Takes on the NGOs: Antifeminism and the New Populismo in Nicaragua," *Latin American Politics and Society* 45, no. 2 (2003).

96. For more on socially conservative U.S. right-wing activists, see Klatch, *Women of the New Right*. For more on the impact of the U.S. Right on Nicaragua, see Whisnant, *Rascally Signs*, 446.

97. Although fundraising is undoubtedly a political activity, it pales in comparison with the kinds of political activities Somocista women were involved in as part of the Somozas' state apparatus. For women who joined the Contra forces in the battlefield and their limited leadership role, see Kampwirth, "Women in the Armed Struggles."

98. Azucena Ferrey, interview by author, Managua, November 24, 1997. Ferrey is one of the few women who participated in the highest decision-making levels of the anti-Sandinista counterrevolutionary forces during the 1980s.

99. See, for example, Graciela Zelaya's article "Un liderazgo liberal con rostro de mujer" in *Mujer Liberal: Boletín Informativo de la Mujer Liberal* 1, no. 1 (May–June [1997?]): 2.

100. Market women (vendors) were among the Somozas' most visible supporters. Like the Somozas before them, Liberals in the late 1990s dedicated their energies to mobilizing this sector of the population. See "Leda Sánchez y las mujeres de los mercados de Managua," *Mujer Liberal: Boletín Informativo de la Mujer Liberal* 1, no. 1 (May–June [1997?]): 4. Leda Sánchez was one of the few members of the "new" Liberal women's movement who had been highly involved in Somocista politics.

101. Gould, *To Die in This Way*, 230.

102. Nicolasa Sevilla, as noted earlier, also attacked middle-class Somocista women in public.

103. Diane M. Nelson, *A Finger in the Wound: Body Politics in Quincentennial Guatemala* (Berkeley and Los Angeles: University of California Press, 1999), 67.

104. Personal conversation with Katherine Hoyt, co-coordinator, Nicaragua Network, Washington, D.C., December 20, 1997.

105. Richard Millet, *Guardians of the Dynasty* (Maryknoll, N.Y.: Orbis Books, 1978), 251.

106. Blee, *Women of the Klan*, 97.

107. Ibid., 77.

108. Nicaragua Network Hotline, September 30, 2008, http://www.nicanet.org/?p= 567.

109. Laura Kipnis, "The Stepdaughter's Story: Scandals National and Transnational," *Social Text* 17, no. 1 (Spring 1999): 65.

CONCLUSION

1. Gould, *To Lead as Equals*, 293.

2. See *Corona fúnebre en recuerdo de la Doctora Olga Núñez de Saballos: Primer aniversario de su muerte* (Managua: Imprenta Nacional, 1972), 69.

3. CPDH, *Los derechos humanos en Nicaragua*, 107.

4. Ibid.

5. Walter, *The Regime of Anastasio Somoza*, 245, 246.

6. Somoza Debayle, *Hacia la meta . . .* , 35.

7. Ibid., 35–36.

8. Vivian Mota, "Politics and Feminism in the Dominican Republic: 1931–45 and 1966–74," in *Sex and Class in Latin America*, ed. June Nash and Helen Safa (Brooklyn: J. F. Bergin, 1980), 274.

9. Somoza Debayle, *Hacia la meta . . .* , 117.

10. Karen Kampwirth and I see support for hierarchical survival strategies and opposition to Communism, class struggle, and state-sponsored imposition of economic equality as defining characteristics of the Right in twentieth-century Latin America. González and Kampwirth, *Radical Women*, 2.

SELECTED BIBLIOGRAPHY

ARCHIVAL COLLECTIONS

Nicaragua

Archivo del Instituto de Historia de Nicaragua y Centroamérica, Managua
Archivo General de la Nación/Archivo Nacional de Nicaragua, Palacio Nacional, Managua
Jorge Eduardo Arellano (personal archive), Managua
Biblioteca del Banco Central, Managua

United States

National Archives, Washington, D.C.
Alice Paul Papers, Schlesinger Library, Harvard University, Cambridge, Massachusetts
Doris Stevens Papers, Schlesinger Library, Harvard University, Cambridge, Massachusetts

NEWSPAPERS AND PERIODICALS

Ala Femenina de Juventud Liberal Nicaragüense (Managua)
El Ateneo (León)
Aurora de Nicaragua (León)
Barricada (Managua)
Boletín de la Unión Panamericana (Washington, D.C.)
Bolsa de Noticias (Managua)
La Gaceta: Diario Oficial de Nicaragua (Managua)
Gente (Managua)
Mujer Liberal: Boletín Informativo de la Mujer Liberal (Managua)
New York Times
Nicaragua: Patria, Arte, Cultura (Managua)
La Noticia (Managua)
Novedades (Managua)
El 93: Diario Político y de Variedades (León)
El Nuevo Diario (Managua)
La Prensa (Managua)
La Prensa magazine (Managua)
Time

OTHER SOURCES

Allen, Judith A. "Contextualizing Late Nineteenth Century Feminism: Problems and Comparisons." *Journal of the Canadian Historical Association* 1, no. 1 (1990).

————. *Rose Scott: Vision and Revision in Feminism.* Melbourne: Oxford University Press, 1994.

Amador, Armando. *Un siglo de lucha de los trabajadores de Nicaragua, 1880–1979.* Managua: UCA, 1992.

Amnesty International. *Informe de Amnistía Internacional: Incluyendo las recomendaciones de una misión enviada a Nicaragua entre el 10 y el 15 de mayo de 1976.* London: Amnesty International, 1978.

Anderson, Leslie E., and Lawrence C. Dodd. *Learning Democracy: Citizen Engagement and Electoral Choice in Nicaragua, 1990–2001.* Chicago: University of Chicago Press, 2005.

Anzaldua, Gloria. *Borderlands/La Frontera: The New Mestiza.* San Francisco: Aunt Lute Books, 1987.

Arellano, Jorge Eduardo. *Héroes sin fúsil: 140 nicaragüenses sobresalientes.* Managua: Editorial Hispamer, 1998.

Armijo, Modesto. *Derechos políticos de la mujer.* León: Tipografía Progreso de Sofonías Salvatierra, 1912.

Arrom, Silvia Marina. *The Women of Mexico City, 1790–1857.* Stanford: Stanford University Press, 1985.

Auyero, Javier. "The Logic of Clientelism in Argentina: An Ethnographic Account." *Latin American Research Review* 35, no. 3 (2000).

————. *Poor People's Politics: Peronist Survival Networks and the Legacy of Evita.* Durham: Duke University Press, 2000.

Babb, Florence. *After Revolution: Mapping Gender and Cultural Politics in Neoliberal Nicaragua.* Austin: University of Texas Press, 2001.

————. "Out in Public: Gay and Lesbian Activism in Nicaragua." *NACLA Report on the Americas* 37, no. 6 (May–June 2004).

Bacchette, Paola, and Margaret Power, eds. *Right-Wing Women: From Conservatives to Extremists Around the World.* New York: Routledge, 2002.

Baker, Suzanne. "Gender Ideologies and Social Change in Revolutionary Nicaragua." Ph.D. diss., Boston University, 1995.

Baltodano Marcenaro, Ricardo. "Ciudadanas por y para la dictadura: El Ala Femenina Liberal de Juventud Liberal Nicaragüense, 1954–1961." *Boletín AFEHC,* no. 34 (February 2008), http://afehc-historia-centroamericana.org/index.php?action=fi_aff&id=1826.

Baracco, Luciano. *Nicaragua: The Imagining of a Nation; From Nineteenth-Century Liberals to Twentieth-Century Sandinistas.* New York: Algora, 2005.

Barberena Pérez, Alejandro. *Estampas de Granada y sus 450 años de fundación.* Managua: Imprenta Nacional, 1974.

Barbosa, Francisco. "July 23, 1959: Student Protest and State Violence as Myth and Memory in León, Nicaragua." *Hispanic American Historical Review* 85, no. 2 (May 2005).

Bayard de Volo, Lorraine. *Mothers of Heroes and Martyrs: Gender Identity Politics in Nicaragua, 1979–1999.* Baltimore: Johns Hopkins University Press, 2001.

Beezley, William H., Cheryl English Martin, and William E. French, eds. *Rituals of Rule, Rituals of Resistance, Public Celebrations, and Popular Culture in Mexico.* Wilmington, Del.: Scholarly Resources, 1994.

Behar, Ruth. *Translated Woman: Crossing the Border with Esperanza's Story.* 10th anniversary ed. Boston: Beacon Press, 2003.

Bergmann, Emilie. *Women, Culture, and Politics in Latin America: Seminar on Feminism and Culture in Latin America.* Berkeley and Los Angeles: University of California Press, 1990.

Besse, Susan K. *Restructuring Patriarchy: The Modernization of Gender Inequality in Brazil, 1914–1940*. Chapel Hill: University of North Carolina Press, 1996.

Bethell, Leslie, ed. *Central America Since Independence*. Cambridge: Cambridge University Press, 1991.

Bickham Mendez, Jennifer. *From the Revolution to the Maquiladoras: Gender, Labor, and Globalization in Nicaragua*. Durham: Duke University Press, 2005.

Blee, Kathleen M. "Evidence, Empathy, and Ethics: Lessons from Oral Histories of the Klan." *Journal of American History* 80, no. 2 (1993).

———. "Reading Racism: Women and the Modern Hate Movement." In *No Middle Ground: Women and Radical Protest*, edited by Kathleen M. Blee. New York: New York University Press.

———. *Women of the Klan: Racism and Gender in the 1920s*. Berkeley and Los Angeles: University of California Press, 1991.

Bodnar, John. *Remaking America: Public Memory, Commemoration, and Patriotism in the Twentieth Century*. Princeton: Princeton University Press, 1992.

Booth, John. *The End and the Beginning: The Nicaraguan Revolution*. 2nd ed. Boulder: Westview Press, 1985.

Borge, Tomás. *The Patient Impatience: From Boyhood to Guerrilla; A Personal Narrative of Nicaragua's Struggle for Liberation*. Willimantic, Conn.: Curbstone Press, 1992.

Borge de Sotomayor, Amelia. *La mujer y el derecho*. Juris Doctorate thesis, UNAN. León: Editorial San José, 1953.

———. "Nicaragua: La condición legal de la mujer y su situación de hecho; Compilación y análisis de leyes que discriminan a la mujer." Unpublished manuscript, Tufts University, 1975.

Bowdler, George A., and Patrick Cotter. *Voter Participation in Central America, 1954–1981: An Exploration*. Washington, D.C.: University Press of America, 1982.

Brenes, Ada Julia, et al. *La mujer nicaragüense en los años 80*. Managua: Ediciones Nicarao, 1991.

Burns, Bradford. *Patriarch and Folk: The Emergence of Nicaragua, 1798–1858*. Cambridge, Mass.: Harvard University Press, 1991.

Bussy Genevois, Daniele. "Mujeres de España: De la República al franquismo." In *Historia de las mujeres en occidente*, edited by Georges Duby and Michelle Perrot. Madrid: Santillana, 1993.

Byron, Kristine. *Women, Revolution, and Autobiographical Writing in the Twentieth Century: Writing History, Writing the Self*. Lewiston, N.Y.: Edwin Mellen Press, 2007.

Campos Ponce, Xavier. *Sandino: Biografía de un héroe*. Mexico City: EDAMEX, 1979.

Cano, Gabriela. *Se llamaba Elena Arizmendi*. Mexico City: Tusquets Editores, 2010.

Cardoso, Ciro F. S. "The Liberal Era, c. 1870–1930." In *Central America Since Independence*, edited by Leslie Bethell. Cambridge: Cambridge University Press, 1991.

Caulfield, Sueann. *In Defense of Honor: Sexual Morality, Modernity, and Nation in Early-Twentieth-Century Brazil*. Durham: Duke University Press, 2000.

Caulfield, Sueann, Sarah C. Chambers, and Lara Putnam, eds. *Honor, Status, and Law in Modern Latin America*. Durham: Duke University Press, 2005.

Chamorro, Amalia. "Estado y hegemonía durante el somocismo." In *Economía y sociedad en la construcción del estado en Nicaragua*, edited by Alberto Lanuza et al. San José: ICAP, 1983.

Chamorro, Emiliano. *El último caudillo: Autobiografía*. Managua: Ediciones del Partido Conservador Demócrata, 1983. Reprinted from *Revista Conservadora*, edición extraordinaria, no. 67 (1966).

Chamorro, Pedro Joaquín. *Estirpe sangrienta: Los Somoza.* Managua: Ediciones el Pez y la Serpiente, 1978.

Cobo del Arco, Teresa. *Políticas de género durante el liberalismo: Nicaragua, 1893–1909.* Managua: UCA, 2000.

———. "Populismo, somocismo, y el voto femenino: Nicaragua, 1936–1955." In *Poder local, poder global en América Latina,* edited by Gabriela Dalla Corte et al. Barcelona: Universitat de Barcelona, 2008.

Cole Chamorro, Alejandro. *145 años de historia política: Nicaragua.* Managua: Editora nicaragüense, 1967.

Collinson, Helen, et al. *Women and Revolution in Nicaragua.* Edited by Helen Collinson. London: Zed Books, 1990.

Comité Permanente de Derechos Humanos (CPDH). *Los derechos humanos en Nicaragua: Segundo informe.* Managua: Comité Permanente de Derechos Humanos, 1978.

Corea Fonseca, Elías. *Historia de la medicina en Nicaragua.* Managua: 2000.

Corona fúnebre en recuerdo de la Doctora Olga Núñez de Saballos: Primer aniversario de su muerte. Managua: Imprenta Nacional, September 12, 1972.

Cott, Nancy F. "Comment on Karen Offen's 'Defining Feminism: A Comparative Historical Approach.'" *Signs* 15, no. 1 (1989).

———. *The Grounding of Modern Feminism.* New Haven: Yale University Press, 1987.

Craske, Nikki. *Women and Politics in Latin America.* New Brunswick: Rutgers University Press, 1999.

Crawley, Andrew. *Somoza and Roosevelt: Good Neighbour Diplomacy in Nicaragua, 1933–1945.* Oxford: Oxford University Press, 2007.

Cruz, Arturo. *Nicaragua's Conservative Republic, 1858–93.* New York: Palgrave, 2002.

Cruz Sequeira, Consuelo. "Mistrust and Violence in Nicaragua: Ideology and Politics." *Latin American Research Review* 30, no. 1 (1995).

Cuadra, Benjamín. *Situación jurídica de la mujer nicaragüense.* Granada: Tipografía de El Centro-Americano, 1905.

Cunningham, Eugene. *Gypsying Through Central America.* New York: E. P. Dutton, 1922.

Cupples, Julie. "Counter-Revolutionary Women: Gender and Reconciliation in Post-War Nicaragua." In *Gender, Peacebuilding, and Reconstruction,* edited by Caroline Sweetman. Oxford: Oxfam, 2004.

———. "Flexible Mothering: Articulating Rights and Negotiating Ideologies in Nicaragua." *Development* 44, no. 2 (2001).

Darío, Rubén. *Poesías completas.* Madrid: Aguilar, 1952.

Debayle, Luis Manuel. "The Status of Women in Nicaragua." *Mid-Pacific Magazine* (Honolulu) 45, no. 3 (1933).

de Grazia, Victoria. *How Fascism Ruled Women: Italy, 1922–1945.* Berkeley and Los Angeles: University of California Press, 1992.

Díaz, Arlene. *Female Citizens, Patriarchs, and the Law in Venezuela, 1786–1904.* Lincoln: University of Nebraska Press, 2004.

Diebold de Cruz, Paula, and Mayra Pasos de Rappacioli. *Report on the Role of Women in the Economic Development of Nicaragua.* Managua: U.S. AID, 1975.

Diederich, Bernard. *Somoza and the Legacy of U.S. Involvement in Central America.* New York: E. P. Dutton, 1981.

Dodd, Thomas J. *Managing Democracy in Central America: A Case Study; United States Election Supervision in Nicaragua, 1927–1933.* New Brunswick: Transaction, 1992.

Dore, Elizabeth. "The Holy Family: Imagined Households in Latin America." In *Gender Politics in Latin America: Debates in Theory and Practice,* edited by Elizabeth Dore. New York: Monthly Review Press, 1997.

———. *Myths of Modernity: Peonage and Patriarchy in Nicaragua*. Durham: Duke University Press, 2006.

———. "One Step Forward, Two Steps Back: Gender and the State in the Long Nineteenth Century." In *Hidden Histories of Gender and the State in Latin America*, edited by Elizabeth Dore and Maxine Molyneux. Durham: Duke University Press, 2000.

Dore, Elizabeth, and Maxine Molyneux, eds. *Hidden Histories of Gender and the State in Latin America*. Durham: Duke University Press, 2000.

Dubois, Ellen Carol. "Comment on Karen Offen's 'Defining Feminism: A Comparative Historical Approach.'" *Signs* 15, no. 1 (1989). *International Forum* 32, no. 1 (January 2009).

Dubois, Ellen [Carol], and Linda Gordon. "Seeking Ecstasy on the Battlefield: Danger and Pleasure in Nineteenth-Century Feminist Sexual Thought." *Feminist Studies* 9, no. 1 (1983).

The Economic Development of Nicaragua: Report of a Mission Organized by the International Bank for Reconstruction and Development at the Request of the Government of Nicaragua. Baltimore: Johns Hopkins Press, 1953.

Enloe, Cynthia. *Bananas, Beaches, and Bases: Making Feminist Sense of International Politics*. Berkeley and Los Angeles: University of California Press, 1989.

Esgueva, Antonio. "El derecho al voto femenino en la legislación de Nicaragua." *Encuentro: Revista de la Universidad Centroamericana*, no. 43 (January 1997).

Exposición del Comité Central Femenino Pro-Voto de la Mujer de Nicaragua (Adscrito a la Federación de Mujeres de América) a la Asamblea Nacional Constituyente, presentado por la Doctora Infieri Srita. Joaquina Vega. Managua: Imprenta Democrática, n.d.

Farnsworth-Alvear, Ann. *Dulcinea in the Factory: Myths, Morals, Men, and Women in Colombia's Industrial Experiment, 1905–1960*. Durham: Duke University Press, 2000.

Fernández Poncela, Anna M. "El abanico organizativo de los grupos de mujeres en Nicaragua." *Fem* (Mexico City) 16, no. 113 (July 1992).

———. "Nicaraguan Women: Legal, Political, and Social Spaces." In *Gender Politics in Latin America: Debates in Theory and Practice*, edited by Elizabeth Dore. New York: Monthly Review Press, 1997.

Fernández Robaina, Tomás. *Historia de mujeres públicas*. Havana: Editorial Letras Cubanas, 1998.

Findlay, Eileen J. Suárez. *Imposing Decency: The Politics of Sexuality and Race in Puerto Rico, 1870–1920*. Durham: Duke University Press, 1999.

Finzer, Erin S. "Poetisa Chic: Fashioning the Modern Female Poet in Central America." Ph.D. diss., University of Kansas, 2008.

Frazier, Lessie Jo. *Salt in the Sand: Memory, Violence, and the Nation-State in Chile, 1890 to the Present*. Durham: Duke University Press, 2007.

French, John D., and Daniel James, eds. *The Gendered Worlds of Latin American Women Workers: From Household and Factory to the Union Hall and Ballot Box*. Durham: Duke University Press, 1997.

Gámez, José Dolores. *Historia de Nicaragua desde los tiempos prehistoricos hasta 1860 en sus relaciones con España, México, y Centro-América*. Managua: Tipografía El País, 1889.

García, Ana Isabel, and Enríque Gomariz. *Mujeres centroamericanas ante la crisis: La guerra y el proceso de paz*. Vol. 1, *Tendencias estructurales: Información estadística por sexo*. San José: FLACSO, 1999.

Gobat, Michel. *Confronting the American Dream: Nicaragua Under U.S. Imperial Rule*. Durham: Duke University Press, 2005.

González, Victoria. "Del feminismo al somocismo: Mujeres, sexualidad, y política antes de la revolución sandinista." *Revista de Historia* (Universidad Centroamericana, Managua), edición especial, nos. 11–12 (1998).

———. "'El diablo se la llevó': Política, sexualidad femenina, y trabajo en Nicaragua, 1855–1979." In *Un siglo de luchas femeninas en América Latina,* edited by Eugenia Rodríguez. San José: Editorial de la Universidad de Costa Rica, 2002.

———. "From Feminism to Somocismo: Women's Rights and Right-Wing Politics in Nicaragua, 1821–1979." Ph.D. diss., Indiana University, 2002.

———. "Josefa Toledo de Aguerri (1866–1962) and the Forgotten History of Nicaraguan Feminism, 1821–1955." Master's thesis, University of New Mexico, 1996.

———. "Memorias de la dictadura: Narrativas de mujeres somocistas y neo-somocistas (1936–2000)." In *Mujeres, género, e historia en América Central, 1700–2000,* edited by Eugenia Rodríguez. San José: Plumsock, 2002.

———. "Mujeres somocistas: 'La pechuga' y el corazón de la dictadura nicaragüense, 1936–1979." In *Entre silencios y voces: Género e historia en América Central, 1750–1990,* edited by Eugenia Rodríguez. San José: Centro para el Desarrollo de la Mujer y la Familia, 1997.

———. "Nicaraguan Feminist Josefa Toledo de Aguerri (1866–1962): Her Life and Her Legacy." *Diálogos: Revista Electrónica de Historia* 5, no. 1, (March–August 2004).

González, Victoria, and Karen Kampwirth, eds. *Radical Women and Latin America: Left and Right.* University Park: Pennsylvania State University Press, 2001.

González-Rivera, Victoria. "Gender, Clientelistic Populism, and Memory: Somocista and Neo-Somocista Women's Narratives in Liberal Nicaragua." In *Gender and Populism in Latin America: Passionate Politics,* edited by Karen Kampwirth. University Park: Pennsylvania State University Press, 2010.

Gould, Jeffrey L. *To Die in This Way: Nicaraguan Indians and the Myth of Mestizaje, 1880–1965.* Durham: Duke University Press,1998.

———. *To Lead as Equals: Rural Protest and Political Consciousness in Chinandega, Nicaragua, 1912–1979.* Chapel Hill: University of North Carolina Press, 1990.

Guerrero, Julián N., and Lola Soriano de Guerrero. *Matagalpa.* [Managua?]: n.p., 1967.

Guevara López, Onofre. *Cien años de movimiento social en Nicaragua.* Managua: IHCN, 2008.

Guido Martínez, Clemente. *Nueva historia de Nicaragua.* Managua: Alba Editores, 2008.

Guy, Donna. *Sex and Danger in Buenos Aires: Prostitution, Family, and Nation in Argentina.* Lincoln: University of Nebraska Press, 1991.

Hagene, Turid. *Negotiating Love in Post-Revolutionary Nicaragua: The Role of Love in the Reproduction of Gender Asymmetry.* Oxford: Peter Lang, 2008.

Hahner, June. *Emancipating the Female Sex: The Struggle for Women's Rights in Brazil, 1850–1940.* Durham: Duke University Press, 1990.

Hershfield, Joanne. *Imagining la Chica Moderna: Women, Nation, and Visual Culture in Mexico, 1917–1936.* Durham: Duke University Press, 2008.

Heyck, Denis Lynn Daly. *Life Stories of the Nicaraguan Revolution.* New York: Routledge, 1990.

Hodges, Donald C. *Intellectual Foundations of the Nicaraguan Revolution.* Austin: University of Texas Press, 1986.

Howe, Cymene. "Undressing the Universal Queer Subject: Nicaraguan Activism and Transnational Identity." *City and Society* 14, no. 2 (2002).

Hoyt, Katherine. "Parties and Pacts in Contemporary Nicaragua." In *Undoing Democracy: The Politics of Electoral Caudillismo,* edited by David Close and Kalowatie Deonandan. Lanham, Md.: Lexington Books, 2004.

————. *Thirty Years of Memories: Dictatorship, Revolution, and Nicaragua Solidarity.* Washington, D.C.: Nicaragua Network Education Fund, 1996.

Institute for the Comparative Study of Political Systems (ICSPS). *Nicaragua Election Factbook.* Washington, D.C.: Institute for the Comparative Study of Political Systems, 1967.

Instituto de Estudios Interdisciplinarios (IEI). *El voto ciudadano: Una perspectiva desde adentro; Significados, memoria, y participación en Granada, Nicaragua.* Granada: Editorial Casa Tres Mundos, 2007.

Instituto Nicaragüense de Cultura (INC). *Catálogo de periódicos y revistas de Nicaragua, 1830–1930.* Managua: Instituto Nicaragüense de Cultura, 1992.

Instituto Nicaragüense de Seguridad Social y Bienestar (INSSBI). *La prostitución en Nicaragua.* Managua: Programa de Rehabilitación del INSSBI, 1980.

James, Daniel. *Resistance and Integration: Peronism and the Argentine Working Class, 1946–1976.* Cambridge: Cambridge University Press, 1988.

Jaquette, Jane S. *The Women's Movement in Latin America: Feminism and the Transition to Democracy.* Boston: Unwin Hyman, 1989.

Jeansomme, Glen. *Women of the Far Right: The Mother's Movement and World War II.* Chicago: University of Chicago Press, 1996.

Jimenez, Michael F. "Class, Gender, and Peasant Resistance in Central Colombia, 1900–1932." In *Everyday Forms of Peasant Resistance,* edited by Forrest D. Colburn. London: M. E. Sharpe, 1989.

Juanita, Testimonios. "Se siente, se siente. Monimbó está caliente. Se siente, se siente, Monimbó aguerrido y valiente." *Casa de las Américas* (Havana) 20, no. 117 (November–December 1979).

Kampwirth, Karen. "Arnoldo Alemán Takes on the NGOs: Antifeminism and the New Populism in Nicaragua." *Latin American Politics and Society* 45, no. 2 (2003).

————. "Democratizing the Nicaraguan Family: Struggles over the State, Households, and Civil Society." Ph.D. diss., University of California at Berkeley, 1993.

————. *Feminism and the Legacy of Revolution: Nicaragua, El Salvador, Chiapas.* Athens: Ohio University Press, 2004.

————. "The Mother of the Nicaraguans: Doña Violeta and the UNO's Gender Agenda." *Latin American Perspectives* 23, no. 1 (1996).

————. *Women and Guerrilla Movements: Nicaragua, El Salvador, Chiapas, Cuba.* University Park: Pennsylvania State University Press, 2002.

————. "Women in the Armed Struggles in Nicaragua: Sandinistas and Contras Compared." In *Radical Women in Latin America: Left and Right,* edited by Victoria González and Karen Kampwirth. University Park: Pennsylvania State University Press, 2001.

Keen, Benjamin. *A History of Latin America.* 5th ed. Boston: Houghton Mifflin, 1996.

Kettering, Sharon. "The Historical Development of Political Clientelism." *Journal of Interdisciplinary History* 18, no. 3 (1988).

Kinloch Tijerino, Frances. *Historia de Nicaragua.* 3rd ed. Managua: IHNCA, 2008.

————, ed. *Nicaragua en busca de su identidad.* Managua: Instituto de Historia de Nicaragua–Universidad Centroamericana, 1995.

————. "El primer encuentro con los filibusteros en Nicaragua: Antecedentes y contextos." *Boletín AFEHC,* no. 36 (June 2008), http://afehc-historia-centroamericana .org/index.php?action=fi_aff&id=1925.

Kipnis, Laura. "The Stepdaughter's Story: Scandals National and Transnational." *Social Text* 58, no. 17 (Spring 1999).

Klatch, Rebecca E. *Women of the New Right.* Philadelphia: Temple University Press, 1987.

Klubock, Thomas Miller. *Contested Communities: Class, Gender, and Politics in Chile's El Teniente Copper Mine, 1904–1951.* Durham: Duke University Press, 1996.

Knight, Alan. "Populism and Neo-Populism in Latin America, Especially Mexico." *Journal of Latin American Studies* 30, no. 2 (1998).

Konetzke, Richard. *Colección de documentos para la historia de la formación social de Hispanoamérica, 1493–1810.* Madrid: Consejo Superior de Investigaciones Científicas, 1953.

Koonz, Claudia. *Mothers in the Fatherland: Women, the Family, and Nazi Politics.* New York: St. Martin's Press, 1987.

Krehm, William. "Call All Trulls." *Time,* August 7, 1944.

Kruckewitt, Joan. *The Death of Ben Linder: The Story of a North American in Sandinista Nicaragua.* New York: Seven Story Press, 1999.

Kühl Arauz, Eddy. *Nicaragua: Historia de inmigrantes.* Managua: Hispamer, 2007.

Ladd-Taylor, Molly. *Mother-Work: Women, Child Welfare, and the State, 1890–1930.* Urbana: University of Illinois Press, 1994.

———. "Toward Defining Maternalism in U.S. History." *Journal of Women's History* 5, no. 2 (1993).

Lancaster, Roger. *Life Is Hard: Machismo, Danger, and the Intimacy of Power in Nicaragua.* Berkeley and Los Angeles: University of California Press, 1992.

Lara de Delgado, Graciela. *Hacia la superación.* Managua: Imprenta Nacional, 1975.

Lauderdale Graham, Sandra. *House and Street: The Domestic World of Servants and Masters in Nineteenth-Century Rio de Janeiro.* Cambridge: Cambridge University Press, 1988.

Lavrín, Asunción. *Women, Feminism, and Social Change in Argentina, Chile, and Uruguay, 1890–1940.* Lincoln: University of Nebraska Press, 1995.

López Miranda, Margarita. *Una chontaleña en la educación nacional: Biografía de Josefa Toledo de Aguerri.* Juigalpa: ASOGACHO, 1988.

MacLean, Nancy. *Behind the Mask of Chivalry: The Making of the Second Ku Klux Klan.* New York: Oxford University Press, 1994.

———. "White Women and Klan Violence in the 1920s: Agency, Complicity, and the Politics of Women's History." *Gender and History* 3, no. 3 (1991).

Mallon, Florencia. *Peasant and Nation: Postcolonial Mexico and Peru.* Berkeley and Los Angeles: University of California Press, 1995.

Marín Hernández, Juan José. "Prostitución y pecado en la bella y próspera ciudad de San José, 1850–1930." In *El paso del cometa: Estado, política social, y culturas populares en Costa Rica (1800–1950),* edited by Iván Molina and Steven Palmer. San José: Editorial Porvenir, 1994.

McGee Deutsch, Sandra. "The Catholic Church, Work, and Womanhood in Argentina, 1890–1930." *Gender and History* 3, no. 3 (1991).

———. "Gender and Sociopolitical Change in Twentieth-Century Latin America." *Hispanic American Historical Review* 71, no. 2 (1991).

———. "Spreading Right-Wing Patriotism, Femininity, and Morality: Women in Argentina, Brazil, and Chile, 1900–1940." In *Radical Women in Latin America: Left and Right,* edited by Victoria González and Karen Kampwirth. University Park: Pennsylvania University Press, 2001.

Mendieta, E. "Evolución de la legislación nicaragüense sobre la prostitución." In *Pensamiento y sociedad.* Managua: n.p., n.d.

Meyer, Harvey Kessler. *Historical Dictionary of Nicaragua.* Metuchen, N.J.: Scarecrow Press, 1972.

Miller, Francesca. *Latin American Women and the Search for Social Justice.* Hanover, N.H.: University Press of New England, 1991.

Millet, Allan Reed. *Semper Fidelis: The History of the United States Marine Corps.* New York: Free Press, 1991.

Millet, Richard. *Guardians of the Dynasty.* Maryknoll, N.Y.: Orbis Books, 1978.

Miranda, Roger, and William Ratliff. *The Civil War in Nicaragua: Inside the Sandinistas.* New Brunswick: Transaction, 1993.

Molyneux, Maxine. "Mobilization Without Emancipation? Women's Interests, the State, and Revolution in Nicaragua." *Feminist Studies* 11, no. 2 (1985).

———. "Twentieth-Century State Formation in Latin America." In *Hidden Histories of Gender and the State in Latin America,* edited by Elizabeth Dore and Maxine Molyneux. Durham: Duke University Press, 2000.

Morales Henríquez, Viktor. *De Mrs. Hanna a la Dinorah: Principio y fin de la dictadura somocista; Historia de medio siglo de corrupción.* [Managua?], [1980?].

Mota, Vivian. "Politics and Feminism in the Dominican Republic: 1931–1945 and 1966–1974." In *Sex and Class in Latin America,* edited by June Nash and Helen Safa. Brooklyn: J. F. Bergin, 1980.

Murphy, John W., and Manuel J. Caro. *Uriel Molina and the Sandinista Popular Movement in Nicaragua.* Jefferson, N.C.: McFarland, 2006

Navas y Barraza, Juan M. *Educación sexual: Estudio de la sexualidad en Nicaragua, Centroamérica, y Rubén Darío.* Managua: Editorial Hospicio, 1967.

———. *La educación sexual y su estado actual en Nicaragua.* Managua: UNAN, 1966.

Nelson, Diane M. *A Finger in the Wound: Body Politics in Quincentennial Guatemala.* Berkeley and Los Angeles: University of California Press, 1999.

Noguera Carazo, Lucrecia. *Evolución cultural y política de la mujer nicaragüense.* Managua: n.p., 1974.

Normas legales de Asociación Nicaragüense de Mujeres Universitarias: Exposición preliminar, acta de fundación, personalidad jurídica, estatutos, reglamento interno. Managua: Editorial Unión Cardoza, October 1968.

Obama, Barack. *Dreams from My Father: A Story of Race and Inheritance.* New York: Three Rivers Press, 2004.

Obando Somarriba, Francisco. *Doña Angélica Balladares de Argüello: La primera dama del liberalismo; Su vida, sus hechos, episodios de la historia de Nicaragua.* Managua: Tipografía Comercial, 1969.

Offen, Karen. "Defining Feminism: A Comparative Historical Approach." *Signs* 14, no. 1 (1988).

———. "Reply to Cott." *Signs* 15, no. 1 (1989).

———. "Reply to Dubois." *Signs* 15, no. 1 (1989).

Olcott, Jocelyn. *Revolutionary Women in Postrevolutionary Mexico.* Durham: Duke University Press, 2005.

Olcott, Jocelyn, et al., eds. *Sex in Revolution: Gender, Politics, and Power in Modern Mexico.* Durham: Duke University Press, 2006.

Osorno Fonseca, Humberto. *La evolución social del liberalismo en Nicaragua.* Managua: Editorial Atlántida, 1938.

Pallais Lacayo, Mauricio. *El periodismo en Nicaragua, 1826–1876.* Managua: Banco Central de Nicaragua, 1982.

Palma, Milagros. *Nicaragua: Once mil vírgenes; Imaginario mítico-religioso del pensamiento mestizo nicaragüense.* Bogotá: Tercer Mundo Editores, 1988.

———. *Por los senderos míticos de Nicaragua.* Managua: Editorial Nueva Nicaragua, 1984.

Palma Martínez, Francisco. *El siglo de los topos: Crítica y enseñanza en plan de ciencia; Filosofía del sexo, psicología, sociología, eugenesia, religión, y arte.* León: Editorial La Patria, [1949?].

Palmer, Steven, and Gladys Rojas Chaves. "Educando a las señoritas: Formación docente, movilidad social, y nacimiento del feminismo en Costa Rica, 1855–1925." In *Educando a Costa Rica: Alfabetización popular, formación docente, y genero, 1880–1950*, edited by Iván Molina Jiménez and Steve Palmer. San José: Editorial Porvenir y Plumsock Mesoamerican Studies, 2000.

Pérez, Justiniano. *Los mitos de la guardia nacional de Nicaragua*. Miami: Orbis, 2007.

Perezalonso, Josefina. *Evolución física y espiritual de la mujer*. Managua: Imprenta Nacional, 1975.

Popular Memory Group. "Popular Memory: Theory, Politics, Method." In *The Oral History Reader*, edited by Robert Perks and Alistair Thomson. London: Routledge, 1998.

Power, Margaret. "Defending Dictatorship: Conservative Women in Pinochet's Chile and the 1988 Plebiscite." In *Radical Women in Latin America: Left and Right*, edited by Victoria González and Karen Kampwirth. University Park: Pennsylvania State University Press, 2001.

———. *Right-Wing Women in Chile: Feminine Power and the Struggle Against Allende, 1964–1973*. University Park: Pennsylvania State University Press, 2002.

Price, Michael David. "Nicaragua and the United States: Policy Confrontations and Cultural Interactions, 1893–1933." Ph.D. diss., University of Houston, 1995.

Putnam, Lara Elizabeth. "The Work and Lives of Prostitutes During Costa Rica's Early Twentieth-Century Banana Booms." Paper presented at the Twenty-Second Annual Meeting of the Latin American Studies Association (LASA), Miami, March 2000.

Quay Hutchison, Elizabeth. *Labors Appropriate to Their Sex: Gender, Labor, and Politics in Urban Chile, 1900–1930*. Durham: Duke University Press, 2001.

Ramírez Mercado, Sergio. *Margarita, está linda la mar*. Mexico City: Alfaguara, 1998.

Randall, Margaret. *Gathering Rage: The Failure of Twentieth Century Revolutions to Develop a Feminist Agenda*. New York: Monthly Review Press, 1992.

———. *Las hijas de Sandino: Una historia abierta*. Managua: Anama Ediciones, 1999.

———. *Sandino's Daughters: Testimonies of Nicaraguan Women in Struggle*. Edited by Lynda Yanz. Vancouver: New Star Books, 1981.

———. *Sandino's Daughters Revisited: Feminism in Nicaragua*. New Brunswick: Rutgers University Press, 1994.

———. "To Change Our Own Reality and the World: A Conversation with Lesbians in Nicaragua." *Signs* 18, no. 4 (1993).

———. *Todas estamos despiertas: Testimonios de la mujer nicaragüense hoy*. Mexico City: Siglo XXI Editores, 1981.

Rich, Adrienne. *Your Native Land, Your Life: Poems*. New York: Norton, 1986.

Rodríguez, Ileana. *Registradas en la historia: 10 años del quehacer feminista en Nicaragua*. Managua: CIAM, 1990.

Rodríguez, Jorge. *Elena Arellano, los salesianos en Centroamérica, y la casa de Granada, Nicaragua*. Managua: Ministerio de Educación, 1992.

Rosemblatt, Karin Alejandra. *Gendered Compromises: Political Cultures and the State in Chile, 1920–1950*. Chapel Hill: University of North Carolina Press, 2000.

Rubio Sánchez, Manuel. *Status de la mujer en Centroamérica, 1503–1821*. Guatemala City: Editorial José de Pineda Ibarra, 1976.

Ruchwarger, Gary. *People in Power: Forging a Grassroots Democracy in Nicaragua*. South Hadley, Mass.: Bergin and Garvey, 1987.

Ruhl, Arthur. *The Central Americans: Adventure and Impressions Between Mexico and Panama*. New York: Scribner's, 1928.

Sánchez Ramírez, Roberto. *El recuerdo de Managua en la memoria de un poblano.* Managua: Dirección de Patrimonio Histórico Alcaldía de Managua, 2008.

Saporta Sternbach, Nancy, et al. "Feminisms in Latin America: From Bogotá to San Bernardo." *Signs* 17, no. 2 (1992).

Scott, James. *Domination and the Arts of Resistance: The Hidden Transcripts.* New Haven: Yale University Press, 1990.

Seligmann, Linda J., ed. *Women Traders in Cross-Cultural Perspectives: Mediating Identities, Marketing Wares.* Stanford: Stanford University Press, 2001.

Selser, Gregorio. *Nicaragua de Walker a Somoza.* Mexico City: Mex Sur Editorial, 1984.

Sevilla Sacasa, Guillermo. *La mujer nicaragüense ante el derecho de sufragar: Por que me opuse a que se le concediera; La verdad sobre mi actitud ante la Constituyente.* Managua: Talleres Gráficos Pérez, 1939.

Solà i Montserrat, Roser. *Geografía y estructura económicas de Nicaragua en el contexto centroamericano y de América Latina.* Managua: UCA, 1990.

———. *Un siglo y medio de economía nicaragüense: Las raíces del presente.* Managua: IHNCA, 2007.

Solà [i Montserrat], Roser, and María Pau Trayner. *Ser madre en Nicaragua: Testimonios de una historia no escrita.* Barcelona: Icaria Editorial, 1988.

Solaun, Mauricio. *U.S. Intervention and Regime Change in Nicaragua.* Lincoln: University of Nebraska Press, 2005.

Somoza Debayle, Anastasio. *Hacia la meta . . .: Mensajes políticos del Gral. Anastasio Somoza Debayle, Presidente Constitucional de Nicaragua, 1967–1972, ante la Gran Convención del Partido Liberal Nacionalista, durante su campaña electoral y toma de posesión.* Managua: Editorial San José, n.d.

Stern, Steve J. *Battling for the Hearts and Minds: Memory Struggles in Pinochet's Chile, 1973–1988.* Durham: Duke University Press, 2006.

———. *Remembering Pinochet's Chile: On the Eve of London, 1998.* Durham: Duke University Press, 2004.

Stoner, Lynn K. *From the House to the Streets: The Cuban Women's Movement for Legal Reform, 1898–1940.* Durham: Duke University Press, 1991.

Tercero de Debayle, Emelina. *Valores femeninos de Nicaragua: Rasgos históricos sobre la mujer nicaragüense.* Managua: Imprenta Nacional, 1966.

Thompson, Wallace. *Rainbow Countries of Central America.* New York: E. P. Dutton, 1926.

Tijerino, Gustavo. *Administración y reforma: Homenaje intelectual en honor al Excelentísimo Señor Presidente de la Republica General Don Anastasio Somoza, ante la vasta obra de progreso que ha realizado en Nicaragua en lo que lleva la administración.* [Managua?]: n.p., n.d.

Tinsman, Heidi. *Partners in Conflict: The Politics of Gender, Sexuality, and Labor in the Chilean Agrarian Reform, 1950–1973.* Durham: Duke University Press, 2002.

Toledo de Aguerri, Josefa. *Al correr de la pluma: Crónicas de viajes, escritas para "Revista Femenina Ilustrada" (de agosto a diciembre de 1920) desde Costa Rica y Estados Unidos de América, pasando por Panamá y La Habana.* Managua: Tipografía Nacional, 1924.

———. *Dramatizaciones escolares.* Managua: n.p., 1939.

———. *Educación y feminismo: Sobre enseñanza; Artículos varios (reproducciones).* Managua: Talleres Nacionales de Imprenta y Encuadernación, 1940.

———. *Personificación de la historia de Managua.* Managua: n.p., 1942.

———. *Puntos críticos sobre enseñanza nicaragüense, 1907–1928.* Managua: Imprenta Nacional, 1933.

————. *Temas pedagógicos.* Managua: n.p., 1935.

U.S. Comptroller General. *Nicaragua: An Assessment of Earthquake Relief and Reconstruction Assistance.* Washington, D.C.: U.S. General Accounting Office, March 1977.

Vannini, Margarita. *Encuentros con la historia.* Managua: IHNCA, 1995.

Vaughan, Mary Kay. "The Construction of the Patriotic Festival in Tecamachalco, Puebla, 1900–1946." In *Rituals of Rule, Rituals of Resistance: Public Celebrations and Popular Culture in Mexico,* edited by William H. Beezley, Cheryl English Martin, and William E. French. Wilmington, Del.: Scholarly Resources, 1994.

Vilas, Carlos M. "Family Affairs: Class, Lineage, and Politics in Contemporary Nicaragua." *Journal of Latin American Studies* 24, no. 2 (1992).

————. *The Sandinista Revolution: National Liberation and Social Transformation in Central America.* New York: Monthly Review Press, 1986.

Walker, Thomas. *Nicaragua in Revolution.* New York: Praeger, 1982.

————, ed. *Revolution and Counterrevolution in Nicaragua.* Boulder: Westview Press, 1991.

Walter, Knut. *The Regime of Anastasio Somoza, 1936–1956.* Chapel Hill: University of North Carolina Press, 1993.

Weber, Clare. *Visions of Solidarity: U.S. Peace Activists in Nicaragua from War to Women's Activism and Globalization.* Lanham, Md.: Lexington Books, 2006.

Whisnant, David E. *Rascally Signs in Sacred Places: The Politics of Culture in Nicaragua.* Chapel Hill: University of North Carolina Press, 1995.

Wilson, Ara. *The Intimate Economies of Bangkok: Tomboys, Tycoons, and Avon Ladies in the Global City.* Berkeley and Los Angeles: University of California Press, 2004.

Wolfe, Justin. *The Everyday Nation-State: Community and Ethnicity in Nineteenth-Century Nicaragua.* Lincoln: University of Nebraska Press, 2007.

Woodward, R. L., Jr. "The Aftermath of Independence." In *Central America Since Independence,* edited by Leslie Bethell. Cambridge: Cambridge University Press, 1991.

Yeager, Gertrude, ed. *Confronting Change, Challenging Tradition: Women in Latin American History.* Wilmington, Del.: Scholarly Resources, 1994.

Zalzman, Philip Carl. "On Reflexivity." *American Anthropologist* 104, no. 3 (September 2002).

Zamora, Daisy. *La mujer nicaragüense en la poesía: Antología.* Managua: Editorial Nueva Nicaragua, 1992.

Zimmerman, Matilde. *Sandinista: Carlos Fonseca and the Nicaraguan Revolution.* Durham: Duke University Press, 2000.

INDEX

Printed in the USA
CPSIA information can be obtained
at www.ICGtesting.com
LVHW041613140124
768977LV00001B/67

9 780271 048710